Cornwall' n
in the F

Torpoint's War Diary 1939-1946

Joe P. Plant

Published by Joe P. Plant
Publishing partner: Paragon Publishing, Rothersthorpe
First published 2010

ISBN 978-1-907611-03-2

Book design, layout and production management by Into Print

www.intoprint.net

01604 832149

Printed and bound in UK and USA by Lightning Source

Introduction
by
Richard Carew Pole. Bt.

I am honoured and delighted to be given the opportunity to write a brief introduction to this remarkable and fascinating book about those, who lived, served or passed through Torpoint during the Second World War. It describes in graphic detail the activities, which took place and those who were involved.

This is a very valuable addition to those books, which have already been written, on the history of Torpoint. It describes in detail the grim and horrifying ordeals, which the local residents had to go through, and their great courage in confronting them.

I can only congratulate Joe on a quite remarkable achievement. This book will provide a permanent insight to this and future generations of the dark days our predecessors had to endure, the contribution they made to eventual victory and the freedoms we enjoy today.

Richard Carew Pole. Bt.

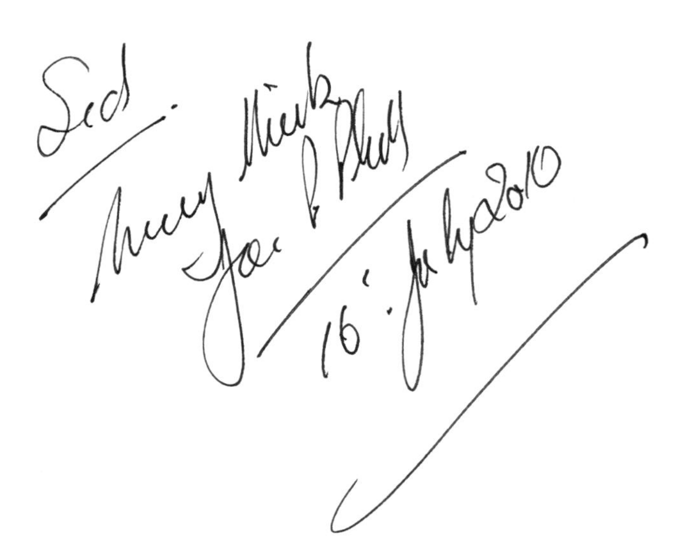

ACKNOWLEDGEMENTS.

In researching this book, I am indebted to the many residents of Torpoint listed below for giving me permission to quote from articles submitted and of recollections of their personal experience throughout the years of the war, all have expressed great interest for its completion. One comment I did receive was. "Why was it not done before"? (Something I could not answer) nevertheless without their input I do not think it could have been possible to create such a historical record of those bygone times in Torpoint's history. The survival of a Town is how it prospers through its people. Torpoint has a history going back over two hundred years its residents like any other town rallied to the war effort during the first World War, sadly 101 servicemen did not survive to see Torpoint again, yet it survived throughout the following years of the depression until the events of the Second World War were to change the face of Torpoint.

An Anonymous Person? - Mr. H. Banks. (deceased).- Mr. J. A. Banham. -
Mr. N. Beaver. MBE. – Mr. M. Bersey. (deceased)- Mr. F. Bolton. –
Mr. Richard (Mel) Bray.- Mrs. I. Bush.- Mrs. J. & M. Carter.-
Mr. A. Corbidge.- Mr. R. Courtier. - Mr. G. Crocker. Cdr. RN.(Rtd).-
Mrs. D. Daws. – Mrs. L. Dawson.- Miss. N. Dunbar.- Mrs. Eady.-
Mr. B. Eady. (Deceased) – Mr. P. Gliddon. – Mrs. M. Harwood.-
Mr. F. Harwood. (deceased) – Mrs. Freda Hawken. – Mrs. B. Hocking.-
Mr. Hoetz.- Miss. K. Johnson.- Mrs. B. Keller.- Mr. K. Lilyman.- Mr. C. Lowings.-
Mr. D. Mitchell.- (script & Photograph)-
Mr. John Peach & Mrs. Jean Peach. (deceased).– Mr. M. Pearn. OBE. ISO. -
Mr. M. Pidgen.- Mrs. W. Plant. - Mr. Jim. Southworth. DFM. –
Mrs. P. Ravensdale.- Mr. J. Smith. MBE.- Lt. Cdr. RN. (Rtd).- Mrs. M. Smith.-
Mrs. C. Stevens. - Mr. F. Timms.- Mr. P. Rolfe.- Miss. C. Sheppard.- Mr. J. Vigus.-
Mrs. Joan Waldron.(nee Goad)- Mrs. K. Wilton. Torpoint Library Manager. –
Mrs. F. Woolcock. – Joan- neice of Herbert Rowe (for specific photographs)
Mr. G. Williams.(American photographs.)

Edited by Mrs. Margaret . R. Roche.
Cover design by Joe. P. Plant and Julian Roche
Photo image by kind permmision of the Imperial War Museum.

THE FIRST CORNISH TOWN IN THE FRONT LINE
TORPOINT'S DIARY 1939-1945

LEST WE FORGET

PROLOGUE

The essence of life has taught us that there is always two sides to every story, so I would like to begin by saying to some degree, this story follows that pattern with a subtle difference. It is not about two individuals, but a township of people who went about their lives in an orderly manner, until a threat from an unseen source turned into a war for over a period of say, six years and beyond, that was quite dramatically to alter their lives. There are stories within stories that can be collated into specific periods and events, of local air-raids or battles that took place in different parts of the world. There are many untold stories, bearing a significant relationship with Torpoint, and sadly resulting in the death of many of its residents. Those persons named within the chapters, subscribe to a story of hardship and sacrifice, endured throughout the years of World War II. In the First World War, 101 Torpoint servicemen paid the ultimate sacrifice for King and Country. Their names are recorded in St. James's Book of Remembrance and on the Plaque affixed to the East Wall of the church. Nevertheless, the passage of time through those unforgettable years of 1939-1946 must not be forgotten, therefore within the following chapters I have strived to indicate and validate the various battles and bombings that took place where Torpoint victims, and I stress victims, perished.

Studying available records, books and newspaper articles, which I must point out due to the census applied during the war, newspapers did not print the name of a town or street where an incident had taken place. Photographs had to be screened before publication, so note should be taken of any newspaper article quoted within the text, indicates, rather than states, the name of a place reporting the situation at that period of time, and therefore can only come close to the conclusion of its name. Those individuals that actually participated, took part, or happened to be on the receiving end of bullets, shells, bombs or any other forms of munitions, have the last answer. However many are no longer with us, and memories have faded with time. Those individuals from Torpoint who took part in the home front bombings, or various battles in different parts of the world, and in some cases on the same day, formulate a jig-saw which can only be reflected upon by recording chronologically, the sequence of events that led up to the loss of a Torpoint residents' life. For example, in March 1942 5 (five) Torpoint servicemen lost their lives, 2 (two) sailors and 2 (two) soldiers in the Far East, and 1 (one) sailor in the Artic Seas. Their names are recorded in St. James's Book of Remembrance. ALL should be remembered with respect. Furthermore, in certain incidents a little bit of detective work has been employed to gather information from various books, to establish a conclusion to the timing, whereabouts and cause of death of named individuals. For every loss there is a story. Their sacrifice is a passage of Torpoint's history, which has long been forgotten. Nevertheless in 1939 it was a thriving community, as illustrated in the following extract taken from Kelly's Directory detailing its location and standing within, together with its list of traders located mainly in Fore Street and its side streets. Due to the intense bombing in the Plymouth Blitz and its overspill, some of these traders would cease to exist.

This is where this story of Torpoint begins. It was necessary to take a step back in time to cover the events during the years of the war, particularly as it became the

'People's War'.

I apologise for any errors or, miss-conceptual comments within the text that were based on facts and or, asssumptions.

[NB:Where appropriate, due to the age and clarity of copies of several documents, details have been transcribed from the originals furthermore, clarity of some photographs are also faded. Also please note that CWG within the text refers to Commonwealth War Graves].

TORPOINT
("GATEWAY TO THE WEST")
(As recorded In Kelly's 1939 Edition)
(by kind permission)

TORPOINT: A small town 2.1/2 miles west from Plymouth Station on the Great West Railway, was created an Urban District and Civil Parish from Antony Civil Parish by Local Government Board Order No. 46041, which came into operation on 1st April 1904. It is in the Bodmin Division of the county, petty sessional division of the South Division of the hundred of East County Court Division of Plymouth, Rural Deanery of East Wivelshire, Archdeaconry of Bodmin and Diocese of Truro. It was formed into a separate ecclesiastical parish in January 1873. It is on the west bank of the River called "Hamoaze," directly opposite the dockyard at Devonport. The river in this part is nearly three-quarters of a mile wide, communication with either side being by a floating steam bridge, established in 1835. Gas and electricity are available, water is supplied by the Torpoint Water Works from springs gathered at Crafthole in the Parish of Sheviock, 5.1/2 miles from Torpoint, and at Eglaroose, about 7 miles west of Torpoint. The Church of St James, in the middle of the town was erected in 1819. In 1930/35 the whole of the church, with the exception of the turret and chancel was reconstructed, it was re-opened for worship on the 20th October 1935. There is a monument in the church to Joshua Rowe esq., (d.1827), as well as to others of this family, including his son Sir Joshua Rowe C.B., Chief Justice of Jamaica. An organ was added in 1901 and two carved oak chairs were given in Memory of 2nd Lt. R. B. W. Vinter M. C. The East Window is a Memorial to C.W. Chubb esq., and the reredos (an ornamental drape) a Memorial to his Wife, there are 500 sittings. The register dates from the year 1819. The living is a perpetual curacy, annual net value £350 (with residence), in the gift to the Vicar of Antony and held since 1932 by the Rev. Bernard Steele Lowe M.A. of Oxford University who is a surrogate. There is a Congregational Chapel erected in 1810 seating 300, and a Methodist Chapel enlarged in 1909 seating 500. The Roman Catholic Church of St. Joan of Arc was erected in 1933, seating 120. The Torpoint Institute contains a large lecture room, and class and reading rooms. The Institution for the St. Germans Guardians Committee Area is about a quarter of a mile from Torpoint. There are pleasure grounds of over 12 acres rented by the council containing a bowling green, tennis courts and refreshment rooms, as well as bathing ponds and sand pits for children. There are no fair's or market's. Sir John Gawen Carew Pole Bart, and the late R.W. Roberts esq., are the principal landowners. The soil is loamy, subsoil, and slate rock. The area of the civil parish and Urban District is 975 acres. The population in 1931 was 3,975 in the civil, and 3,907 in the ecclesiastical Parish.
Post, M. O. & T. Office letters, should have Cornwall added.

TORPOINT URBAN DISTRICT COUNCIL OFFICES
York Road

Meets at the Council Offices on the first Thursday in every month, at 7.p.m.
Chairman: M. Light.
Vice Chairman F.H. Roberts
to Retire April 1939.
W. Collins, E. Martin, S. Martin, D.O. Peacock, and W. Turner
to Retire April 1940
P. P. Herod, H. E. Jago, E. J. Maddaford, W. G. Pearce, and F. H. Roberts
to Retire April 1941.
W. H. Horswell, G. Jones, A. E. Leggatt, M. Light, and W. Peach.
Officials.
(Address: Council Offices, York Road Torpoint, unless otherwise stated)
Clerk, Alfred N. F. Goodman LL.B, St Aubyn Street Devonport.
Collector, William T. Horton.
Treasurers, Lloyds Bank Ltd. Fore Street Devonport.

Medical Officer of Health, Francis P. Lauder. L. R. C. P & S. Edin., D. P. H.

Surveyor & Sanitary Inspector, Geo. Rodley. M. I. M. C. E.

COUNTY MAGISTRATES FOR THE PETTY SESSIONAL DIVISION OF THE SOUTH DIVISION OF THE HUNDRED OF EAST.

(For addresses of magistrates see complete list at the front of the book)

Boger Alnod. John - Bowhay. T.T. - Brown C.H. - Gill. Lt. Col. John Wallis. – Grenfell. Henry Osbourne. - Kittow Mrs. - Menhinick Edwin. - Oliver. Robert. - Pooley John Henry. - Price. Ms. Helena. M. - Rashleigh W.S. - Roberts Col John Debree Anderson. R.A. - Rogers. Thomas H. - Tamblyn. Thos. Cobden. – Webster. Ernest. - Weeks Arthur.

The Mayor of Saltash, the ex Mayor of Saltash (who sits at Saltash only) & the chairman of the St Germans Rural & Torpoint Urban District councilors are ex officio magistrates.
Clerk to the Magistrates is C. D. McDonald 4, Ker St. Devonport.

Petty sessions are held at the Council Chambers Torpoint, the second Tuesday in the month at 11.a.m. & Saltash the last Tuesday in the month at 10.30 a.m.

The following places are included in the petty sectional divisions:
Antony Botusfleming Maker, Millbrook, Rame, Sheviock, St. John, St, Germans, St Steven by Saltash, Torpoint, Landulph, & Lan, with St Ernay.

PUBLIC ESTABLISHMENTS

County Library Branch - Urban District Council Offices R. H. Groves Librarian
Fire Station, Albion Road.

Ministry of Labour Employment Exchange, Elm cottage Maj. W. J. Hart, Branch Manager.
Police Station, Tamar Street

Torpoint Institution, William A. Pattenden Master:-: Mrs. H. Pattenden, Matron. A. L. Davies. M.A., M. R. C. S., L.R. C. S. Medical Officer, Rev. B. S. Lowe. M.A. Acting Chaplain.
Torpoint Institute, Tamar Street, Ernest Cocks, Hon. Sec.

Water Works, William T. Horton Collector, Council Offices, York Road.

PUBLIC OFFICES

Registrar of Births, Deaths, & Marriages St. Germans District, John Morley Tamblyn (attends Monday 5 to 6 p.m. & Friday 6-7 pm.) Council Offices, York Road.

Carriers: Harry Downing to Plymouth, Stonehouse & Devonport, daily except Wednesday
&
Walter John Lee from Looe to Plymouth on Wednesday, Friday & Saturday returning same day.

Western National Omnibus Co. Ltd. Services: Torpoint to Antony & to Looe & Polperro.

Water Conveyance - Steam Ferry to Devonport every 15 minutes.

COMMERCIAL

FORE STREET

Street	Description	Tel.
1 Fore st	Nodder Thos. Ernest D. draper	T.N 57
1a Fore st	Williams Bertie confctr.	
2 Fore st	Gidley & Wilcox Sol .(attend 2.30 –5. p.m.)	
2 Fore st	Hancock Wilfred Undertaker.	
3 Fore st	Stimpson Wlm. Bootmender	
4 Fore st	O' Gorman Arthur . E.	
6 Fore st	Lt.W.J.Griffin.R.NShipwright	
7 Fore st	Electric Power Co.	T.N 40
8 Fore st	Electric Power Co.	T.N 40
9 Fore st	Redding Hardware Stores	
10 Fore st	Standard Inn (Saml. Emery Brown)	
11 Fore st	East Wine & Spirit Stores (Sml. Jones propr.)	T.N 32
13 Fore st	Harrison Wm. Boot repr.	
14 Fore st	Smith Charles shoe maker	
16 Fore st	Gosling's Stores grocers	T.N 23
17 Fore st	Jubilee Inn (Saml.Rosevearse)	
18 Fore st	Slee's Butcher	T.N 56
18 Fore st	Williams Thos. hairdresser	
19 Fore st	Bradford Fearnley Jn. Dairy	
20 Fore st	Toms Wm. Jn hairdressr	T.N 71
21 Fore st	Jory Hugh. Dist. Chemist	T.N 51
22 Fore st	Gliddon Fredk. Albt. Butcher	T.N 23
23 Fore st	Vinton Wm. grocer	
24 Fore st	Tyler Alfd J hairdresser	
25 Fore st	Browning Mary (Miss) knitting wool repository	
27 Fore st	Morgan Wm. H. motor garage.	
29 Fore st	Torpoint Liberal Society (Fredk Roberts sec)	
	Downing Harry carrier Fore St.	
37 Fore st	King's Arms P.H. (Mrs. Margt. E Gibbs).	
39 Fore st	Leach. Willm. H. (H.W.J C Lockyer man)	T.N 19
40 Fore st	Banks Eliz. (Mrs.) grocer.	
43 Fore st	Parker. Albt. A. J..	
46 Fore st	King Enst. J. butcher	T.N 14
47 Fore st	Granger J. & Son bakers	T.N 28
48 Fore st	Wheeler's Hotel (Geo. A Crinks prop.)	T.N 16
49 Fore st	Jago Cecil Oliver baker	
50 Fore st	Plymouth Mutual Co-operative & Industrial Society Ltd	T.N 29
51 Fore st	Davis Mrs. Fishmonger	T.N 76
52 Fore st	Medlin Wallace .Jas. dairyman.	
53 Fore st	Plymouth Mutual Co-operative & Industrial Society Ltd. & Harvey st.	
54 Fore st	Barclays Bank Ltd. (sub branch to Devonport) (F. G. Lyon Man.)	
55 Fore st	Crowte Maurice Wm. W/less eng	T.N 61
56 Fore st	Haydon Thos F. draper	T.N 7
57 Fore st	Lloyds Bank Ltd. (branch)	
58 Fore st	Hacker Mary (Mrs.)fried fish dlr.	
59 Fore st	Kingdom Geo. fruitr.	
60 Fore st	Nodder Jas Harold fruitr	T.N 75
60 Fore st	Fox-Taylor Jn. B.D.S. L'pool, dental surgn Ollis W.S. L.D.S. dental surgn. (attends).	
62 Fore st	Evans Iris	
63 Fore st	Pengelly Albt.	
64 Fore st	Stevens Alfd. R. shopkeeper	
65 Fore st	Greenaway Arth.Edwin boot rep	
66 Fore st	Worms Geo. Vivian newsagt.	
71 Fore st	Vigus Rd. fruitr	T.N 95
75 Fore st	Post Office Sheppard. Mrs. E. Sub Postmist	

TAMAR STREET

Street	Description	Tel.
2 Tamar st.	Fras. E. drapers	
3 Tamar st	Hoskins J taxi proprietors	
5 Tamar st	Hoskins J.& Son radio dealers	T.N 13
6 Tamar st	Parkins Edith (Mrs.) fruitr	T.N 35
8 Tamar st	Norman Alice J. (Miss) café	
	Torpoint Institute (Ernest Cocks hon sec)	

ELLIOT SQUARE

Street	Description	Tel.
1 Elliot sq	Andrews Jn shopkeeper	
2 Elliot sq	Blackler Ernest newsagt	T.N 34
3 Elliot sq	Western National Omnibus Co. Ltd.	T.N 47
5 Elliot sq	Norsworthy Frank shkp.	

BEATRICE TERRACE

Street	Description	Tel.
1 Beatrice ter	Eustace M. W. (Mrs.) confectr	
7 Beatrice ter	Drew Amy (Mrs.) shopkpr	
8/11 Beatrice ter	Devonshire Arthur, motor garage	T.N 2

ANTONY ROAD

Street	Description	Tel.
3 Clarence Pl	Smith Doris. (Miss) A.L.C.M. teacher of music.	
Chalk's Garage	(H. Redwood proprietor) Motor engr. Antony rd	T.N 58
	Peoples Palace- Regal Cinema Edward Ives. Proptr.	
	Torpoint & District Comrades & United Services Club (Geo. H. Jones hon. sec.)	
	Webster Geo. F motor proprietor. Antony rd.	T.N 24

CLARENCE ROAD

Street	Description	Tel.
40 Clarence rd.	Shepperd Percy. D, shopkpr	
58 Clarence rd.	Blake Irene (Miss) A.T.C.L. teacher of music (Isaac Cornish sec) 26 Victoria st.	
65 Clarence rd. & Antony	Ancient Order of s (Wolsdom No 9,099) (F.W. Woodhouse sec) No 9,545)	
Clarence rd	Sleeman Arthur bldr	

OTHER ESTABLISHMENTS

Name	Description	Street	Tel.

Andrews Jn. fried fish shop Harvey st.
Beaver Freda. (Mrs.) shpkpr. 2 Florence ter.
Bowden S. 3 Navy ter.
Davies Arthur Llewellyn M.A. , M.R.C.S.,
L R.C.P physcn. & surgn.& medical officer
to the Institution, St. Germans area,
East Guardians Committee
& examining factory surgn. 1 Carlton ter
Horton William. rate collector.
Torpoint Urban District
Council Offices York rd. T.N 10
Jolliff Elsie (Mrs.) district nurse 4 Gordon ter.
Jones Fredk, Jn. Felix. L.M.S.S.A.Lond
physcn & surgn. Port Rouge T.N 4
Lean Wltr. L.D.S.Eng. Dental surgn.
(attends Thurs10.am. to 8 pm) 6 Coldstream ter.
Menhencott. Geo. Arth. shopkpr Albion rd.
Ministry of Labour Employment Exchange
(Maj. W.J. Hart .branch man.) Elm cott.
Mitchell Minnie (Mrs.) grocer 12 Merrifield ter North rd.
Morris Harold W. newsagt 16 Ormond ter.
National Deposit (Approved) Friendly Soc.
(H .J. Wagg sec.) 27 Liscawn ter.
Oddfellows Independent Order of
Manchester Unity – Pride of Lodge No. 4083
(F.W. Short – Sec.) 8 Uplands ter. T.N. 93

Parkin Geo. Laity. Dairy farmer Carbeile T.N 74
Paul Chas. Undertaker 5 Carew ter.
St. Johns Ambulance Brigade
(C Humphreson supt.) Union rd.
Sleep Leslie decrtr. 2 King st.
Stimpson Wm. R. boot repr. Ferry st.
Templars' Hall (W.A. Collins sec)
.Torpoint (The) Coal & Gas Co Ltd.
(H.R. Anderson sec & mangr) Ferry st.
Torpoint and District Unionist Club Ltd.
(W. A. Lowings Sec) Antony rd.
Torpoint & District General Supplies,
Agricultural, builders, & coal & coke
Merchants. Carew wharf. T.N 36
Torpoint Meat Supply (H. J Hamlin proptr)
Butchers 16 Victoria st
Torpoint Water Works (Wm. Horton collector)
Council Office York rd.
Watts Mary (Miss) L. L C.M., AL. C.M.,
Teacher of music 21 The Crescent
Webb Fredr. Chas. Coal mer. Barossa pl.
Weighill Allan Andrews shopkpr 9 Hillsborough ter.
Williams Dorothy (Miss) district nurse.
5 Coldstream ter.
Woodhouse & Son plumbers 8 The Crescent T.N 78
Worth Jn. Dairyman 15 Ormond ter.

Below is a list of Telephone numbers that were listed in the GPO Telephone Red Book for the South West Region March/April 1939. That identifies the number of Business/Residents that had line communication installed (note the numbering system).

GENERAL POST OFFICE
Telephone numbers

Name	Tel. No.	
AMBULANCE		
Ambulance Service (St. Johns Ambulance Assn)		
Torpoint District	Torpoint	69
Antony Call off	Torpoint	67
Antony Estate	Torpoint	60
Atkins, W.B.G. OBE Old vege Antony	Torpoint	41x4
Automobile Association Roadside Telephone.		
Rytha Fork	St Germans	246
Baker. B,A, 13 Wellington st	Torpoint	96
Barclays Bank		
54 Fore st	Torpoint	65
Barker Mrs. Ben, Minnadhu cott	Millbrook	96
Barker, Henry C.D. (Engr.-Captain Retd.)		
Cliff Ho. Kingsand	Millbrook	78
Bate. Miss. E. 4 Beechfield	Downderry	43
Benskin Rev. B.W. MA.		
The Rectory St John	Millbrook	34
Bersey A.W. Cattle Del.		
Up on the hill	Downderry	234
Bersey W. Farmr. Manor farm	Millbrook	48
Bersey. W.C. Farmr. Minard Polbathic	Downderry	37
Cockler E. Nwsagt. 2 Elliot sq	Torpoint	34
Boger. A..J. Woolston Antony	Millbrook	213
Bounsall. S. Kelvin ho. Cawsands	Millbrook	71
Bradford F.J. Dairyman 19 Fore st	Torpoint	72
Brittan A. Island cott. Kingsand Cawsand	Millbrook	69
Broad N. E. Agricultural .Mcht	Downderry	55
Broad R. Clift Farm Antony	Torpoint	41x5
Broad W. S. Motrs. Bay cott	Downderry	7
Broom Lt. A. 43 st	Torpoint	12
Busbridge. C.E.G. Clifflands	Downderry	26
Carne Rex. G. Rame Barton Cawsand	Millbrook	305
Carne Roy. Cross Park farm Cawsand	Millbrook	306
Carter. E.H. Whitehall Wilcove	Torpoint	94
Cawsand Post Office	Millbrook	23
Chalk's Garage	Torpoint	58
COASTGUARD H.M:-		
Coastguard Stations.		
Rame Head	Millbrook	39
Cole . A. Scarsden farm	Torpoint	41x6
Coleman A. E. Wentworthy	Downderry	36
Collier. E. J.Woodside cott. Cawsand	Millbrook	289
Collings A.C. 5 Road	Torpoint	80
Collings C..G.W. Bldrs Island ho	Millbrook	58
Collins W.C. Bldr & Undtkr	Torpoint	102
COUNTY COUNCIL-		

Name	Tel. No.	
Children's Home Anderton	Millbrook	40
Ferry Office	Torpoint	33
Poor Law Institutions.		
Torpoint	Torpoint	25
Electric Power Co.		
Torpoint 8 Fore st	Torpoint	40
Ditto	Torpoint	30
Cousins Miss C.E Forder Rame Cawsand	Millbrook	79
Crabb E. Treggelly Antony	Torpoint	97
Cremyll Ferry. Cremyll Plymouth	Millbrook	12
Crinks G.A. Wheelers Htl	Torpoint	16
Criterion Hotel & Tea Lounge Cawsand	Millbrook	44
Crowte M. Wireless Dir. 55 fore st	Torpoint	61
Currie Mrs. A. Coombe end Cawsand	Millbrook	76
Daniel W.J.&S Blds. Hardware Strs	Downderry	57
Davies Dr. A. L.I. Physn, Srgn.1 Carlton vls.	Torpoint	15
Dent J.H. Uplands North rd	Torpoint	55
Devonshire's A.A Motrs. 8 Beatrice ter	Torpoint	2
Devonshire R. C. 21 rd	Torpoint	3
Dobson C.J. Warleigh	Downderry	58
Down H.L West st	Millbrook	43
Down H.L Dairy Frmr Tregonhawke	Millbrook	55
Downing W. Gen Carrier 7Chapel row	Torpoint	50
Driscall Bros Irmgrs. West st	Millbrook	16
Driscall H. H. Plmbr. West st	Millbrook	315
Driscall T. W. Belle Vue Blindwell	Millbrook	86
Eddystone Hotel Seaton beach	Downderry	21
Edgecumbe R. S. No 1Flat Cawsand	Millbrook	36
Edwards Nelson Commercial Hotel	Millbrook	53
Ekins Cannon. H.C.W.		
Rame Rectory Cawsand	Millbrook	14
Elliot Miss W.M. Wide Sea ho	Downderry	48
Elworthy Fred. Grcr. 1 Fore st	Millbrook	25
Eteson Fred. Ship Inn Cawsand	Millbrook	107
Eustace E.E. Confctur. 1 Beatrice ter	Torpoint	54
Fawcett Mrs. G.M. Cawsand pk. Cawsand	Millbrook	100
FIRE STATION –		
Torpoint	Torpoint	20
Fox G. R. Seaton	Downderry	38
Frazer Mrs. G. The Grey House Cawsand	Millbrook	321
Furze Miss A. Algoma The Green	Millbrook	311
Gardner C. W. Tremorhan	Downderry	3
Giles F.W. Frmr. Maker farm Maker Plymouth	Millbrook	35
Gilbespy Payr -Captain J.W.E. Maryfield cott	Torpoint	22
Gillespie Col. R. St. J.C.I.E. O.B.E.		
Pato ho. Wilcove	Torpoint	99

Name	Exchange	No.
Gliddon F. A. Meat Purveyor 22 Fore st	Torpoint	53
Goldsmith Lieut. F.R.N. Hillside Seaton	Downderry	41
Goslings Stores Grcrs. 10 Fore st	Torpoint	23
Granger A. Bkr. 47 Fore st	Torpoint	28
Gregory E.F. Forda Cawsand	Millbrook	93
Griffin Shiprwright-Lieut. W.J. R.N. 6 Fore st	Torpoint	103
Haddy E.S. Anderton ho. nr. Plymouth	Millbrook	3
Haddy E.S. & Son Garage Proprs.		
Kingsand Cawsand	Millbrook	13
Hancock Mrs. E.C. Cawsand ho. Cawsand	Millbrook	83
Harding A.H. Devlock farm	Downderry	59
Harper Rev. C.J. Summer court	Downderry	54
Haydon T.F. Drpr. 56 Fore st	Torpoint	7
Heath F.T. Frt, Grwr. Seaton vily. Gdns	Downderry	11
Heath J. P. Rock cott	Downderry	18
Henwood A. B. Prven. Mcht. 29 West st	Millbrook	62
Herbert Rev. S. Maker vergo		
Mt. Edgecumbe Nr. Plymouth	Millbrook	94
Hill A.E. Bkr. Grcr.		
Fore st. Kingsand Cawsand	Millbrook	7
Hill F.R. 2 Coryton villas	Torpoint	11
Hinton J.A. Devonport Inn Kingsand	Millbrook	90
Honey H. Wringford fm. Rame Cawsand	Millbrook	87
Honey M. Nwsagt. Fore st Kingsand Cawsand	Millbrook	22
Hoskin E. J. Car Hire Square Cawsand	Millbrook	41
Hoskin R.B. Horson fm	Torpoint	41x5
Hoskin Stephen Frmr. Home fm	Torpoint	9
Hoskin T. A. Hendra St. Grmns	Downderry	25
Hoskins E. Sub-Postmistress PO	Torpoint	5
Hoskins J & Son Taxis st	Torpoint	13
Humphrey J. Fcy. Goods PO Cawsand	Millbrook	23
Hutchings H. Frmr. Borough farm	Torpoint	26
Jones Felix Physn. Srgn. Port Rouge	Torpoint	4
Jones Rev. Harold J. Parsonage ho	Downderry	252
Jones S. East Wines & Spirit Store	Torpoint	32
Jordan Hugh Dspng. Chemst. 21 Fore st	Torpoint	51
Jordan R. Hay Farm Antony	Torpoint	79
King E. J. Btch. 46 Fore st	Torpoint	14
Kneebone Miss. B. 7 Waterloo st	Torpoint	63
LABOUR, MINISTRY OF –		
Employment Exchange		
Elm cott	Torpoint	39
Langdon Engr Lt. Cmdr. J. B. Private Hotel		
The Woodland Cawsand	Millbrook	18
Lawson –Smith M. Lyner villa Antony	Torpoint	31
Lebour Miss M. V. Kean hill. Cawsand	Millbrook	103
Lock A.E. J. Wheelwright-Uundtkr.		
Lyner villa Antony rd	Torpoint	41x1
Lind L. M. Bungalow Tea ho.		
Treganhawke cliff	Millbrook	75
Lloyds Bank Limited.		
Fore st	Torpoint	19
Locke R Freathy bungalow	Millbrook	11
Lovesgrove F. E Bkr. 8 West st	Millbrook	6
Lowe Rev. Bernard. The Vicarage	Torpoint	18
Lyne A. E. Frmr. Innesworke Barton	Millbrook	38
McGilkdowny Miss. E.M.		
The Balcony Cawsand	Millbrook	92
Macnair- Smith Col. J. Mount Brionl	Downderry	4
Maddever R. Trelay Antony	Torpoint	41x3
Maker Camp		
(Plymouth Ju.venile Council)	Millbrook	70
Marina Café Cawsand Nr. Plymouth	Millbrook	85
Mashford Bros.		
Shipbldr. yard Cremyll Plymouth	Millbrook	33
Masters Miss. D.		
The Glass ho. Kingsand nr Plymouth	Millbrook	29
Matthews A. W. Btchr.. The Parade	Millbrook	318
Matthews E P. Grcr. Square	Millbrook	57
Matthews H.T. Blerrick Antony Torpoint	Millbrook	97
Maunder J. H. Bldng Contr. Victoria st	Torpoint	27
Miles Capt. R. T. R.N. Trevol ho	Torpoint	91
Millbrook Steamboat & Trading Co. Ltd	Millbrook	2
Miller Mrs.F.F.M. Derry ho	Downderry	49
Mitchell F.W. Carrier. 1 Terrace	Downderry	2
Mount Edgecumbe Estate Office Plymouth	Millbrook	30
Mount Edgecumbe Ho. (Butler),		
Mount Edgecumbe Plymouth	Millbrook	56
Mount Edgecumbe Kitchen Gdns. Plymouth.	Millbrook	72
Mullen J. Hillcrest Seaton	Downderry	33
Nancarrow A. Gwadalam		
The Green Kingsand	Millbrook	312
Nelson Pay -Capt. D. H.		
Sunnyside Cawsand	Millbrook	314
Newcombe W. Devon & htl	Millbrook	320
Nodder J. H. Gngrcr. 60 Fore st	Torpoint	75
Nodder T. E. D. 1 Fore st	Torpoint	57
Norgate R. C. H. Mdel Prctner.		
The Main ho Nelson st	Torpoint	38
Northcott Lt-Col. W. A. E.		
The Cabin Cawsand	Millbrook	274
OFFICERS MESS-		
Tregantle	Millbrook	210
Page A. C. Haulage Contr. Antony	Torpoint	66
Palmer & Parsloe Motr. Engrs.		
Downderry Garage	Downderry	14
Parken G. I. Fmr. Carbeile farm	Torpoint	74
Parsloe E. A.	Downderry	19
Peake Mrs. Ronald Downderry lodge	Downderry	17
Pearce S. W. Café Seaton fm	Downderry	12
Pienlger O. M. Dahinda Anderton Plymouth	Millbrook	24
Perkin W.S. Treliddon	Downderry	27
Perkins E. A. Frtrs First 6 st	Torpoint	35
Phillips Mrs. K. 1 Osbourne villas	Millbrook	322
PLYMOUTH CO-OPERATIVE SOCIETY Ltd.		
Grocery & Butchery		
Millbrook	Millbrook	19
Torpoint	Torpoint	29
Pole Carew Miss. F. J. Maryfield ho	Torpoint	62
Pole Sir. J. G. Carew Antony ho	Torpoint	6
County Constabulary-		
Antony	Torpoint	86
Kingsand Cawsand	Millbrook	31
Millbrook	Millbrook	8
Torpoint	Torpoint	20
Priest W.H.J. Cabin	Downderry	8
Prowse Mrs. M.J.T. P.O. St. Johns	Millbrook	68
Redding A.W. Inmgr. 9 Fore st	Torpoint	77
Rendle Lt-Comr.. W.W.B. R.N. (Retd.)	Downderry	56
Reynolds W.. J. Admiralty Contrs.		
Loch Lomond	Torpoint	8
Richards A. Rose cott. Greenlands	Millbrook	37
Richards C.D. J. Chums cott. Freathy	Millbrook	73
Ridge-Jones I. Physn. Srgs.		
The Cleave Kingsand Cawsand.	Millbrook	9
Roberts C.H. Coombe Park	Torpoint	70
Roberts J.W. 2 North Hill ter	Torpoint	44
Rogers S.G. Pothorn Cove Cawsand	Millbrook	66
Roseveare T.S. Frmr. W. Antony farm	Torpoint	52
Rundle J.R. Higher Tregantle farm Torpoint	Millbrook	45
St. Johns Ambulance Association		
(Torpoint Section) 16 Clarence rd	Torpoint	69
St. Johns Call Office	Millbrook	68
St. Margaret's Home of Rest.		
Kingsand Cawsand	Millbrook	110
Sea View Hotel	Downderry	10
Sharman John. C. Grower Westleigh	Downderry	42
Short F. W. 8 Upland ter	Torpoint	93
Skinner F.J & Son Ltd. Parade garage	Millbrook	5
Slee's Purveyors		
8 fore st	Torpoint	56
Smith P. Garrett st Cawsand	Millbrook	277
Sneyd G.S. Watch ho	Downderry	5
Sparks M.V.3 The Battery Cawsand	Millbrook	259
Spoor Drs. W.H. & S. Medical Practns		
Oak cott	Downderry	13
Staple W.G. Genl..Dlr. Parade	Millbrook	46
Swain F.M. Freathy Huts Hire Whitsands	Millbrook	50
Tapper W. D. Wireless Dlr.		
Garrett st. Cawsand	Millbrook	91
TERRITORIAL ARMY (DEVONSHIRE)		
4TH. Coy Devon & Royal Engineers		
Church ho	Torpoint	49
Thompson Mrs. W.I. Appledore	Downderry	240
Toms A. Dairy	Downderry	46
Toms W.J. Ladies Hairdrsr. 20 Fore st	Torpoint	71
Torpoint Call Office PO	Torpoint	5
Torpoint Coal & Gas Co. Ltd	Torpoint	64
Torpoint & District General Supplies		
Gen. Mchts. Carew whf	Torpoint	36
TORPOINT URBAN DISTRICT COUNCIL		
Council offices Buller rd	Torpoint	10
Toys Major. A. M. 2 Anderton villas Anderton	Millbrook	81
Tregallas Alfred. Triffle farm	Downderry	24
Trethowan N Grcr Dairy		
Market st. Kingsand Cawsand	Millbrook	65
Treverrow W. 18 Tremayne ter	Torpoint	73
Ridney A.C	Downderry	44
E. Withue Barton	Millbrook	317
Vann Rev. A.G. S. Vicarage Maryfield	Torpoint	98
Vigus R. J. Gngrcr 71 Fore st	Torpoint	95
Waller D.D. Keti Kaa Rame Cawsand	Millbrook	4
Warde R.W Btchr	Downderry	53
Watson W.H. Edgecumbe Arms Hotel		
Cremyll Plymouth	Millbrook	99
Watts J.F. Hounster farm	Millbrook	319
Webster G. F. Motr. Engr.		
Garage		
Antony Road.	Torpoint	24
Wenmoth D.T. Chmst. The Stores	Downderry	32
West A./ C. Dodbrook ho	Millbrook	20
West M. C. Stone fam	Millbrook	67
West S.R. Btchr. 9 West st	Millbrook	42
Western Counties Brick Co. Ltd. Southdown	Millbrook	17
Western National Omnibus Co. Ltd.		
8 Elliot sq.	Torpoint	47
Wevell J.B. Cair	Downderry	16
White Mrs. G. Kenwood Cawsand Plymouth	Millbrook	84
Whitsand Bay Hotel Ltd Crafthole	Millbrook	27
Wilcocks R.K. Firliegh Merifield	Torpoint	90
Wilcocks T. Beechfield Cawsand	Millbrook	63
Williams Mrs. E. Ring o' Bells Antony rd	Torpoint	41x4
Williams Capt. F.McClure		
Wood park Anderton	Millbrook	26
Wilton J.P. Penmillard Rame Cawsand	Millbrook	82
Woodhouse S.J. Plmbr. Beacon ho		
The Crescent	Torpoint	78
Worth S. J. & Son Boats Hire		
88 Moleworth terr	Millbrook	51
Young Rev. Gilbert C.E. Millbrook Vicarage	Millbrook	

As a point of interest, in March 1939 the above list was issued by the General Post Office (GPO). It records the number of telephones in use as approximately 240 rental telephones, six months later there might have been a few more added to the above list. Communication during the period of the war, was more by 'word of mouth' than by telegraphic cable means, obviously it caused somewhat of a problem when information was passed on from one person to another and so on. The original message must have been slightly distorted, or greatly exaggerated, by the time it reached the very last person?

The Regional Telephone exchange was located in Plymouth, and the above listed numbers have been extracted from a GPO Telephone List covering the Plymouth Exchange system. This entailed some 45 pages of user numbers and in comparison to the modern day telephone list, is just a mere fraction of the current list of user numbers. The Torpoint Telephone Exchange was managed by the Chadwick's at Number 3 Wellington Street (as quoted by Cynthia Sheppard), another Telephonist was Mrs. Matilda Crocker (as stated by her son Gordon Crocker).

In the above list of telephone recipients addresses and throughout the following chapters, certain Terraces are mentioned as located in the residential part of the town. After the war these names were phased out, but have been reverted to the name of a street or road where they still stand, therefore, it might be of interest as to where these Terraces were located.

Antony Road :		Clarence Place (opposite Sparrows Park)
	L.H. side towards Antony:	Ormond - Beatrice – Grosvenor Terrace's
	R. H. side " "	Hillsboro - The Cresent - Monpellier,
North Road:	L.H. side:	North Mill - Moresworth - Trelawney – Merrifield Terrace's.
	R. H. side:	Uplands - Florence Terrace's.
	(Carbeile end).	Mt. Edgecombe Terraces
Modder Road:		Moor View Terrace.
Wellington / Waterloo Street :		Cambridge Terrace.- opposite Cambridge Fields was Green Banks (Now St James Surgery)
Nelson Street	L.H.side far end:	Coldstream Terrace.
Barossa Road:	R.H. side:	Arthur Terrace
Union Road/ Now Marine Drive;		
	L.H. side:	Navy Terrace.
	R.H. side:	Cremyll - Harbour View - Alexander Terrace's. Then : the Public Institute. (Old Poor House)
Lower Carbeile	L.H. side:	Chapeldown - Gordon Terrace's (opposite North Road)
	R.H. side:	Pembroke Terrace,
York Road from North Road		
	L.H side:	Coryton Terrace
	R.H. side:	Tremayne Terrace.
Buller Road	L.H.side:	Pole - Littleton Terrace's.
	R.H side:	Cowen Terrace.
Sconner Road:	L.H. side	Waverlley Terrace.
	R.H side	Killarney Terrace.

The Torpoint UDC Chairperson's throughout the war were:

1939/40	Mr. Frederick Roberts
1940/42	Mr. D.B. Peacock
1942/44	Mr. H.B. Jago
1944/45	Mr. D.B. Peacock

Other units were:

Special Police:	Special Sgt. Elliott - Mr. G. Row - Mr. William Houghton – Mr. W. Toms – Mr. William Crop - Mr. Ernie Eustace – Mr. Percy Herold
ARP. Post:	Mr. D. Mallet - Mr. C. Paul
First Aid Post:	Mr. Eddy - Mr. Major - Mrs. Swann
Ambulace Drivers:	Mr. Henry Banks -- Mr. Frank Bolton - Mr. Bowden – Mr. Jack Fisher - Mr. Frank Downing - Mr. Brian Hobbs – Mr. Mahoney.- Mr. Timms
Ferry:	Mr. G. Mills - Mr. Mahoney

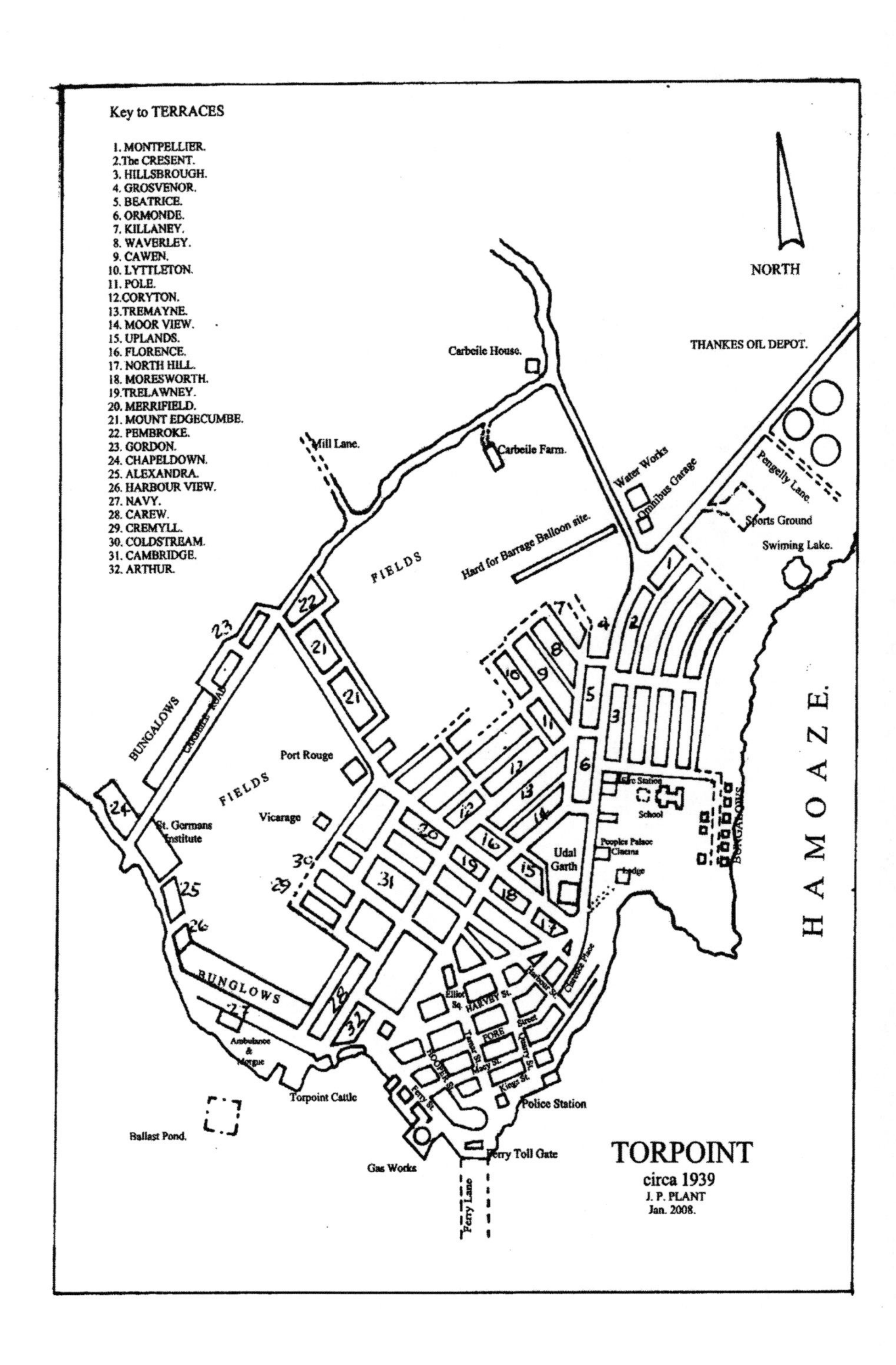
Key to TERRACES
1. MONTPELLIER.
2.The CRESENT.
3. HILLSBROUGH.
4. GROSVENOR.
5. BEATRICE.
6. ORMONDE.
7. KILLANEY.
8. WAVERLEY.
9. CAWEN.
10. LYTTLETON.
11. POLE.
12.CORYTON.
13.TREMAYNE.
14. MOOR VIEW.
15. UPLANDS.
16. FLORENCE.
17. NORTH HILL.
18. MORESWORTH.
19.TRELAWNEY.
20. MERRIFIELD.
21. MOUNT EDGECUMBE.
22. PEMBROKE.
23. GORDON.
24. CHAPELDOWN.
25. ALEXANDRA.
26. HARBOUR VIEW.
27. NAVY.
28. CAREW.
29. CREMYLL.
30. COLDSTREAM.
31. CAMBRIDGE.
32. ARTHUR.
NORTH
THANKES OIL DEPOT.
Carbeile House.
Mill Lane.
Carbeile Farm.
Water Works
Omnibus Garage
Pengelly Lane
Sports Ground
Swiming Lake.
Hard for Barrage Balloon site.
FIELDS
BUNGALOWS
Port Rouge
FIELDS
Vicarage
St. Germans Institute
School
Udal Garth
Peoples Palace Cinema
Lodge
BUNGALOWS
HAMOAZE.
BUNGLOWS
Elliot Sq.
HARVEY St.
Harbour St.
Clarence Place
FORE Street
Tamar St.
Quarry St.
HOOPER St.
Macey St.
Kings St.
Ambulance & Morgue
Torpoint Cattle
Ferry St.
Police Station
Ballast Pond.
Ferry Toll Gate
Gas Works
Ferry Lane
TORPOINT
circa 1939
J. P. PLANT
Jan. 2008.

Torpoint's Entertainment.

Motion Pictures at the Peoples Palace Regal (The Rat Pit) now know as 'The Garden'. This local cinema was one of a chain of cinemas under the control of a Mr. Taylor who owned quite a few throughout the south west. During the war the Manager of the Regal was a Mr. Johnston, assisted by his wife. The Ticket Lady and Usherette was Miss Cynthia Sheppard. The sequence of film shows were run twice daily, Monday/Tuesday/Wednesday, then the programme changed to a new film for Thursday, Friday and Saturday. The cinema was closed on Sunday.

The cost of entry was 1/- front row seats, 1/9p middle row seats and 2/3p for the rear seats. There was an interval during which, I understand, ice cream was sold. The seats were not very comfortable, some had springs coming through the threadbare fabric and I am informed that some were just wooden tip up seats. However the entertainment that was provided on the silver screen was enjoyed by all patrons, except when the film broke down, then there was plenty of hissing, booing, and jeering going on until the film was repaired and restarted, much to the satisfaction of the paying customers.

Films with movies stars such a Victor Mature, Betty Grable, John Wayne, Humphrey Bogart, Ronald Reagan, Charlie Chaplin, The Marx Brothers, Laurel & Hardy, George Formby, Arthur Askey, Will Hay, Tommy Trinder, Noel Coward, Michael Redgrave, John Mills, Celia Johnson, Trevor Howerd along with many more of that period, and not forgetting the Pathe News films keeping everyone up to date with what was going on in the outside world. A list of films that might have been shown is:
Gone with the Wind - Stage Coach - Wizard of Oz - The Grapes of Wrath –
Mr. Smith Goes to Washington - Rebecca - His Girl Friday – The Philadelphia Story - Down Argentina Way - Tin Pan Alley - The Shanghai Gesture - Citizen Cane –
The Maltese Falcon - Knite Rockin All American - Yank in the RAF –
Kings Row - The Big Shot - Suspicion - Moon Over Miami - I Wake Up Screaming – Casablanca - Sweet Rosie O'Grady - Song of the Island - Footlight Serenade - Hellcats of the Navy - The Day of Wrath – A Guy Named Joe - Bedtime for Bonzo - Shadow of a Doubt - Coney Island - Spellbound - Springtime in the Rockies - Minister of Fear - Brief Encounter - To Have and Not Have - The Woman in the Window - Pin Up Girl –Scarlet Street - Diamond Horseshoe - and many others.

[Authors Note: The film 'In Which We Serve.' -
Some scenes were filmed at HMS *Raleigh.*]

also

The following exert is a recollection of what most school children experienced going to the Saturday Picture Show for Children and highlights the enthusiasm of that time as related by:]

Mr. Norman Beaver MBE. born in No. 1 Trelauney Terrace, Torpoint on the 20th Sept. 1928, son of Mr. Herbert Henry & Mrs. Edith Olive Beaver, recalls in 1939:

I joined the St. John Ambulance Cadets at Albion Road School. Although the Cadet Superintendent had been called to the colours, the division was still functioning, and I was dreaming of being an Ambulance Driver.

As my home town was Torpoint, the Cinema is also memorable. It was re-opened sometime during the pre-war years. One could always be sure of seeing the films as the floor angle was steep and one could easily look over the head of the person in front.

During the war it was used on a Sunday evening as a Concert Hall, this was on the occasions when we were urged to save money for Warship Week or, buy a Spitfire Week. It was packed to capacity and although there was a war on, it was a first class show with local talent and helped by service people stationed in the area.

As a family we used this place of entertainment throughout the war years. After the war the cinema sported a "Commissionaire" who wore a green uniform with medals and all the regalia that went with it. Again we had two films and news plus adverts, all for a shilling or one and nine.

The Millbrook Kinema:

I will always have fond memories of the cinema in Millbrook. It was indeed the first "Pictures" I was allowed to go to on my own. Being 9 years old at the time, it was quite something to buy one penny's worth of sweets and be the carrier of a twelve sided three penny bit, which was the price of a show that many children in the village of Millbrook looked forward to on Saturday afternoon.

The cinema was situated in the main street (West Street opposite Rosson's Barbers shop). It was, as I remember, the old Liberal Hall which was used solely as a Picture House on Wednesday and Saturday Evening's, with a Matinee on Saturday afternoon. The word Kinema was to be seen on the end of the building facing West Street.

The inside consisted of a hall with the screen at one end and a stage at the other which had real cinema seats and were of course the most expensive. The other seats were ordinary chairs and I would estimate the place held about 100 patrons.

The business was run buy a family called Strutt. And Mrs. Strutt was the person in charge. On a Saturday Matinee she would position herself In front of the screen (after collecting our three penny in a biscuit tin), and call all us children to order. She would clap her hands and warn us that if we did not stop talking she would not show the picture!! Well that was enough for us all to settle down. Mrs. Strutt would then signal to "Ronnie" who was the projectionist, to start, and if we should dare show excitement she would shout to Ronnie to stop the film and we would have the rough edge of her tongue.

One of the most exhilarating parts of the show was the serial "Jungle Jim". This was most sought after, some weeks it would not be shown, it must have got lost in the system, and to us children it was a disaster. There were two films and the news, no adverts, but it was wonderful show and not to be missed

ooOoo

Other forms of entertainment:

The Institute located in Tamar Street was the place to go to attend meetings, dances, meet friends and generally enjoy oneself. However during the bombing raids of 1941 the Institute was bombed and partially demolished. A better example of the type of entertainment that was provided later, and detailed in the Torpoint 'Wings For Victory' Programme. The main features were held in Torpoint beginning on Saturday May 22nd. Some details as follows:

Opening Day	3.00 pm.	Parade of various branches of the services headed by the Band of HMS. Raleigh .	
Opening Ball	7.00 pm.	Council Chambers; Music by the RAF Orchetra.	
Sun. 23rd:	3.00.pm.	Regal Cinema; Concert by the Royal Marines Plymouth.	
	6.30. pm.	Service at Parish Church.	
Mon. 24th.	6.00. pm.	Council Hall.	W.V.S. Dance
Tue. 25th.	2.30. pm.	Council Hall.	Co-op Society Guild Whist Drive .
	6.00.pm.	Council Hall.	Co-op Society Guild Dance
Wed. 26th.	2.30. pm.	Church House.	British Legion Whist Drive.
	7.30. pm.	Council Hall.	British Legion Dance
Thur. 27th.	7.30. pm.	Council Hall.	Services Concert
Fri. 28th.	2.30. pm.	Church House.	Civil Defence Whist Drive
	7.00.pm.	Council Hall.	Civil Defence Dance
Sat. 29th.	3.00.pm.	Fancy Dress.	Carnival and Parade.
Final Ball	7.30.pm.	Council Hall	Council Hall.Metro Dance Band.

Other similar entertainments were staged throughout the week at different parishes for different monetary Targets

Millbrook	Target £5, 000.
Maker & Rame	Target £5, 000.
Antony	Target £2, 000.
Sheviock	Target £2, 000.
Downderry & Seaton.	Target £3,000.
Hessenford	Target unknown.

Whether the full Target of £40,000. was ever met is not known. But possibly other similar entertainments that were staged throughout the years of the War did swell the kitty? Thus Torpoint did possibly achieve its Target

1939
YEAR 1

PREPARATION FOR WAR.

Torpoint was "The Gateway To The West". It was a thriving small town with a nucleus of Cornish folk, born and bred to the way of the seas. This included a strong work force of "Dockyardees" working in the Royal Devonport Dockyard who traveled to and from Devonport on the Torpoint Ferries. Nearly all were employed in various shipbuilding trades dating back before King Charles I, however the surrounding urban area of Torpoint was vastly rural and under the control of the **Torpoint Urban District Council**. Throughout the late twenties, un-employment in Great Britain was at its highest - remember the Jarrow March by the Miners? - nevertheless, Britain wasn't the only country suffering during the depression. Germany, led by of the Third Reich Field Marshal von Hindenberg, was also in dire straights. Lack of commercial stability caused un-employment and unrest, a period of time ripe for a change in power. Adolf Hitler seized the opportunity in the thirties to become the prime person in opposition to Hindenberg.

Adolf Hitler: Austrian by birth - during World War One served his time in the German Army as a Corporal. Awarded the Iron Cross (very much a debated mystery as too how?). He organised his own political party, the National Socialist (Nazi) party. Hitler's sudden rise in power prompted Von Hindenburg in 1933 to appoint him as the Reich Chancellor. Thus upon the death of Hindenburg the following year, Hitler became a self appointed Fuhrer who's policy and aim was to set Germany on a course to become a total Arian race. So began a dictatorship that was to lead to the almost annihilation of countless Jews in various European countries. During the following years, Hitler gradually built up his Army, Navy, and Air Force, together with vast munitions of war which developed into the strength of his Great War Machine. Hitler's ever-increasing power was openly flaunted by himself and his political party. It even spread to Great Britain when in 1934 the infamous fascist leader of the British Union of Fascists, Sir Oswald Mosley took the side of Hitler and spoke of a "modern dictatorship". His movement dressed in black shirts and black belts wore the arm band of the Nazi Swastika.

The British Government under Prime Minister the right Hon. Neville Chamberlain, condemned his party but were aware of the increasing dominance and strength of the Third Reich. He put into operation many plans that would be implemented without delay in the event of a war. In March 1938, Hitler took over the control of Austria as a German State and in September, he claimed that part of Czechoslovakia, known as the Sudetenland, was German. Upon this new revelation, and fearing war was about to break out, Neville Chamberlain accompanied by Edouard Daledier of France met Hitler and Mussolini the Italian Dictator in Munich to try and persuade Hitler against it. As an act of appeasement, they agreed to Hitler's demands and signed the Munich Pact. Prime Minister Chamberlain flew home to a rapturous reception and waved a sheet of white paper above his head quoting "Peace in our Time". However for Hitler that meant nothing. He continued with his plans and in March 1939, his army seized the remaining territory of the Sudetenland, and in doing so broke the agreement of the Munich Pact. Realising that Hitler could not be trusted, Neville Chamberlain began implementing the major plans already prepared for in the event of a war. Selected reservists were recalled to the colours, unlike World War 1 when men volunteered in their thousands. The National Service Act was approved and conscription for men began. It was to become a People's War raged by Nazi Germany upon not only Great Britain, but also the whole of Europe including later the Soviet Union and subsequently spread to other continents.

Torpoint's men, like everywhere else in Britain, either volunteered or were conscripted into the forces and its residents prepared for war, unsure of what could or would happen in the years ahead. Nothing happened, apart from the introduction of Identity Cards, Ration Books and the issue of shelters and other precautions including propaganda posters. At the end of August 1939, Three such posters were issued to offer the public reassurance for the dark days which lay ahead. They were distributed throughout the land to convey a message from the King who wished to assure his people that all necessary measures were being taken to defend the Nation. They were printed in stark Red & White with the only graphic at the top the Crown of King George VI, below was the following Statements:

(a) 'Your Courage, Your Cheerfullness,
 Your Resolution will Bring us Victory'
(b) 'Freedom is in Peril'
(c) 'Keep Calm and Carry on'

They soon appeared in shop windows, Billboards and Railway Stations, all advertising the point as made. Later various other posters were issued e.g., 'Dig for Victory' encouraging people to grow there own food in the garden and allotments, they appeared in parks and on any Common or Park were un-used grassland was available. These posters were issued at various times throughout the war.

Not until after the Evacuation of Dunkirk did the war spread itself on the seas and in the skies over Great Britain. Subsequently, every man, woman and child, whether taking part in a military action or as civilians, regardless of whether they lived in a Hamlet, Village, Town or City became involved in action, working on the land, in munitions factories, service industries or being bombed from the skies. Everyone suffered hardships through the imposed rationing that lasted throughout the war and well into the nineteen-fifties. It became the normal way of life. Not so for the dwindling number of senior citizens who experienced that period of time. Rationing restricted many luxuries to go without, but so long as you had your health, and had escaped yet another bombing attack, it was a small price to pay under such demanding circumstances.

It is now seventy years on when a majority of the residents of Torpoint who lived through the war years, have now departed this world, or have either forgotten or do not wish to remember. It is hard to pinpoint those who did lose sons, daughters, relatives or friends. They are casualties of war nevertheless, and to put the story together of the hardships, deprivation and sacrifices that were endured throughout that period, can often be related back to maybe a decade before the outbreak of war. A rather uneasy time for Great Britain, fraught with uncertainty, misgiving, and unbelievable trust in the political correctness that was employed at that time. It is true to say that the period of unrest during the thirties finally resulted in war. The end of the war brought with it many scars, with the loss of life of both service men and women, including vast numbers of civilians and children. World War 1, which did happen to have very few bombing raids, carried out by the Air Ships and very slow Gotha bombers that bombed London as early as June 1917 causing a number of civilian causalities, cannot be compared to the fatalities and casualities, that the bombing inflicted on the civilians throughout the United Kingdom during World War II. By force of circumstance it became a war, and all civilians became deeply involved. The march of time over a period of twenty-one years since the 1920's had changed the world in the field of advanced technology such as medicine, electricity, radio, television, transport, aviation, radar and not forgetting munitions and armaments to name but a few. All these had a formidable bearing on what was to happen at a later date. Therefore it is necessary to recap on a brief history of how and why the Urban District of Torpoint, involuntarily became involved in the Second World War with such disastrous results. A time when women were employed in the Royal Naval Dockyard to learn different trades, to replace men who were called up in the face of adversity. They were also employed by the Torpoint Ferry Company to collect the tolls, and during the night time Naval personnel helped man the ferries. For the employment of these women, the Land Army girls who came to work in the fields around Torpoint, unfortunately no records could be found. Torpoint was to become;

"Cornwall's First Town in The Front Line."

After my appeal for memories and experience's about the War Years in Torpoint, several people did respond and contributed their accounts, and in some cases photos, and gave their permission to include them within this manuscript. The first person to respond was a lady from Wilcove, Freda Hawken, who provided her hand written memory's of her experiences during the war. Freda was one of the women who worked in the Royal Naval Dockyard (as stated above). Another was excerpts taken from a life story of a policeman by the name of 'Doug Mitchell' and although not a Torpoint man, he was posted to Torpoint during the war years. For the extracts from that time, like all the other accounts that have been submitted in brief or in full, it appears logical to take those descriptive paragraph's out, and place them in the appropriate narrative, within the sequence of events e.g. Freda's account. This should provide the various incidents with evidence and authenticity of those events as seen through the individuals eyes.

PC Doug Mitchell

ooOoo

My War Memories by Freda Hawken (nee Spears):

My war started for me the day my dear brother was called up to fight for his country. He joined the Royal Engineers, then there were just the two of us left at home, mum and me. My elder brother was married and was called up into the Army and my sister's husband was also in the Army, the Royal Tank Corps. He was lucky to be the last one away from Dunkirk but one of the first to go back on D-Day.

We lived at number 5, Pato Point Wilcove. Before he left, my brother Bill said he would build us an air-raid shelter and he looked around the garden to find a suitable place but found nowhere. So he went in next door and saw a lovely spot right underground. Mr. Webber our neighbour said it would be good, so Bill began digging and re-enforced it making it into a underground shelter. He put a small iron bed and seats inside and went away happy. It later saved lives.

After his training, when Bill was due to leave these shores, we received a letter from a lady in Exmouth inviting us to her house to have tea with Bill before he went overseas. As my mother was not up to the journey, Bill's friend Bill Knott accompanied me and we went by train. When we arrived at this lady's house, she welcomed us and the told us that she had met Bill at their church meetings. She was quite a beautiful lady and said that she never met anyone who cared for his mum and sister like Bill did. When it was time to leave I felt very sad when I had to say my farewells to dear B

We travelled back by train and upon arriving at Devonport we got off the train in the middle of an air raid. The pair of us ran like mad down through Devonport Park, down the ferry approach and into the ferry waiting room where we sat until the air raid siren sounded the 'All Clear'. Bill Knott was in the Fire Service and did good service for his country. He also promised my brother that he would keep an eye on us and look after us, which he did. Now it was my turn to do my bit. I very much wanted to join the WAAF's, but my mother did not enjoy very good health and I did not want to leave her on her own. She had already been though the 1914-18 war in which my dad had been killed (Charles Spear), so I was fortunate to gain a job in the Royal Naval Dockyard in Devonport in the main electrical workshop. I started at engraving, then coil winding and due to sickness of some of the Foreman's staff, he sent for me and I did a short period of time in his office, until his staff recovered. I did work on all the ships that had to be repaired, most of which got sunk at the beginning of the war. I did asdic work for Submarine detection. I remember well when RADAR came about, it was a wonderful invention and we were told "walls have ears." So we kept very mum in those days. No way would we cause any trouble for the lads.

ooOoo

As early as 1935 the Government were looking into methods of protection from Air Raids. They published a circular entitled 'Air Raid Precautions' that was distributed to all local authorities. By April 1937, the formation of the Air Raid Wardens took place, and local volunteers joined up to be trained in the ways of First Aid, Rescue Work and Raid Policing. Within the space of a year some 200,000 were recruited. During 1939 until the start of the war, over 200,000 men volunteered for the Territorial Army and thousands of Naval reservists returned to there mustering places such as Portsmouth, Devonport, Chatham and many other areas. County Council's then divided the County into 19 sub areas from West to East, designating Torpoint's urban area as **Area 14**. It's borders extended from the boundaries of Saltash, along the shores of the Lyner River around the coastline of the Rame Peninsular, as far as half way towards the borders of Looe (Area 16), northwards to join up with the borders of Liskeard (Area 13) and Saltash (Area 15). Within these areas, the respective Council's would become responsible for any necessary controls brought in by the Government throughout the war. Torpoint's Urban District Council, under the Chairmanship of Mr. M. Light took all necessary steps to prepare Torpoint in the event of a war. The civilian side of things took on a similar role when the so called 'too old to volunteer veterans' of the previous war were only to pleased to be back in some form of uniform. They became members of the Home Guard, Air Raid Warden's and other voluntary services. In the case of the threatened aerial bombing by gas, the issue of Gas Masks, Identity Cards and Ration Books was instigated. From February of 1939 the supply of Anderson Air Raid Shelters began, which came as a giant construction kit with flat and curved sheets of galvanized metal complete with nuts, bolts and washers to secure the sheets together. These were issued to individual homes and in addition, Communal Air Raid Shelters were dug-out and built.

Air Raid Shelters

With the limited supply of Anderson Air-Raid Shelters to all homes, this was the time when the building of Communal Air Raid Shelters began. County Council's had approved proposals for the construction of four Communal Air Raid Shelters in Torpoint located at:

Antony Road - Opposite the Regal Cinema
Macey Street - Below the school
Ferry Street.
Cambridge Fields - (The mound at the Wellington Street end is still visible)
Albion Road Junior School
Antony House. (Occupied by The Admiralty)
Maryfield House. (Home to the Royal Dutch Navy)
Wilcove.
Elliot Square.
Plus others.

Extracts from a letter dated the 27th February 1940 Issued by Cornwall County Highways Division refer to the progress and cost during the construction of several air-raid shelters within Torpoint The following is a SAMPLE copy from the County Surveyor

Quote:

Dear Sir,

A.R.P. Shelters at Torpoint:

The estimated cost of these shelters which I have already forwarded to you, were based on the cost of £3.10.0 per person, for the trench type shelters, £2.15.0. for the Ferry Street Surface Shelter, the Macey Street Surface Shelter was estimated for by taking out quantities.

On these bases the following estimated cost were obtained.

Site	Structure	Accommodation Works	Total
	£.	£.	£.
Antony Rd.	800.00	230.00	1030.00
Macey Street	220.00	50.00	270.00
Ferry Street	365.00	175.00	540.00
Cambridge Terrace	486.00	154.00	640.00
Totals	1871.00	609.00	2480.00

As the Regional Officer seems desirous of keeping the cost down to a minimum by limiting the expenditure on accommodation works to 6/-per person. I suggest that if this allocation is not sufficient to provide for the whole of the seating, you spend up to this limit, and any deficit in seating be left over in accordance with previous instructions contained in a letter from the Regional Officer, stating that the provision of seats is desirous but not essential.

In view of this please arrange to keep a separated cost for:

(a) Structural Works
(b) Accommodation Works

Signed E.H. Cullcutt

[Authors Note: There was other correspondence dealing with this matter, but the final letter reads as follows]:

Dear Sir,

A.R.P. Shelters at Torpoint

As it seems likely, from figures of actual expenditure already submitted by you in your last monthly report, that some over expenditure may be incurred in item (a) due to high cost of excavation mainly in rock and various other items, over the original estimate of £1871.00, the money will have to be obtained from the Regional Officer in order that it can rank for grant.

I have been advised that a rate of 6/- per person should suffice for seating and sanitary accommodation including equipment.

The cost of gates would be about £37 and of the hurricane lamps about £13, the total should then not exceed £290.

In these circumstances, I am authorized to convey approval to the proposal,
subject to the limiting cost of £290, reasonable expenditure up to that figure will rank for grant, subject to the terms of the relevant financial regulations.

Site	Structure	Accommodation Works	Total
	£.	£.	£.
Antony Rd.	800.00	105.00	905.00
Macey Street	220.00	42.00	262.00
Ferry Street	365.00	75.00	440.00
Cambridge Terrace	486.00	68.00	554.00
Totals	1871.00	290.00	2161.00

Signed W.N. Wilmott
Regional Officer
'Unquote.'

[Authors note: From the above example it illustrates that Councils were able to definitely control the expenditures, particularly during times of cut-back, unlike today when gross expenditure out-way's initial estimated proposals].

ooOoo

Norman Beaver MBE. recalls:

The first shelter I remember was built in the Cambridge field. It was a 'Heath Robinson' arrangement, as it was just a trench dug out of the top of the park which used the wall and was covered by galvanized sheets and covered with sandbags - a poor effort, until a permanent one was built later.

We had an Anderson Shelter at home in Lyttleton Terrace which we used up until we moved to Millbrook after the destruction of Coryton Terrace. I can remember that dreadful night.

When we were children and during the later part of the war, we used to gather outside Andrews Fish and Chip shop in Harvey street as Polly Akers in Fore Street only opened for short periods, I seem to remember, as we were always chasing the girls! Also there was a brick built air–raid shelter in Elliot square.

ooOoo

His Majesties Stationery Office: (HMSO) Issued a Training Pamphlet No.3 at the cost of 1 penny. This was directed at all A.R.P. personnel on what to do in an Invasion. Within the Pamphlet, under each section, were a list of questions followed by instructions. The following are the list of subjects appropriate to specific requirements, and what or, how the actions were to be given and taken.

ADVISING THE PUBLIC IN THE EVENT OF INVASION:

1. What to do if fighting breaks out in my neighbourhood and I receive the instructions STAND FIRM:
2. What do I do in areas which are some way from the fighting? CARRY ON:
3. Will certain roads and railways be reserved for the use of the Military, even in areas of action?
4. ADVICE AND ORDERS: Whom shall I ask for advice?
5. From whom shall I take orders?
6. Is there any means by which I can tell that an order is a true order and not faked?
7. INSTRUCTIONS: What does it mean when the church bells are rung?
8. Will instructions be given over the wireless?
9. In what order will instructions be given out?
10. FOOD: Should I try to lay in extra food?
11. NEWS: Will normal services continue?
12. MOTOR-CARS AND CYCLES: Should I put my car, lorry, or motor cycle out of action?
13. How should a car be put out of action?
14. THE ENEMY: Should I defend myself against the enemy?

The Pamphlet finished with the following instructions.

YOU SHOULD GIVE ALL THE HELP YOU CAN TO OUR TROOPS

DO NOT TELL THE ENEMY ANYTHING

DO NOT GIVE HIM ANYTHING

DO NOT HELP IN ANY WAY.

There were other Pamphlets issued covering separate subjects
(not covered within this book)

Pamphlet No. 1: Price 3 Pence.
Notes on the 'Detection and Reporting of Unexploded Bombs and Shells'

Pamphlet No. 2: Price 3 Pence.
'Objects Dropped from the Air'

The Plymouth Blitz has gone down in the annals of history as one of the City's most horrendous periods of its time, during which it was besieged from the skies above Plymouth and became a target for the German bombers. Torpoint being such close neighbours, a mere 1.746 yards across the Hamoaze, were to endure and suffer many hardships and subsequently did not go unscathed. The Germans, in an attempt to put out of action not only the Royal Naval Docks at Devonport, but also the Torpoint Ferries (a crucial link to the transport of ammunition to the gun emplacements surrounding Torpoint, which received more than their share of bombs scattered throughout the locality), described as a few incidents, which could not be further from the truth, remembering that of Saltash further up the river. However, theirs may well be a different story.

The mention of Plymouth within the text does occur many times, nevertheless, does not undermine the status of Torpoint which took quite a beating during that period of war. Many of it's residents were to sacrifice their lives not only in the services, but also during the bombing raids. Excerpts of memories, dedicated by those mentioned within the text, can only qualify those incidents as this story unfolds in a chronological sequence. So as the preparations continued in and around Torpoint, the clouds of war were gathering momentum when the inevitable happened.

POLAND
September 1st 1939

Unlike the First World War when the invading infantry marched to the front, this time the German Luftwaffe were to strike first with their Blitzkreig tactics (Lightning strikes) that destroyed the Polish Air Force with little loss to themselves. Thus began the march of the German Army into Poland to take over the country, and the beginning of the :

SECOND WORLD WAR.

TORPOINT
THE ENEMY & PLYMOUTH'S SOUTH WEST DEFENCES

THE ENEMY
THE GERMAN LUFTWAFFE

The German Luftwaffe was the principle cause of all the devastation that was inflicted upon the civilian population of Great Britain with their bombing raids, either in single hit raids, or by concentrated waves of aeroplanes in formation, which on occasions seemed endless. During the hours of daylight when the first warning wail of the air raid siren began, signaling an imminent attack, had everyone running, seeking the protection of the nearest shelter, until as time progressed they became accustomed to the warning wail before the bombers eventually began their bombing raids. It was the constant night-time raids which began after dark, and ended nearer to dawn, which took their toll on the defenseless civilians down below. The bomber aircraft which carried out the raids, dropping thousands of tonnes of bombs, were mainly the following types of aircraft.

Dornier 17. Do17. Commonly known as the Flying Pencil, a twin engine night fighter/bomber plane with a compliment of four crew members. It was very fast with a speed up to approx 250 mph. Capable of carrying a 1,000 kg bomb load, it was armed with a 20mm cannon and three machine guns.

Heinkel 111. HE 111 The muscle and backbone of the Luftwaffe. A twin engine night bomber with a crew of five. It was also fast, with a speed of 270mph, capable of carrying one 500kg bomb externally and one 500-kg bomb internally, or eight 250 kg bombs, it was armed with one 20mm cannon and a max of 9 small caliber sub machine guns.

Junkers 88. Ju. 88. The Stuka single engine night-time dive-bomber with a crew of two max speed 170 mph, capable of carrying two external bombs under each wing, armaments were two cannons and one sub machine gun.

The latter two types were the principle aeroplanes used by the Luftwaffe on air raids carried out on Plymouth and the surrounding areas. Maybe there were other types used, for dropping mines into the shipping lanes off shore, but these are not noted.

The bombing raids over South West England did not commence until June 1940 when the Germans had occupied France. Very quickly the Luftwaffe located their airfields in the region of South West France suitably sited for their bombers to make a return trip from their bombing raids over the South West of England. The airfields which were normal farm fields, confiscated by the over-running German forces and turned into airfields, during rainy periods many of the aeroplanes would get bogged down in the mud, until the Germans laid concrete runways and parking areas for their planes using enforced French slave labour to carry out the construction. Similar to the Royal Air Force the Luftwaffe had an operational structure e.g. Gruppe (Gr) Operational unit (approximately equivalent to a Wing Commander in the RAF.)

Normally comprising of three Staffel (squadrons) of nine aircraft and a Stab (Staff) Flight with a total compliment of thirty aircraft. Any order of a wing would consist of:

Stab/KG55 - I/KG55 - II/KG55 - III/KG55

An independent bomber Gruppe was prefixed Kampf hence Kampfgruppe (KGr) e.g. KGr. 126. The wings (Gruppe) that were used for coverage of the South West of England were from the following airfields in France. Notated with type of plane and Officer in Charge:

Gruppe	Airfield	Plane	Commanding Officer
Stab/KGI	Rosieres-en-Santerre	HE 111	Obstltn. Exss
I/KG1	Montdidier	HE 111	Maj. Maier
II/KG1	"	HE 111	Obstln. Kosch
III/KG1	Rosieres- en- Santere	JU. 88	Maj. Fanelsa
Stab/KG26	Gilze	HE 111	Obstltn. Fuchs
I/KG26	Moerbeke	HE 111	Maj. Busch
II/KG	Gilze	HE 111	"
Stab/KG27	Tours	HE 111	Obrstltn. Behrendt
I/KG27	Tours	HE 111	Hptmn. Aschenbremmer
II/KG27	Dinard	HE 111	Hptmn. Eschenauer
IIIKG27	Rennes	HE 111	Maj. Frei Herr von Steinburg
Stab/KG55	Villacoublay	HE 111	Obstltn. Korte
I/KG55	Dreux	HE 111	Maj. Roeber
II/KG55	Chartres	HE 111	Maj. Kless
IIIKG55	Villacoublay	HE 111	Maj. Schlemmell
Stab/KG77	Laon	JU. 88	Obstltn. Von Wuhlisch
I/KG77	"	JU. 88	"
II/KG77	Asch-Norde	JU. 88	"
III/KG77	Laon	JU. 88	Maj Kless
KGr100	Vannes	HE 111	Hptm. Aschenbrenner

'BLITZ ' LITERALLY MEANS LIGHTNING:

KG.	Kampfgeschwader - Bomber group.
KGr Kampfgruppe.	Bomber wing.
Luftmine	Seamine dropped by parachute - LMA 500KG &1000KG.
Nachtjadgeschwader	Nightfighter.
Stuka (Sturzkamffugzeng KG87).	Dive Bomber.
Stab.	Staff KG.
SKG (Schnellkampfgeschwader)	Fast Bomber Group.
'Seerauberangriff'	Literally 'Pirate' known by the British as tip and run or Scalded cat raids.

BOMBS

The type of bombs that were used were:

HE (High Explosive) types: SC, SD, LZZ and Incendiary Bombs.(I.B's)
SC (Sprengbombe-Cylindrisch), thin cased general purpose bomb designated by the weight of the bomb e.g. SC50 was a 50 kilogram bomb. Also called Minenbombe. It had a high charge ratio for blast effect 55% explosive and they were primarily used for demolition purposes. A device called "the trumpets of Jericho" made out of black cardboard tubes 14" in length and 1'' inch in diameter, were more often than not fitted to the tail units of the SC50 and SC250 size bombs, shaped like organ pipes they surrounded the bomb, as the bomb dropped and gathered mementome, the wind blew through the tubes and made a loud shrieking noise. Their sole purpose was primarily used as a morale breaker for civilians and troops alike.

SD (Splintterbombe Dickwandig) Usually a drawn or forged casing in one piece similar in design to the SC type, but their fragmentation effect was far superior. Usually distinguished by a red stripe painted on their tail fins.
LZZ was a type of fuse fitted to some of the different sizes of bombs (Langzeitzunder)
Long time delay bomb fuse:

Incendiary Bombs: (Sprengbrandbombe), Explosive Incendiary Bomb the same shape and size as a SC50 bomb but filled differently. The nose section contained 10kg of TNT, behind was a silk bag containing black powder that served as the igniter, expelling charges for the middle section of the bomb where the incendiary units, six fire pots and sixty-seven small triangular metal incendiary units were located. Upon impact the incendiary elements were ejected over a radius of approx 100yds.

Another type of incendiary bomb was the **(Phosphorbrandbombe),** phosphorus bomb similar to the SC50 & SC250 kg HE bombs

As illustrated below: *with Kind permission of Before and After the Battle*

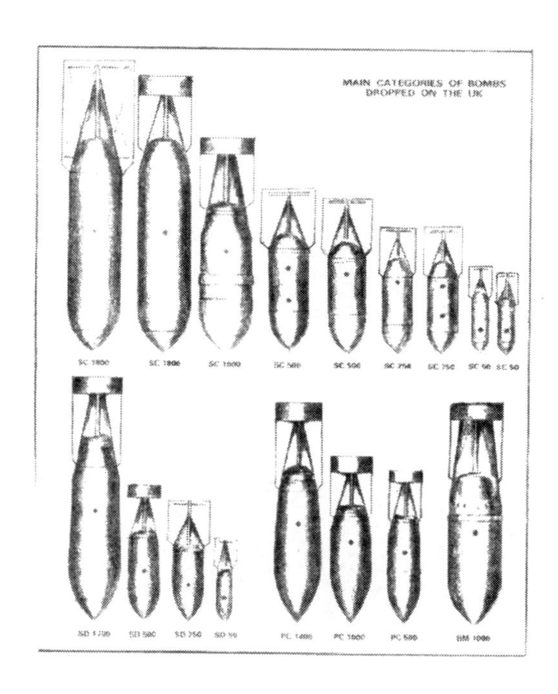

Various Sizes & Weights of Bombs

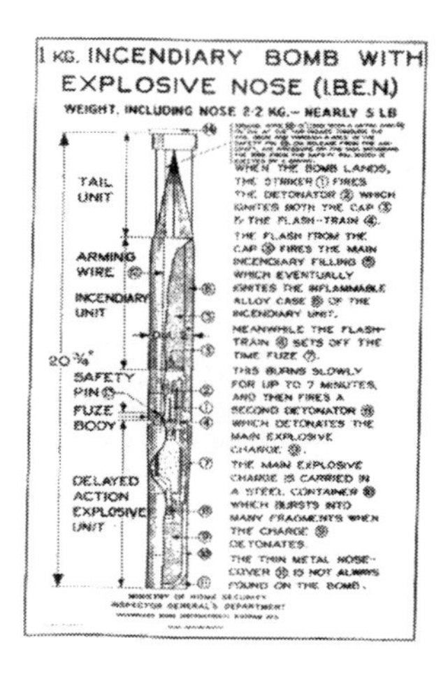

Description of Incendiary Bomb

The below plate is a copy of a German Reconnaissance Photograph date unknown, but either before 1939 or early 1940?, that illustrates the vulnerability of **TORPOINT** as a named Target. *By kind permission of the Imperial War Museum.*

GB 14 33 bc Geheim	Torpoint Truppenlager	Karte 1 : 100 000 Engl. Bl. 36 c

Bild Nr. 594 Z 14 **Geogr. Lage** 4° 13' W, 50° 22' N, **Höhe ü. d. M.** 30 m Stand IX. 40

Maßstab etwa 1: 13 500 (1 cm = 135 m)

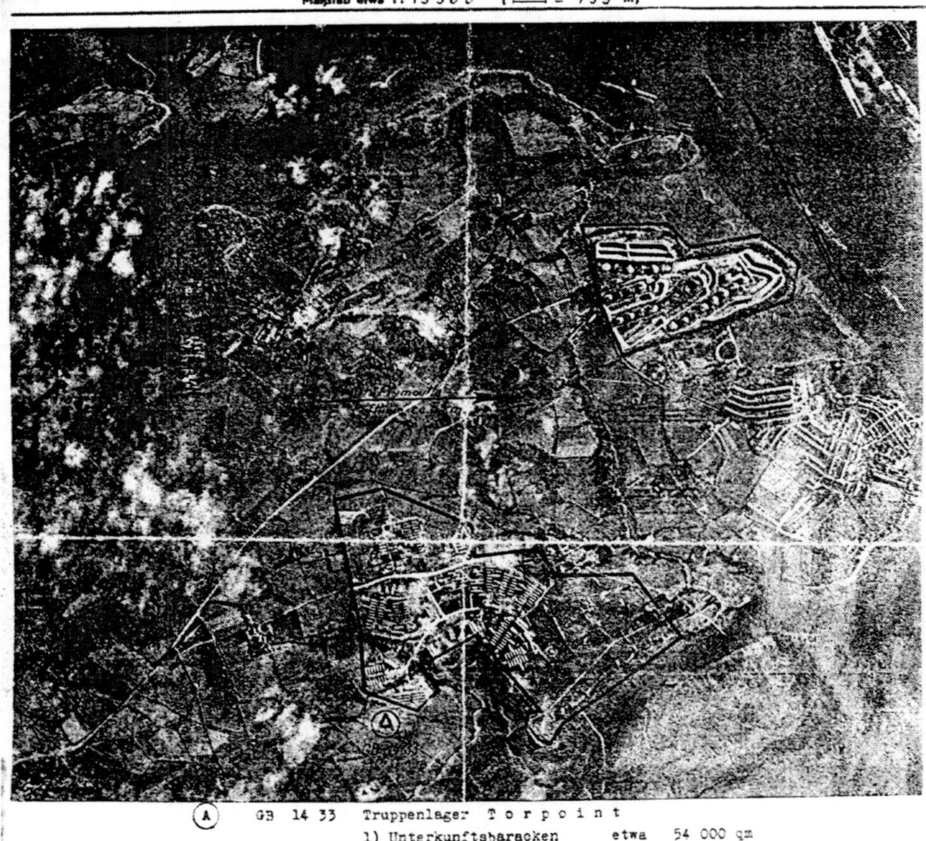

Ⓐ GB 14 33 Truppenlager T o r p o i n t

1) Unterkunftsbaracken	etwa	54 000 qm
2) Zeltlager (50 kleine und 10 große Zelte)	etwa	500 qm
bebaute Fläche	etwa	54 500 qm
Gesamtfläche	etwa	600 000 qm

Ⓑ GB 21 41 Tanklager Plugelly Plantation

It was inevitable that when the German war machine decided to make raids on strategic military targets in England, Plymouth with the Devonport Royal Naval base and the Radar station on Rame Head, became vital targets for many aerial bombing raids, which ment that any town or village within the vicinity and flight path of the Luftwaffe's dropping zone (DZ) would not go unscathed. Therefore Torpoint and its surrounding area could not be avoided. In the book 'The Making of a Cornish Town' by Gladys & F. L. Harris, Published in 1976, mentions only the amount of damage and destruction to Torpoint, caused by the bombing during the war, and leaves the story for someone else to build upon, however, as discovered by the Author, when piecing together its events the Official Records of Torpoint's involvement during the war, have either been lost or destroyed, therefore the Author can only rely on the facts as found in the sparse remains of Official Records, various books, paper clippings or, as presented by personal accounts of those days, remembered with nostalgia. As time progressed each snippet of information that they came to light, gathered from various sources, collaborated with others and within reason, confirmed the incident as it happened, developing into a fascinating record of a forgotten way of life during the time of war, and hopefully will portray to the young people of the town, the privation and hardships thrust upon their forefathers and elders of the town who had to endure and, in many cases sacrifice their lives in the fight for freedom. However, what must never be forgotten is the many service members and women including civilians of Torpoint who gave their lives. In the case of the civilians, unwittingly paid the ultimate sacrifice. Nevertheless they became embroiled within the savagery of a new kind of war, a war against civilians. Due to a **'lunatic'** hell bent on revenge, trying to put the books right because of the defeat of the German Nation in the First World War, so called 'A War to end all Wars'? and create a world full of German raised Arian people. The following events have been logged in chronological order principally to record the demise of those service men, women, and civilians wherever they were at that time, due to the consequences of events over the period 1939/46.

THE SOUTH WEST COMMAND

THE ROYAL NAVY

Based at Devonport Royal Dockyard a homeport for part of the Southern Fleet, were to be come heavily involved in the defence of the Southwest Seaways, Atlantic Sea, and the Mediterranean Sea. Situated within the Dockyard was *HMS Drake* with another two establishments of *HMS Fisgard* and *HMS Raleigh* both in Torpoint. All were Shore Bases and Training Depots, *HMS Fisgard* was an Apprentice Training School teaching young intakes to become Artificers and Junior Officers on the other hand *HMS Raleigh* was a purpose built camp previously known as Trevol Camp with wooden huts and the usual facilities for the training of young ratings. Later in 1944 it became the home for many American servicemen waiting to be shipped out on D-Day. All three Shore Bases were to become targets for the Luftwaffe's bombing raids. The Senior Commanders of the Royal Navy took over the Premises of Antony House, where all communications and directives were issued. One such lady from Torpoint provides the opening and setting to the many stories related within the following chapters.

Quote as typed.

WAR MEMORY'S as recounted by Delsey Dawe (nee Edwards):

I joined the 'Wrens' in 1939 when there was a crisis. We wore armbands with WRNS on them. When war broke out, we eventually received our uniforms of serge suit and black lace-up shoes. I lived at home and was therefore classed as immobile. The girls whose homes were up country were mobile and billeted at Antony House and HMS Raleigh. Oddly enough, my home was in a terrace called Navy Terrace which is now Marine Drive. I joined HMS Raleigh in 1940 and although there was a war on, I enjoyed my WRNS appointment. We were lucky enough to have Princess Marina inspect us in the early part of the war. She looked lovely in her WRNS Uniform, and we admired her and envied her as she wore silk stockings and court shoes, whereas we had thick black stockings and laced up shoes, and our skirt had to be so many inches below the knee.

My mother, my sister and her baby, and myself were evacuated from Navy Terrace as there was an unexploded bomb in the vicinity. We then lived out at Freathy in a Chalet and I would cycle into Raleigh when on duty. One such morning as I arrived at the gates at about 6.30 a.m, a bomb exploded in front of the Ward Room sending boulders and cars into the air. I grabbed my bicycle and ran behind the NAAFI shop until it was all clear.

We also wanted to get out of Torpoint during the Blitz as we were never able to sleep. I befriended the batman of the Major I was assigned to when we were awaiting the D Day landings. The batman's name was Billy Eagle and he came from London, he also drove an Army lorry and used to give us lifts to town. My mother would invite him to have meals with us at times. One day she asked him if he would drive my father's car out to the Two Bridges Hotel at Princetown, where we had family. He agreed and we started out with my mother, sister and her baby, and me. We got lost as there were no signposts because of the war, and with Billy not knowing this part of the country, we ended up at St. German's where my mum had a friend who put us up for the night. The next morning we could not start the car, and we all had to push it up the hill before we could get it going. We just managed to get to work by 6.30 a.m, only to find out that the tanks had been bombed the night before.

The R.M. B andmaster produced a pantomime 'Cinderella' in which I took part. We opened the panto with the 'Fleets In' and then I had to perform a little tap dance number. I also had to come out on stage in front of the curtains dressed as a harem girl, with an Arab chasing me across the stage. I was supposed to scream but could hardly do it as all the sailors in the audience were 'wolf whistling!'. Our costumes were lovely and were on loan from Drury Lane Theatre.

I was married in Torpoint on 28th March 1942. We had a wonderful wedding with a 'Wrens' guard of honour, and plenty of brass hats attended, including Commander Skinner who I was assigned to look after. Captain 'Tiny' Dalton, who was Captain of the 'tiffies', Surgeon Captain Mccloud, and 1st Officer of the Wrens Hilary Williams. When the guests arrived to the reception at the Masonic Hall, they were amazed at the food and said that *you would not have thought there was a war on. The Wrens served on the tables and when we left the reception to go on honeymoon to London it was late at night and they all linked arms over to the ferry singing 'I'll be with you in apple blossom time'. We were on the top deck of the ferry and heard the singing all the way over to the Devonport side. I felt very touched and had tears in my eyes, a moment I shall never forget.*

We had a very strict Chief Petty Officer Fenton, who took us for drill on the parade ground and if he saw sailors making fun of us he would pick them out and make them march with us. Very embarrassing for them! HMS Raleigh was visited by Noel Coward, Evelyn Laye and Michael Redgrave, who was my idol at that time. Evelyn Laye performed for the troops and Noel Coward was at Raleigh because he was producing the film 'In which we serve'. I met Michael Redgrave when he came to my Commander's Cabin with a message. He was wrapped in oilskins as it was pouring with rain. I had just finished polishing the floor when he arrived and I looked up into his lovely blue eyes. He apologised for leaving pools of water on the floor, but I didn't mind as I was so excited just to see him.

I left HMS Raleigh when my daughter was due to be born.

ooOoo

Recollections of my war experience by HENRY BANKS:

When the war started I was a dustman working for the Torpoint Urban District Council. My mother, just like a lot of people started to take in lodgers who were working for the war effort. One of the lodger's was a London man who was the foreman of the steel erector's working at HMS Raleigh and HMS Fisgard. He wanted a reliable man to train as a steel erector. (I was that man) so I changed jobs and one day while working up a loft, I fell about fifty feet, fortunately I landed on a pile of sand that had been delivered the day before, even so I was off work for two weeks with concussion. In those days we could see the air-raid flags at Mount Wise. There were three flags and we kept a sharp eye for any air raid warnings, but usually the planes were over and upon us before the correct flags were hoisted.

ooOoo

ROYAL ARTILLERY: Ack Ack Defence Units G.D.A (GUN DEFENDED AREA) Ref : AA COMMAND

by Colin Dobinson

The Heavy Ack-Ack defences that surrounded Plymouth were in several cases, non-static and dependant on the changing policy of Ack-Ack defences. Some Batteries were moved but the following gives some idea of where they were locatated.

No.	Name	Map Ref.	Torpoint UDC	Battery No.	Gun

1	Rame	SX436493	yes	203 HAA 4x 3.7
2	Down Thomas	SX506492	-	201 HAA 4x 3.7
3	Torpoint	SX419557	Burough Farm	91 HAA 4x 3.7
4	Seaton Barracks	SX493590	-	165 HAA 4x 3.7
5	Higher Tregantle	SX405529/SX395529	yes	203 HAA 4x 3.7
6	Billacombe	SX525540	-	201 HAA 4x 3.7
7	Carkeel	SX414605	-	301 HAA 4x 3.7
8	Staddon Heights	SX490514/SX504516	-	91 HAA 1x 3.7
9	Maker Barracks	SX438514	yes	203 HAA 4x 3.7
10	Home Park	SX473557	-	
11	Norton	SX556464	-	
12	Bere Alston	SX452662	-	
13	St Winolls	SX341554	yes	
	Penlee	SX441489/SX435516	yes	
	Picklecombe	SX449514	yes	170 HAA 1x40
	Bofors Renny	SX492489		91 HAA 1x 3.7

In addition to the guns, 12 x 90cm Searchlights manned by 483 Battery, operated around Plymouth and these were located at:
Cross Linkerne, Trifle Crafthole, Maker, Rame, Coomber Merton, and Abbot St. Dominick.

Of the 19 HAA batteries allocated to the defence of Plymouth, 8 HAA Battery Units were located within the Cornish area designated 14. (Torpoint Urban District Council).

The type of AA gun utilized were 3.7 static, 3.7 mobile and 3.0 case.

The first guns to be established within the GDA (Area 14) by the end of May 1940 were: 4 - 3.7 mobile and 8 - 3.0 Case type guns making a total of 12 guns. These were gradually increased in numbers until 3.7 static units were put in place, this happened round about the middle of July1940. These HAA units were sited and built until the middle of September, when 24 units had been set up (as per above listing) and were to remain in action throughout the war. Once the 3.7 static gun emplacement's was completed, both the 3.7 and 3.0 case mobile HAA guns left the GDA, in addition to those land based AA Guns, supporting fire was provided from any of the Naval ships docked in the Hamoaze, or, in Devonport including the Polish ship *Gydinia*

In addition to the above there were thirty gun emplacements using 32 - 303 Lewis guns, and in the Dockyard there were 12 - 3 inch non-rotating launches used by 102 AA 'Z' Battery.

Later in March 1944 with the pending build up to Operation Overlord, additional guns were cited increasing the number of 3.7's to 48, and by the 6th June, those numbers had been increased to 64. Later in July 5.2 Static Guns were installed but were deemed non-operational. By August the number of operational units had been reduced to 50, and as the events of the invasion over in France progressed the gun sites became non-operational and with the 3.7's being required elsewhere, only 12 - 5.25's guns were left as non-operational up until May 1945, the end of the war in Europe.

With all these AA gun emplacement's the Torpoint Ferry was to become a vital link in the delivery of much needed ammunition shells for the manning of the guns by the Royal Artillery gunners in the defence of Plymouth and the surrounding area.

Freda recalls:

We had Ack Ack guns and troops in the woods behind us and in the fields around Wilcove. The Pioneer Corps came with their smoke screens and placed these tubes starting at the end of Torpoint, right along the roadway to the end of Pengelly Lane, they worked hard and their efforts saved the Tanks. The Barrage Balloons were dotted around the sky. There were troops everywhere, I was on my way to work one morning when I got near the little shop in Wilcove somebody shouted. "Halt who goes there"? I stopped and said in my squeaky voice. "Its only me on my way to work in the Dockyard", then a torch was flashed on me and seeing who I was, the voice came from out of the darkness "OK. on your way".

ooOoo

Norman Beaver MBE. recalls:

I remember the Pioneer Corps placing those Smoke Jacks with their tall black funnels along the Antony Road, stationed in accordance with the wind direction, to provide a covering screen for the Dockyard and Tanks.

ooOoo

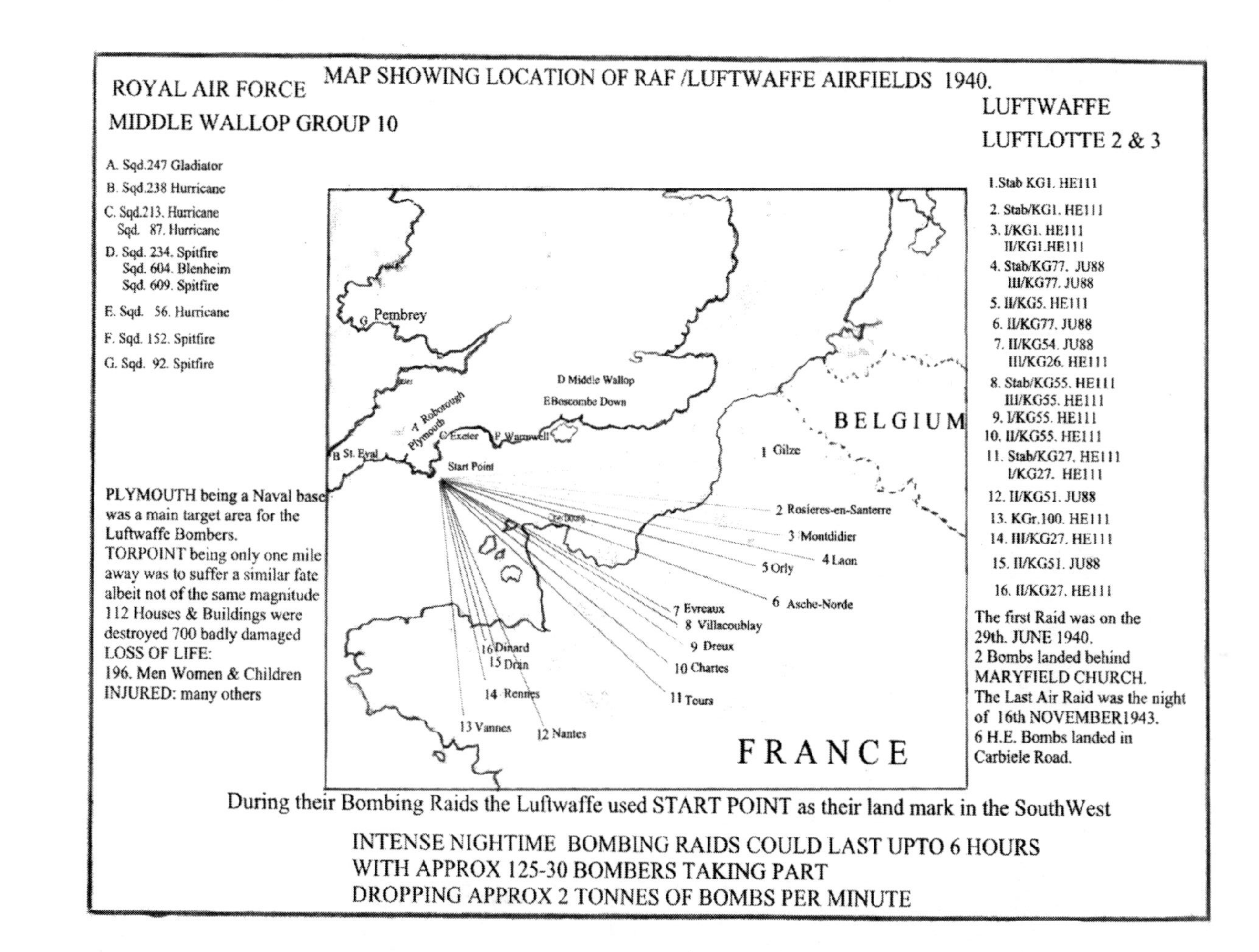

MAP SHOWING LOCATION OF RAF /LUFTWAFFE AIRFIELDS 1940.
ROYAL AIR FORCE
MIDDLE WALLOP GROUP 10
A. Sqd.247 Gladiator
B. Sqd.238 Hurricane
C. Sqd.213. Hurricane
Sqd. 87. Hurricane
D. Sqd. 234. Spitfire
Sqd. 604. Blenheim
Sqd. 609. Spitfire
E. Sqd. 56. Hurricane
F. Sqd. 152. Spitfire
G. Sqd. 92. Spitfire
PLYMOUTH being a Naval base was a main target area for the Luftwaffe Bombers.
TORPOINT being only one mile away was to suffer a similar fate albeit not of the same magnitude
112 Houses & Buildings were destroyed 700 badly damaged
LOSS OF LIFE:
196. Men Women & Children
INJURED: many others
G Pembrey
B St. Eval
A Roborough
Plymouth
C Exeter
F Warmwell
D Middle Wallop
E Boscombe Down
Start Point
BELGIUM
FRANCE
1 Gilze
2 Rosieres-en-Santerre
3 Montdidier
4 Laon
5 Orly
6 Asche-Norde
7 Evreaux
8 Villacoublay
9 Dreux
10 Chartes
11 Tours
12 Nantes
13 Vannes
14 Rennes
15 Dran
16 Dinard
LUFTWAFFE
LUFTLOTTE 2 & 3
1.Stab KG1. HE111
2. Stab/KG1. HE111
3. I/KG1. HE111
II/KG1.HE111
4. Stab/KG77. JU88
III/KG77. JU88
5. II/KG5. HE111
6. II/KG77. JU88
7. II/KG54. JU88
III/KG26. HE111
8. Stab/KG55. HE111
III/KG55. HE111
9. I/KG55. HE111
10. II/KG55. HE111
11. Stab/KG27. HE111
I/KG27. HE111
12. II/KG51. JU88
13. KGr.100. HE111
14. III/KG27. HE111
15. II/KG51. JU88
16. II/KG27. HE111
The first Raid was on the 29th. JUNE 1940.
2 Bombs landed behind MARYFIELD CHURCH.
The Last Air Raid was the night of 16th NOVEMBER1943.
6 H.E. Bombs landed in Carbiele Road.
During their Bombing Raids the Luftwaffe used START POINT as their land mark in the SouthWest
INTENSE NIGHTIME BOMBING RAIDS COULD LAST UPTO 6 HOURS
WITH APPROX 125-30 BOMBERS TAKING PART
DROPPING APPROX 2 TONNES OF BOMBS PER MINUTE

ROYAL AIR FORCE - GROUP 10 COMMAND

In 1939 Air defences in the South West were supported by Fighter Squadrons of Number 10 Group, with Air Vice Marshal Sir Quintin Brand in command of operational sectors at Pembrey, Filton, St Eval, and Middle Wallop at the following airfields.

Squadron Number	Aircraft	Airfield
92	Spitfire	(Pembrey
87	Hurricane	(
213	Hurricane	(&
125 April 43	Beaufighter	(Bilbury
238	Hurricane	St Eval
247 (one Flight)	Gladiator	Plymouth/ Roborough
234	Spitfire	(
609	Spitfire	(Middle Wallop
604	Blenheim	(
56	Hurricane	Boscombe Down
152	Spitfire	Warmwell

Mountbatten Island was a Seaplane Base flying Sunderland Flying Boats.

When the incoming waves of bombers were identified on the radar, the order "Scramble" was given to those airfields controlling their individual sectors. The Squadrons would take off into the vast area of the skies above to seek out the enemy, destroy them over the range and area available to the pilots, in many cases they returned with success. Spitfire and Hurricane Pilots from all different Squadrons became engaged in hunting down the bombers, either on the incoming flight or on their return flight, within the text, mention is made of the many battles which were fought, and these kills have been stated by Squadron Nos. under Group 10's Command, patrolling in the various sectors, and not to individual pilots, illustrates a limited account of the battles fought high above in the sky, which in the end saw victory over the Luftwaffe Pilot's. However many kills by other Squadrons have not been entered.

Barrage Balloon Units operated under the control of the Royal Air Force No. 13 Balloon Centre R.A.F Station Collaton Cross Yealmton Devon, with four different Flight Group H.Q's:

'B' Flight Wolsdon, Antony Torpoint.
'C' Flight Harredge House, Plymouth
'D' Flight The Vicarage, Torpoint
'E' Flight Ferry House Inn, Saltash Passage

Balloon Sites:

Alexander Park
Antony Park
Barn Barton
Beaumont House
Block House
Bull Point

Cremyll	Ham House	Trevol Road
Devonport Park	Mountbatten	Weston Mill Cem.
Eaton Kings	Plymouth Hoe	Wilcove
Emcacombe	Torpoint Car Park	

Barrage Balloons were also attached to each of the Torpoint Ferries for added protection, but if they broke away from their moorings, their trailing wires caused more damage to the ferry chains and had to be shot down. Other sites were at Antony Gate opposite Burroughs Farm.

The Barrage Balloon was a passive form of forcing aeroplanes to fly at a much higher altitude, thus with the accuracy of the then bomb aiming equipment available during that period, proved to be useful in ensuring the bomb was provided with much less accuracy on their intended target. However, the balloons were also lethal to our own fighter aircraft. The Barrage Balloon was approx sixty-six (66) feet long and thirty (30) feet high and was nicknamed 'PIG'. On their steel mooring cable they were capable of being let out to a height of 10,000 feet thus forcing the enemy bombers to heights of up to 20,000 feet which was the normal altitude for bombing. Because of its size and silver colour, floating about on their steel mooring cable, they were obviously extremely vulnerable to attack. They were far more useful during the night-times or during days when visibility was bad. Strategically sited around the perimeter of an area, is when they became an aid in the defence of a Town or City, and most needed by the AA guns and fighters. One such airman who was drafted to the Torpoint Barrage Balloon Unit was Jim Southworth, who spent many months in Torpoint before he volunteered for more active service in Bomber Command as a Rear Gunner. For his gallantry, he was awarded the Distinguished Flying Medal DFM.

A short story as told to the Author by Jim:

Jim relates that when he arrived in Torpoint to start his service time with the Balloon Squadron, it was after two in the afternoon and as he had come down from Preston where the Public House's normally stayed open until three o'clock, He decided to pop into the King's Arms Public House. He recollects that it was about quarter after two as he entered the pub, there was nobody about except the Landlady who incidentally he remembers as Mrs. Maggie Gibbs. He wandered in and she asked what he wanted.

"Pint of ale please" Jim asked.

"No you can't have one were closed" says she sternly.

Puzzled by this Jim began to retrace his steps out through the door, upon which Mrs. Gibbs called him back and said,

"OK you can have a pint, but none in the future after we have called "Time Gentleman Please".

'Oh. Right'o thank you Mrs'. Grateful for the pint of ale, Jim enjoyed his pint and thanked Mrs. Gibbs again before he left.

[Authors Note Apparently Jim was the only person in Torpoint not only to get a free pint, but served after hours by the Landlady herself Mrs. Gibbs. She was as he recalls, a stickler for pub time keeping]

Norman Beaver MBE. recalls:

There was a Barrage Balloon Site in what was then a field, and is now built on. This field was bordered by Pole and Lyttleton Terrace on the south side and Coryton Terrace on the east side. Another site was situated in a field, which faced the front of Carew Terrace. This field is now part of Hamoaze and Cremyll Roads. Another site I remember was at Wiggle Farm at Rame.

ooOoo

R. D. F. (Radio Detection Finding)

Later classified as Radar and referred to hereon in.

R.D.F. was discovered by Robert Watson Watt (later Sir Robert Watson Watt) in 1936. Its capabilities proved it a useful detection system in the location of any unwanted invaders approaching the British Isles from the sky. This was put on the secret list as part of the new 'early warning system'. The network of Radar Stations was established and set up at predominant places around the coast of Britain including Devon, and those sites were: West Frawle, Hawks Tor, Rame Head, Dry Tree and Carnanton on the North Coast. The site at Rame Head was a CHL (Chain Home Low) Station, that was integrated with all the other Stations around the coast. Unlike the very high steel tower construction that had been built at other sites, it was, nevertheless, what they called a bedstead construction, a gigantic bed set of wires & antennas, above which was a 15 foot steel structure. The operators brick-built hut was located a short distance away from the CHL, a steel fence with added protection of barbed wire fencing surrounded it. Situated on top of the cliffs at Rame Head, it was completed just before the outbreak of war in 1939 and later became a target for the Luftwaffe. However, it played its part in the defence of Plymouth and Cornwall.

THE FIRE BRIGADE

Those men who volunteered to fight fires, were to become legends throughout the war with their constant vigilance and attendance to the numerous fires that were caused by the falling bombs and incendiaries, raining down from the planes high above. In 1939 Auxiliary Fire Service (AFS) Detachments were formed and the Home Office provided trailer pumps to be towed by any available vehicle. Following the outbreak of war, Fire Station's were manned during the night-time to ensure the quickest possible turn-out of men and machines in the event of any incendiary bomb attacks. During the early 1940's as the war progressed, the strain on the men, machines, and the system increased. Throughout those early months of the war, urgent calls for newly trained personnel and for further recruits were constantly made to aid the "old volunteers". Due to the intensive bombing of Plymouth, it was necessary to call upon re-enforcements. Fire pumps were required from Torpoint, Saltash, Liskeard, Looe, Callington and as far away as Bodmin. Because of their close proximity to Plymouth and the Devonport Dockyards, Torpoint and Saltash were to be at the forefront of the battle against the Luftwaffe's Incendiary Bombs. On 8th August 1941, the Fire Services (Emergency Provision) Bill came into force instigating the National Fire Service, which combined the AFS with other Brigades. The whole of Plymouth and parts of South West Devon became Fire Force Area 19.

AFS Units under Borough and District control, were integrated and renamed the National Fire Service (NFS) and so remained until after the war had ended.

The Air Raid Precautions (ARP) Civil Defence (CD):

As early as January 1938, a recruitment campaign was organised by the Government for the beginning of the Air Raid Precautions (ARP) Organisation. It required various people from different walks and trades of life, to volunteer for the Forces or one of the following Categories: Police, Fire Service, Nursing Service, Women's Land Army & ARP Service, Wardens, Ambulance Service, First Aid Post Service, Rescue and Demolition and Decontamination Service. Age limits were also imposed, 18 or over 40 in the Report Centre's and Communications Services, and 25-30 age group not required for Military Service, Wardens or any other service required. When the war did break out, the Wardens distributed gas masks amongst the populace, with instruction on how to use them. Area 14 TORPOINT HQ was located on the corner of Rowe Street and Church Row. (Now St. John B&B). It was manned by two (2) whole-time personnel. On the ground floor was a Message Room and a separate Map Room. On the first floor, three rooms were allocated to Local ARP Officers. However, due to the lack of Torpoint Records, a typical Fire Guard's Duty Instructions from St. Mawes, were as follows:

'Quote:'

CIVIL SERVICES Part IV:

Location & Phone Numbers of Control and/or Report Centres, Wardens Posts, Rescue and Decontamination parties.

C8 Post (Captain Jones)   Phone St. Mawes 278

Names and addresses of Wardens (as at 28/10/1942)

G.Jones	Seacliff Warren	St. Mawes	phone 178
C. Willmore	Andennis	St. Mawes	phone 282
G. Nind	Trelawney Road	St. Mawes	phone 284
G. Betton-Foster	Tresullian	St. Mawes	phone 285
H. Harris	Marine Parade	St. Mawes	
D. Hooper	Polvarth Terrace	St. Mawes	phone 221
C. Cory	Bohella Cottages	St. Mawes	
G. Stone	Laurel Villa	St. Mawes	phone 235
J. Wallace	The Bungalow	St. Mawes	
R. Cocking	White City	St. Mawes	
H. Couch	St. Just Lane	Porthecatho	phone 41

Method of Calling:

Miss Horridge on her way to the First Aid Post, will call Harris and G. Stone who will then call Wallace and Cocking. All Wardens have been instructed to warn First Aid Personnel in their sector, and each First Aid person will immediately proceed to First Aid Post, calling up other members of First Aid Party on their way.

1. Outline of Duties (copy of orders issued to wardens).
2. You will patrol your beat in an emergency.
3. Inform C8 Post (phone St. Mawes 278) of any incident, such as dropping of H.E. or Incendiary Bombs, parachute landings, fires etc., and immediately return to the incident and render what aid you can until help arrives.
4. Anyone rendered homeless by enemy action must be taken to Church Hall, where W.V.S. (Women's Voluntary Service) personnel will feed and take care of them. Walking casualties that occur WEST of Ship and Castle will be directed to RAF (Polvarth).
5. After an incident has been reported, First Aid personnel will be sent if necessary, to the incident but on no account must serious cases be moved without doctor's orders unless exposed to enemy fire.
6. Stretchers are kept at First Aid Post (Church Hall) & H. Harris Marine Parade, C. Cory (Bothella), R.A.F. (Polvarth) and C8 Post.
7. You can demand entry into any house to phone in an emergency.
8. It must be understood that wardens, in a very grave crisis, must use their own judgement and report to C8 Post, otherwise there will be complications and compensation.
9. You should find out all houses with phones in your sector.
10. If telephone communications are cut between you and C8 Post call for the ambulance St. Mawes 206, for the doctor St. Mawes 241, RAF (Polvarth) or First Aid Post (Church Hall). If possible, send message by hand to C8 Post.

'Unquote'

DECLARATION OF WAR
London 1939

On the 1st of September 1939, orders for the blackout were announced. The Royal Navy prepared for War. Operation "Pied Piper" was put into operation, the plan so named for the evacuation of London's children that lived in areas designated as 'Evacuation Area' and the children living within those areas, were classified under the following four distinctive groups:

a) school children accompanied by their teachers
b) mothers with children under five
c) pregnant women
d) certain categories of disabled people

Over the next four days London was engaged in transporting approximately one and a half million 'evacuees' as they were called. They were loaded onto trains at the main line stations and sent to those places identified as "so called safe havens", in the Home Counties and in the South West. That included Towns and Villages throughout Hampshire, Somerset, Cornwall, Devon and Dorset. Quite a few of the evacuees had to be housed in Torpoint and the surrounding villages. Mrs. Phylis Mudd who lived in Wilcove had a family of five evacuees, plus another brother and sister billeted at Wilcove. Later in 1941 during the Blitz of Plymouth, children were evacuated from Torpoint. Peter Rolfe then a young resident of Wilcove remembers being evacuated, as did Gordon Smith, Margaret Tresider [who later married Gordon], along with her sister and others, were sent to Newquay. [Also note that during 1944 when the doodlebugs began to rain down on London and the South East another evacation was undertaken under the Code Name of "Operation Rivulet" referred to later in the chapter headed 1944].

ooOoo

But first a description of the days event as recalled by:
Norman Beaver MBE.

When war was declared on the 3rd September 1939, I remember hearing the Broadcast by the then Prime Minister Mr. Neville Chamberlain in our Sunday School room at Torpoint, which had been made into a Canteen for servicemen who had already been called up. At the time I was eleven and was too young to realise the seriousness of the situation. At school Air Raid Shelters were built at the bottom of the school playground, and at first we took shelter when there was a 'Yellow Warning', which was a yellow flag flown at the flagstaff steps of the Royal Dockyard this being visible from Torpoint, enabling a fireman in the nearby fire station to then warn the school. However, complacency soon set in and it was not until a red flag was flown did we scamper for shelter. Col. R. Gillespy OBE., was the Officer in Charge of the Torpoint Civil Defence (TCD) very much an ex-army Officer who was a man of few words, but when he spoke it was a directive that had to be complied with, real discipline, and as boy messenger's he scared the life out of us.

Sun. 3rd Sept. **LONDON**

At 11.15 a.m. BMT [British Mean Time], after the chimes of Big Ben had sounded on the wireless, The Prime Minister The Right Honorable Neville Chamberlain announced over the radio. 'That Britain was at War with Germany', within half an hour of his announcement, the first wail of the air raid sirens were heard, luckily it was a false alarm. That very same day at approx 11 a.m. a wireless transmission was sent to the British Liner *Athenia* bound for Montreal Canada, advising her of the outbreak of war. The ship had sailed from Glasgow the previous day the 2nd with 1,103 passengers on board, amongst them some evacuees. At that time she was approximately 250 miles out into the Atlantic to the west of Inishtrahull Island. At 9.o'clock that evening in the fading light, a German submarine a U-30, fired torpedoes at the *Athenia,* it's fate: doomed to the bottom of the sea, with the loss of 112 civilian passengers, amongst those, were evacuees, members of the crew including 28 Americans. President Roosevelt of America denounced the attack, nevertheless, declared America neutral and so they remained. With the sinking of the *Athenia*, the battle of the Atlantic had begun.

Another submission provided by Mrs. Jean Peach,
by her late husband
WAR YEARS REMEMBERED BY
JOHN PEACH

I was about four years old when war was declared on the 3rd September 1939. Our house was 12 Victoria Street, where I lived with my parents Leonard and Lillian Peach and my older brother Geoff. On March 13th 1940 my sister Marjorie was born. Soon after we moved to 9 Trelawney Terrace (now York Road). There was no Air Raid shelter, so like many others we would seek safety by crouching in the big cupboard under the stairs. When dad was working night shift in the Dockyard, we would spend the night at 1 Kempton Terrace, where Granny Hambly lived, she did have a shelter, so we would spend many hours huddled together waiting for the all clear.

Mon. 4th Sept. **GERMANY - WILHELMSHAVEN:**

In retaliation to the atrocity of the sinking of a civilian Liner, 10 RAF Blenheim bomber plane's took off from their bases in England, to attack and bomb the shipyards of Wilhemshaven at the entrance to the Kiel Canal, their targets, Germany Warships and installations. At the same time, advance parties of the British Army Expeditionary Force landed in France, ready to set up General Head Quarters (GHQ) in preparation to take on the might of the German Army. Possibly some *Torpoint Soldiers?* That very same day in a Government Reshuffle a 'War Cabinet' was announced and Winston Churchill was made First Lord of the Admiralty. An excited signal was sent to the Fleet. "Winnies Back". Other New Departments announced were: Food, National Service, Information, and Economic Warfare. The original plans became reality and were instigated immediately. Conscription of civilians into the forces began. It was the beginning of the 'Blackout', street lighting became almost non-existent, and heavy black cloth was needed to make blackout curtains. In Torpoint this material was probably obtained from the drapers shop Hayden's at 56 Fore Street. That shop later was to became the local Food Office.

SOUTH WEST ENGLAND:

Sat. 16th Sept.

Petrol was put on ration.

TORPOINT:

Freda recalls:

I loved dancing, and would have lovely times at the dances on the Plymouth Hoe with Nancy Astor. Who used to say 'Come on girls they only want to dance they don't want to marry you'. Later we had American Bands but my goodness it was hard on your shoes. How we kept going I don't know but we did. We had dances at Torpoint to raise money for airplanes, for soldiers, for the Red Cross and many more we saved a lot of money for them.

My evenings I spent writing to my dear brother, sending snaps of us, and parcels of little things, also to my boyfriend to whom I was engaged. I knew him at school, he joined the RAF, had been in France, and was sent to Talika in Malta "Hell Fire Post 2 as it was called. He was there for four years. My brother was in the Middle East at first when things were bad there, but then we heard they wanted Engineers in the Far East and he was sent to Burma he was one of General Wingate's 'Chindits'. He had an awful time and was away for years. He was a young man when he went away and he returned home with grey hair. My elder brother was sent home because he was ill, and after that never enjoyed good health.

Mrs. Marjorie Harwood (nee Thom) recalls:

Looking back over the years, and living In Wilcove during World War 2, how many serving their country survived, and are still alive? I know Freda Hawken (nee Spears), Betty Willis (nee Rice), Eileen Smart (nee Spencer), Muriel Coles (nee Rice) did as well as myself.

For the 'War Effort' we gave up our jobs if they were not important. I was working at 'Maryfield Cottage', with Captain and Mrs. Gillespie as Cook-General. I volunteered with many other women from Torpoint to work in the NAAFI Canteen at HMS *Raleigh.* We were issued with a uniform and shown where the 'Rest Room' was, where we left our belongings and had a cup of coffee when off duty, Mrs. Eddy our Charge-hand sorted out our duties morning or afternoon. We cleaned the canteen in the morning and helped in the Kitchen. There were Doughnuts to be made, Rock buns, Apricot tarts, Sandwiches to be cut, we melted the margarine and 'Brushed' it on the bread to make it go further. Other foods were brought in. but all were rationed.

The canteen was prepared for opening at I p. m, the sailors rattled the shutters for us to open 'I suppose they were hungry'? I cycled to and from the camp from Wilcove, sometimes taking a short cut through the cemetery. Our work in the canteen was very hard and Mrs. Eddy was a taskmaster for work.

ooOoo

Sun. 17th Sept. **ATLANTIC:**

Fourteen days after the beginning of the war, the aircraft carrier HMS. *Courageous,* already engaged in the battle of the Atlantic, was sailing off the South West Coast of Ireland during the night when it was torpedoed and sunk by the German submarine *U-29.* Five hundred and eighty (580) sailors on board were drowned. Amongst those were two sailors from Torpoint:

D/MX 57261. E.R.A.El/Art. 4th. Cl. JOHN JAMES NETHERCOTT. Age 22
Panel 35 Col. 1.

and

D/K 25206. STO. EDWARD WILLIAM RILEY. Age 45
Panel 34 Col. 3.
BOTH THE ABOVE AT CWG. PLYMOUTH NAVAL MEMORIAL

Torpoint had suffered its first casualties of the war.

TORPOINT:

Norman Beaver MBE. recalls:

A survivor of "HMS *Courageous*" was C.P.O. Shipwright James Hyslop, his family lived in Salamanca House in Elliot Square. Later in his life he related how this tragedy happened. The ship was manned by many retired Royal Navy men who had been recalled, and many young men who were serving on their first ship. He recalled that the Life Rafts had been painted over for many years and were not able to be released. Jim became a devout Christian after his rescue, he was a gentleman and always willing to give help where needed.

I also remember when "HMS *Gloucester*" sailed from Devonport, it was to be the last we would see of her. My parents and I were with W.O. Ernest Household's wife to wave farewell to that Great Ship that was built in Devonport.

Another ship that sticks out in my mind was "HMS *Cambletown*", the ex-American four funnel Destroyer that had been converted to resemble a German Destroyer. She was off to St. Nazaire to ram and destroy the dock and deprive the Germans from using it for their Capital Ships, never again to return to Devonport, I was 11 or 12 at the time.

ooOoo

Fri. 29th Oct. **TORPOINT:**

Registration began for the issue of Identity cards and Ration Books. Everyone had to register.

Sat. 1st Oct.

Compulsory Conscription. A further 250,000 men are called up, amongst them was quite possibly a number of Torpoint men.

Sat 14th.Oct. **SCOTLAND - SCARPA FLOW:**

A German U-Boats without being detected, torpedoed and sank HMS *Royal Oak,* at anchor in her home base of Scarpa Flow, with the loss in excess of 800 seaman, only 396 of its crew survived.
(During the month Ration Books were issued to every man, women and child).

Wed. 8th Nov. **GERMANY - MUNICH:**

An attempted bomb assassination on Hitler, visiting the Burgerbrau Bier Kellar in Munich fails. What '**IF**' he had been killed is a big question?
[Authors note: This, the first attempted assassination was carried out by Johann Elser, a lone assassin. Although the bomb did explode, Hitler escaped by leaving the Bier Keller 13 minutes earlier. The explosion killed eight people, including the father of Hitler's mistress Eva Braun. Johann Elser was arrested interrogated, transported to Sachsenhausen concentration camp and later confined in the notorious concentration camp of Dachau where he spent the rest of the war. During the period of the war there were 19 planned attempts by various top military leaders to assassinate Hitler, all failed including the Rastenburg attempt on July 20th 1944. This was Lt. Colonel Count Claus Schenk von Stauffenberg's third and final attempt between August 8th. 1944 and April 9th. 1945. 19 persons were executed for their part in the attempted coup. The SS executed Johann Elser on the 9th April 1945. The extent and horrors of these notorious Concentration & Extermination camps were not discovered until after the death of Hitler, when Allied troops discovered approximately twenty (20) camps that had been purposely built to encaserate and exterminate 6,000,000 Jews.]

ooOoo

Wed. 13th Dec. **SOUTH ATLANTIC - URUGUAY:**

The Battle of the River Plate came to an end after a long range running sea battle between the German Battleship *Graf Spee* and the British ships HMS *Exeter, Ajax, & Achilles* during the battle although they each sustained damage themselves they caused severe damage to the *Graf Spee,* that was forced to carry out repairs, her Captain Hans Langdorf had to seek shelter in the Capital of Uruguay and permission to enter its port of Montevideo. Uruguay was then a neutral country. The three British ships lay a few miles off shore surrounded the exit approaches of the mouth of the River Plate, therefore preventing the *Graf Spee* from leaving. For the three waiting British Ships, it was a case of wait and see what her Captain was about to do?

Three days later Captain Langsdorf ordered her to sail before scuttling her, then Captain Hans Langsdorf shot himself.

1940
YEAR ONE

Another collection of war time memory's:

SCOTLAND - ROSYTHE:

J. A. Barnham Telegraphist on board HMS. Speedwell, Rosythe. Entry in diary:

1st Jan. Left harbour 7.30 a.m fog too thick, so returned again by 11a.m, going aft heard we were going south but no more made. Got to wait. Sent letter saying we were going south.

2nd Jan. Left harbour 7. 30. a.m found out we were going north heading towards Aberdeen. At night anchored, rolling quite a bit during the night.

ooOoo

SCOTLAND - ORKNEYS:

Charles E. Lowings recalls:

In 1940 I was a coder on the staff of the Assistant Chief of Staff (ACOS) at Lynees on the Orkneys.

My brother George came off the "Neptune" to claim me, as they wanted a coder on his ship. I was in my bunk and had a bad pain in my stomach, so said I could not go as I was awaiting passage to Aberdeen on the Isle of Jersey, a Hospital Ship.

He called again and saw me on the Hospital Ship and said he could take me as a cot case, but I refused and he took a coder by the name of Pat Cleary in my place. When a doctor saw me on the ship and I gave my name, the chap next to me asked, had I got a brother on the "Neptune"? and told me he had got off the ship pretending he had got stomach trouble as he had a funny feeling about the "Neptune".

I arrived at HMS Drake after getting extra leave from my doctor, and going through the gate heard a Chief P.O. say 'What did I tell you Jan? I was right'. Incidentally I got a job answering phone calls from the Post Office and the first call I got was " Request further whereabouts of son Pat Cleary DGX signed mother. To add to this story when I joined barracks at Drake, I was piped on the Tannoy to report to the Drafting Office. On the way I met a draft of mine and had a quick yarn to a coder I knew, and he said they were off to the Prince of Wales. When I got my draft the Chief said 'Where have you been'? I told him my own doctor had given me an extra week at home. The Chief replied that he had me down for the Prince of Wales a big ship, very safe'.

Eventually I got a ship called HMS Pangbourne which, when I got to Harwich found it to be a Minesweeper, one of last war's coal burners called the "Smokey Joe's ". How much we earned that one-shilling a day extra, escorting Collier's and Tanker's up and down the East Coast and in the Faroes trimming our own minefields.

My uncles, six of them, were all on active service, one Horace Hender died on the "Furious" another was on the "Lively" trying to find survivors, of which there was only one from the "Neptune". I knew after all this, that someone up above was watching over me for the rest of the war.

ooOoo

TORPOINT:

Fred Timms recalls:

During the early months of 1940 it was very quiet in Plymouth, East Cornwall and the surrounding area.

When FRANCE threw in the towel, Devon and Cornwall became vunerable to the Luftwaffe, who carried on their emerging bombing raid operations over a wider area of the South West.

I was sixteen years old, employed by a firm called Cease Trading and was then learning a trade as a Building Contractor. Being eager to volunteer but too young for the Armed Forces, I was recommended to apply for a job with the NAAFI, as a Canteen Assistant on a land based job until my seventeen birthday, when I would officialy become available to serve in the canteens aboard H.M. Warships. This came about, and I was drafted into the kitchens of HMS. Raleigh, a new Military Naval Establishment, who were then engaged in receiving men called up for naval duties. I started my employment as a Kitchen Hand and gradually worked my way up until I became a Shop Assistant working behind the counters serving the navies seamen with all their requirements, which were quite meagre because there was rationing on.

ooOoo

The beginning of the year brought with it the rationing of food. This is when Ration Books became a major part of the weekly shopping. There were different coloured books for different ranges of age. A buff coloured one for adults above a certain age, a blue coloured one for children above a certain age and a green one for minors and babies below a certain age. The purpose of rationing food was introduced to stop people panic buying. It was always going to be a massive problem to feed a nation at war, the ships that brought food to the shores of Britain would come under attack and quite possibly sunk. Plans had already been draw up to turn parklands and gardens into workable allotments, so that essential and nutritious vegetable crops would be grown to feed everybody (hence the later 'DIG FOR VICTORY' programme). A force of Land Army girls was created so that they could take over the menial task of the farm labourer, to replace those farm workers called up to do Military Service. Everyone was allowed a certain amount of food per week but you could only buy food if you had enough coupons in your Ration Book. Each time you bought the allotted amount, the shopkeeper would either cut out the coupon or mark it with a crayon pencil that could not be rubbed out. The purpose of which was to stop people from buying more than what they were entitled too. So on the 8th of January Rationing began, and the weekly allowance per person per week was:

4oz (100g) of	Bacon or,Ham,
12 oz (350g)	Sugar
4oz (100g)	Butter.
2 oz (50g)	Cheese
2oz (50 g)	Tea
4 oz (100g)	Margarine
4oz (100g)	Cooking Fat

Milk was 3 pints per week: adults expectant mothers 7 pints, infants 14 pints, children up to 7 pints, invalids were allowed 14 pints. 4 eggs per month, (except for expectant mothers). Infants and children were allowed 12 eggs per month. Two oranges for children per month, plus fruit juice, and Cod Liver Oil.
Meat to the value of 1s-2d. (7 new pence), could buy 4 sausages or, 2 lamb chops.
A chicken would cost about 5s. (25 new pence).
Sweets per month 12 oz (350 g)
Obviously the bigger the family, the more was purchased, but certainly those times were extremely hard.

ooOoo

TORPOINT:
Norman Beaver MBE recalls:

Some war news was bad, but some good news that reached us was that a Devonport warship *HMS. "Exeter"* had engaged the German Battleship the "*Graf Spee", Exeter* had been badly damaged the day before she returned to Devonport, we were all informed. Mr. Peacock (Head Master) paraded the whole school in the playground and when *HMS. "Exeter"* made her way triumphantly up the Hamoaze he raised his hand and we all gave three hearty cheers. [Author's note circa Jan- Feb 1940]

Tue. 19th Mar. **SOUTH WEST ENGLAND.**

An un-identified aircraft was reported off Plymouth. A yellow warning was issued to the docks and dockyard area.

Sat. 13th Apr. **NORWAY - ANDALSNES:**

British Troops landed at Andalsnes and Namsos. Hitler alarmed by this, ordered the evacuation of his troops from Narvik. During the Battle of Narvik, British Warships, amongst them HMS. *Punjabi, e*ngaged and sank the remaining eight German destroyers. HMS. *Punjabi* was hit by six shells and badly damaged, but waback in action an hour later, during that action a Torpoint sailor was killed.
D/K 63826. C/Sto. RICHARD GEORGE LAUNDRY. Age 33.
CWG. PLYMOUTH NAVAL MEMORIAL Panel 40 Col.3.

Sun 15th Apr. **NORWAY - NARVIK**

British Troops landed in Norway and recaptured Narvik, a small Norwegian fishing town inside the Artic Circle in Northern Norway, which had been occupied by the Germans earlier in the year.

Sat. 11th May.**LONDON:**

Prime Minister. Neville Chamberlain Resigns. Winston Churchill is appointed Minister of the newly formed Coalition Government, and takes on the role of Head of the Government.

SCOTLAND - ROSYTHE:

Arthur Corbidge relates his war time experience:

I was one of the lucky few for the five years of war. From the 18th May 1940 to the 6th April 1946, I served on 2 happy and efficient ships, my first was the *HMS. Renown,* a Battle Cruiser sister ship to *HMS Hood and* until 19th August 1944 when I was posted to a Town Class Frigate HMS Falmouth.

18th May. I joined *HMS. Renown* in Rosythe Dockyard, where she was undergoing a refit. When the refit was completed, we sailed for Scarpa Flow, for I month we were working, after which we sailed for Gibraltar, carrying the flag of a Rear Admiral. We took over with *HMS Ark Royal* and two Destroyer Flotillas, also *HMAS Sydney* who was only with us for one month and we formed Force H. We used to spend a lot of time patrolling the Atlantic, escorting the Carriers with Aircraft to fly off to Malta. We were on patrol in the Atlantic when we spotted a British Merchant ship, which looked suspicious, so we boarded her and found she was manned with a German Prize Crew with a British crew as their prisoners. We took the Germans aboard and the British crew sailed her into Gibraltar. We couldn't get anything out of the Germans as there were 3 "S.S" men among them, we soon found out who they were, on board we had a young electrician who was half German, his father and brother were German, but his mother was English and she brought him back with her to England in 1930, he joined the Navy in 1936. He could speak fluent German, so the Captain put him down in the Cell Flat, and separated the 3 "S.S" men from the others, he was then able to listen to the rest of the mens conversations. We found out a lot of things about another 3 Merchant ships.

ooOoo

TORPOINT.

Henry Banks recalls:

When all the steel erecting was finished, I got a job as a carpenter with the Contractors WIMPY and the first job of work was laying the screed boards for the road at the gun site at Millbrook. I was in charge of six Gypsies, I don't mind telling you that it was a real test of wills. When that job was finished we moved to Radford Dip Valley. I along with others was laying the foundations for the fuel storage tanks. While working in the rain and the deep water, I trod on a piece of wood that was stuck in the mud unfortunately, a nail pieced my foot, needless to say my foot became poisoned, off work again. During that period of sickness I remember one day, it was a Wednesday afternoon and a lovely clear day at that, I was up at my father's garden tending the poultry and his two incubators, suddenly "ALL HELL BROKE LOOSE" every gun around Plymouth was banging away and the next thing there was a terrific roar, there must have been two Squadrons of German Aircraft coming right down the river from the north. They were so low that I could see the men inside. Strangely enough I felt no fear, just stared in wonder and surprise.

ooOoo

Fri. 24th May. **NORWAY - NARVIK:**

The raid on Narvik was successful, but a decision had already been made to evacuate the troops fighting there. (if there were any Torpoint soldiers involved it has not been recorded).

Sun. 26th May.**BELGIUM - DUNKERQUE:**

Evacuation of Dunkerque (Dunkirk) begins. One cannot imagine the mayhem that followed during the next week, when the evacuation of the retreating British and French armies were cornered and trapped at Dunkirk. So began a rescue that was to be recorded in the Annuals of History. It had to be a combined effort of the Army, Navy and Air Force, to ensure that the evacuation proceeded with maximum resources and effort. The Army was to fight a rear guard action, the Air Force to attack and down any of the Luftwaffe planes that patrolled the skies above, and the Navy to take off and ferry the soldiers back to safety across the Straits of Dover, so that the beleaguered and dis-organised British Expeditionary Force (BEF) could be regrouped and organised into an Army ready to fight another day. Amongst the Armada of Ships of approximately 1.000, plus vessels that were commandeered to take part in Operation Dynamo was HMS. *Bideford* the only Sloop type ship that was part of the Royal Navy's force of Cruisers, Destroyers, Corvettes, Gunboats, plus many other types of ships. Others were made up from RAF Seaplane Tenders, French, Polish, and Dutch Warships, and masses of small sailing boats of all sorts of shapes and sizes, that came from all seaside resorts, ports and rivers around the South Coast of England. Such was the make up of the Armada, all to play a vital role in the ensuing Evacuation.

Mon. 27th May.

The beaches at Dunkerque were crowded with troops. Overhead the air battle began and 50 German aircraft were shot down with a loss of 14 RAF planes. 14,000 troops were lifted in the first 24 hours and still the bombing, shelling and strafing continued.

Tue. 28th May.

The Belgian Army surrendered, and a further 25,000 British troops were evacuated and shipped back to Dover.

Wed. 29th May.

In the evacuation, along with many others supporting ships, HMS. *Bideford, Locust, Mosquito & Wakefield* were attacked by Ju.87. Stuka dive bombers. Unfortunately HMS. *Wakefield* was bombed, and sank with great loss of life.

HMS. *Bideford* had her stern blown off, sustaining casualties and one fatality which was a Torpoint sailor:

D/JX 140849. L/S. FREDRICK JOHN CROCKER. Age 21 was killed.

CWG. DOVER. (ST JAMES) CEMETERY.

[Authors Note: HMS *Bideford* was saved from a worst fate by being towed from the beech by HMS *Locust.*]

Thu. 30th May. **ENGLAND – St. MARGARETS BAY**

French ships had joined in the rescue and the French destroyer *Bourrasque* was dive-bombed and sunk, the same fate was to happen to HMS *Wakefield,* despite the aerial bombardment during a period of one hour, 4,000 troops were lifted from the beaches. The following day the 31st. approx 68,000 troops had been taken away from the beaches and still the aerial bombardment continued. With the whine of Stuka Bombers diving from high above in the sky, before they aimed their bombs and jettisoned them on the lines of troops winding there way to the waters edge. Then flying in low they strafed them with machine gun fire. With bullets whizzing about the crunch of exploding bombs, the smoke and stench of cordite mixed with burning fuel, rubber tyres and any other type of combustible items. The thin lines of troops still managed to make there way to the waters edge before wading into the sea towards the waiting flotilla of small boats. As the incoming tide became deeper some of the soldiers drowned whilst others, possibly up to their necks in the water before they were hauled out and ferried out to the waiting larger ships, then across the open seas to the shores at Dover and St Margaret's Bay. But not all survived a number of the Naval ships including many of the flottila of small boats were sunk.

ENGLAND - KENT:

Royal Marine, Fred Harwood recalls:

Whilst attending the wounded, one of the other musicians and I were travelling on an East Kent Bus from Folkstone to Deal taking the wounded to the sickbay at Deal. Painted on its top was a big red cross, there were no seats but stretchers suspended from the roof. On one trip a German fighter flew over us, we had all been given rifles to use in an attack that never came thank goodness. That afternoon was the first time I had had a rifle in my hands, things were altering now. The school was looking for a new home, but on the 7th June it was back to sea for me, just in time to see the detachment arrive back from leave.

[Authors note Fred Harwood was at the time stationed at the Royal Military School of Music, Deal].

Sun. 2nd Jun. **NORWAY - NARVIK:**

Throughout the Evacuation of Dunkerque, other British forces involved in the landings at Narvik, were being evacuated. Ships of the Royal Navy were there in place to commence and assist in their evacuation.

Tue. 4th Jun. **ENGLAND – DOVER:**

The Dunkerque Evacuation was completed with over 350,000 soldiers of the British Expeditionary Force being saved including many French and Belgium troops. All these troops over the previous five days had been taken by train to London for onward dispersal at various Barracks throughout the British Isles for reassembly into British Army Battalions. Nevertheless reminants of the BEF were left to fight a rearguard action and were either killed or taken prisoners to finish the war as POW's

Sat. 8th Jun. **NORWAY - NARVIK:**

The Evacuation of Narvik was in its last phase, the last of the 25,000 deployed troops were evacuated. Throughout that period of time the battles at sea, between the German and British Navy had continued.

ooOoo

TORPOINT:

Henry Banks recalls:

Of course I was still in Torpoint when The Dunkirk Evacuation took place and afterwards Trevol Road was packed with hundreds of survivors of all countries and they were in a shocking state.

ooOoo

Sun. 9th Jun. **NORWEGIAN SEA:**

After the Evacuation of Narvik, the Aircraft Carrier HMS. *Glorious* with RAF planes on board, along with escort destroyers HMS. *Acasta & Ardent w*hilst steaming on their homeward voyage, the German battle cruiser *Scharnhorst* and her escort opened fire, HMS. *Glorious* sustained severe shelling, resulting in fires, she received further severe damage aft and began to list heavily, before she rolled over and sunk. In the ensuing engagement, the *Scharnhorst* and its escort ship, sunk the two other ships. The total loss of officers and men drowned that day were 2,203.
HMS. *Glorious w*as to lose 1,515 officers and men, including RAF personnel. Amongst those sailors drowned on board HMS. *Glorious*, were four sailors from Torpoint:
D/JX 131337. L/S. DANIEL EDWARD HEALY. Age 27
Panel 37 Col. 1
D/KX 115164. P.O. FREDRICK VICTOR LEACH. Age 31
Panel 36 Col. 3
D/JX 139859. L/S. ARTHUR LESLIE MILLETT. Age 22
Panel 37. Col. 1

&

D/MX 47135.E.R.A. 2nd/Cl. THOMAS FREDRICK NETHERCOTT Age 38
Panel 42 Col. 1 [Authors Note: Brother of James Nethercott who lost his life just ten months before when HMS. *Courageous* was sunk].
ALL ABOVE CWG. PLYMOUTH WAR MEMORIAL.

Mon. 17th Jun. **NORTH AFRICA - EYGPT :**

A Torpoint soldier, became the first soldier to be killed from Torpoint.

1882097. SAPPER. CHARLES JOHN MUDGE. Age 22

Royal Engineers 2nd Field Sqd,

CWG. El ALEMEIN WAR CEM XB3 g17.

Wed. 19th Jun. **CHANNEL ISLANDS:**

Once France fell to the Germans, with the close proximity of the Channel Islands to France, it was inevitable that the Germans would invade and take over the Islands, the decision was made to evacuate as many as possible, thus the Evacuation of the Channel Islands began. Within 5 days 22,656 British citizens were evacuated. It was to become the third major British Evacuation within a matter of weeks.

Fri. 21st Jun. **FRANCE - PARIS:**

France capitulates to the Germans and the surrender negotiations were arranged to take place in the same railway carriage that had been used at the end of the last war, when it was Germany's turn to sign the documents of surrender. Since that day the railway carriage had been kept by the French as a Museum Piece that had become a proud French exhibit to its victory over Germany. Now Hitler as a point of humiliation to the French, used the same railway carriage and venue for the French to sign the Document of Surrender. After this last signing of surrender, Hitler had become the Master of Czechoslovakia, Poland, Norway, Denmark, Holland, Belgium and France, six of which had surrendered to the Germans within the last nine (9) months. But Hitler had not forgotten his determination to bring Britain to her knees. On the other hand, Winston Churchill was equally determined that would never happen. That same night Churchill made his famous speech declaring: "His Majesty's Government believe, that whatever happens, they will be able to carry the war, wherever it may be, on the seas, in the air, and on the land, to a successful conclusion" Operation "CATAPULT" the code name given to the blockade of all French Warships, docked in various ports in France and French North Africa. The operation was to ensure that the Germans could not capture the French Navy and be used against the isolated British. Many ships from the Northern French Ports and the Mediterranean Ports, upped anchor, sailed to the Ports of Southern Britain and over to North Africa in particular the port of Mers-el Kabir.

PLYMOUTH:

Part of the French Navy sailed into Plymouth. The battleship *Paris*, a Cruiser *No. 141* and the largest Submarine at that time *Surcouf*, plus one or two other smaller craft, entered Plymouth and sailed up the Hamoaze, and either anchored in mid-stream or tied up in the north basin off Devonport Royal Dockyard. At that time suspicions were very high as to what the French Navy, and of course their Army, were likely to do, either take sides with the Germans or, remain allies to the British forces. Surveillance and security took over and the French Naval vessels were kept under guard at all times.

ooOoo

TORPOINT:

Norman Beaver MBE. recalls:

1940 were the 'dark years of the war' although as schoolboys, we did not realise the seriousness of it. France had fallen and in the first instance many frenchmen made their way to

England. As boys we were excited when so many ships of the French Fleet arrived at Devonport, headed by the French battleship *Paris*. The Submarine *Surcouf*, the largest Submarine in the world also arrived. It had 8" inch guns and carried a seaplane - this was a great attraction for us lads.

ooOoo

Sun. 30th Jun. **TORPOINT:**

Approximately at 0100 hrs, what the Americans called '*the phoney war'*, came to an abrupt end. The wail of Plymouths "Alert" sirens sounded off, an unidentified aircraft, possibly on a reconnaissance mission, flew over Plymouth & Devonport Dockyard, across the waters of the Hamoaze, towards the Oil Tanks at Thanckes Farm. It released 2 (HE) high explosive bombs. This incident was voiced by Freda Hawken (nee Spear) who lived in No. 5 Pato Point Wilcove. Her recollection was:

Freda recalls:

"I remember the first bomb that fell in the back lane near Maryfield House. We were sat on the floor at the back of the house, when we heard this plane coming over, then this almighty bang. The next day we went up to see the big craters and picked up pieces of shrapnel. Now it really was war! "

ooOoo

The two HE bombs, which missed the tanks by half a mile, landed in the grounds of the Antony Estate, just off the lane leading up from Wilcove, towards the old school (now Maryfield House, behind Maryfield Church). The damage caused was mainly to trees and surrounding stonewalls, there were no casualties. Obviously the roar from the overhead plane engines, and the following explosion of bombs, certainly created a lot of interest. Many of the local dwellers from Wilcove, made their way to the bomb craters to see the damage. At that point in time, little did they or anyone else know or understand, what they and the inhabitants of Torpoint and the surrounding district, were in for?

[Authors Note: During the war, newspapers & pictures were censored, so names of specific places etc., were never printed. Signposts were removed in the event of an invasion, and were not replaced until after the war. An extract from the Cornish Times dated Friday 5th July 1940 refers to this incident].

'Quote:'

NEWSPAPER REPORT ON FIRST 2 BOMBS TO LAND IN CORNWALL:

A. S. W. AIR-RAID

PHLEGMATIC RESIDENTS NEAR BOMB CRATERS

On Saturday night the South West of England was to experience the first of many air raids when two bombs were dropped in a grass field just outside the town. The net result of the explosion, apart from leaving two moderately sized craters, was to demolish a few yards of fencing, and to cause one of a herd of cows in the field to give premature birth to a calf.

Although there are a number of houses and a church not far from the spot where the bombs fell, none of them were damaged in the slightest degree and the occupants for the most part did not even stir from their beds, and certainly were not unduly alarmed.

Typical of the reactions to this early-morning visitation of enemy aircraft were those of Mr. R. J. Mathews a farm worker who lived in a cottage 200 yards away, and was the first to discover the bomb craters. Mr. Mathews told the "CORNISH TIMES" Reporter that he and his family were in bed when they were aroused by what they believed to be the report of a gun. They went downstairs, and checked around and all seemed well, then there was a knock on the front door and a woman neighbour who lives alone in a house nearby, asked if she could stay with them for a while until the raid was over. And all the time the two children remained asleep in bed.

SURPRISED TO FIND CRATERS:

The next morning at about 6 o'clock, when he went out into the field to bring in the cows for milking, he was surprised to see two newly-created cavities in the earth, right at the very edge of the field where it is divided from a coppice by a metal fence. Most of the cows had wandered over to the craters to gaze inquisitively at them, as all cows are want to do when anything untoward happens around them.

"It is a wonder that some of the cows were not killed," said Mr. Mathews, but as far as I could see they were not hurt in any way, except that one of them licked a calf, probably due to shock.

Soon afterwards schoolboys and others began to arrive for the purpose of seeing what damage had been done, or pick up a relic, strictly against official injunction, and by the afternoon the souvenir hunters had gone over the ground so thoroughly that not a single fragment of metal or trace of any bombs remained. So keen was the desire to take home a scrap of German "HE" to display before marveling eyes, or perhaps to adorn a private museum, that one small boy with marked business acumen, was able to dispose of a piece to a grown up for the non-profiteering sum of sixpence.

Spectators became more numerous during the day, and for a period the Police mounted guard and refused admittance to the field. Measurements were also taken, one of the craters was found to be 29ft wide by 10ft deep, and the other rather smaller. From one to the other was a distance of about 50 yards.

NEARBY CHURCH SAFE:

The explosion was also heard by a clergyman whose house was situated about 400 yards away from the field. Only a few minutes previously he had been looking out of the window, suddenly he heard two dull thudding explosions, followed by a heavy crash and two lighter ones, anxious for the church, the clergyman examined it on the following day to find out whether the bombs had caused any ill effect. No damage whatever was evident, and although a twisted piece of metal was picked up near the door, the woodwork had not been touched.

LITTLE SLEEP LOST:

Miss Q. Willcocks, who lives with her parents less than a quarter of a mile away from the scene of the explosions, related to a "CORNISH TIMES" Reporter how they were all in bed when they were awakened at about 12.50. a.m. by the sound of the explosions, which they all thought to be a gun being fired. The vibration was such that it shook the house like others in the vicinity. However they did not lose much sleep as a result of the incident.

Two soldiers doing guard duty about 100 yards away heard a plane overhead and the shriek of the falling missiles, which seemed to have been released directly above their heads. One of them an old soldier fell down flat in the 'approved manner' while the other took cover in a nearby shelter.

Several people in the town were awakened and hurried in various stages of dress and undress, to public air-raid shelters. Others peacefully slept through it all, and were surprised to hear next morning that there had been an air raid.

A sailor claimed to have caught sight of an enemy plane for a split second and later heard the explosions. He estimated the plane a solitary raider was flying at a height of about 26,000 feet.

'Unquote'

Keith Lilyman, who lived in Antony, was 8 years old when he refers to this incident.

When we heard about the bombs being dropped behind the church at Maryfield, me and my mate got on our bikes, and peddled like hell, to see where the bombs had dropped, we went down the Antony drive and turned down the rutted School Lane towards the Old School, getting off our bikes, we left them in the old playground, well it was just a patch of rough ground. Some people were in the next field so we clambered through the hedge and made our way to where a group of people stood looking at a big hole with piles of mud all around it. It as quite deep and nothing really to see, but further along there was a copse where other people were coming out of, so we went into the wooded area where another bomb had landed, and had blown a big hole in the stone wall and felled some trees. We started looking for bits of metal to take as mementoes of the bomb.

He also relates the fact that he went to school in Saltash, cycling into Torpoint to catch the ferry across to Devonport, then the train from Devonport Station via St Budeaux, across the bridge into Saltash where they got off and cycled to school.

[Authors Note: Was Keith that certain little boy who sold on his piece of bomb for sixpence? Also was the twisted piece of metal the Clergyman found shrapnel? During the following months that extended into years, only parts of the experience, suffering and depravity of many, can only be described in the following sequence of bombing raids that occurred around the area of Plymouth and the Urban District of Torpoint, it can also be stressed that with its close proximity to Plymouth, Torpoint shared in the 'alerts' and the bombing raids that happened throughout those dark and dismal days. Along with many other events that had a direct bearing on the lives and environment of so many, and to say the least must not be misread or misleading?]

The night-time bombing raids by the Luftwaffe were repetitive, there was always the constant sound of the threatening drone of Wooom Wooom Wooom, that became associated to the sound of German aircraft overhead. Not necessarily making attacks on Plymouth or Torpoint, but by virtue of the German airfields located in

France, the bombers would be flying overhead nightly towards other parts of, Bristol, Wales, and other regions of the South West. With the wail of the air-raid siren, the systems surrounding Plymouth, would swing into action. The intense beams of the search lights, would cut through the blackness of the night sky, in their attempt to light up and pinpoint an invading aircraft. Once success was achieved, it became the turn of the Observers and Artillery Gunners to identify the range and open fire with their Ack-Ack guns. Round after round would be discharged in a vain attempt to hit the intruders, some with success. Not forgetting the role the Air Force Pilots who attacked the incoming raiders, spitting bullets from their guns, in a lot of cases being successful. With all this noise and mayhem going on night after night, a normal nights sleep, never seemed possible, but people did, and soon got used to this constant interruption, and got on with their lives.

Sun. 30th Jun. **CHANNEL ISLANDS – JERSEY:**

Such was the speed of the advance of the German Army across France that German troops landed on British soil 'The Channel Islands'. The German Occupation had begun and the Islands became isolated and within easy reach of the mainland of England. Strange as it may seem but the uniformed British 'Bobby' were still permitted to patrol the streets? The Germans also issued everyone with Identity Cards dual printed in German and English that included a photograph of the recipient.

Mon. 1st Jul. **NORTH AFRICA - ALGERIA :**

Operation "CATAPULT" began, on the 3rd of July it was put into force. British Navy Warships blockaded Mers- el Kabir where most of the Mediterranean Fleet had fled. The British gave the French four choices:
a) To sail to British Harbors and 'fight with us'
b) To sail them into a British port and hand them over to British crews.
c) To demilitarize them, or
d) To scuttle them in such a way that the Germans could not use them.
The French refused. Britain then gave a fifth choice: To sail them to the French West Indies, where they would either be disarmed, or handed over to the United States and held until after the war had finished.

Wed. 3rd Jul.

The French again refused. The British warships opened fire. The bombardment lasted for five minutes destroying the ships in the port.

PLYMOUTH:

On the 3rd of July under the Operational Code Name of **"CATAPULT",** a contingent of armed British Troops, surrounded the Destoyer No. 141 and the *Paris.* The French sailors surrendered without any hesitation. Not so with the Submarine *Surcouf,* as the British boarding party approached, 2 officers were shot dead, and in the return fire a British Officer was shot and killed by a French Officer, who was very rapidly overpowered, clubbed down and subsequently died. The Submarine's crew were disarmed and marched ashore under strong escort and interned. All the other French vessels received the same treatment. Maybe this side of the story relates strongly to Fred Timms account of what happened to some of the French sailors who were interned at HMS. *Raleigh.* (See Page 67, German aerial reconnaissance photo plate, taken on the 21st. July 1940).

TORPOINT:

Fred Timms recalls:

With the fall of France, about 300 Frenchmen who had escaped the advancing German Army were landed at Trevol Pier, there they were surrounded by Royal Marines and marched to HMS. Raleigh every man being spaced three meters apart in single file. As I was on duty at six o'clock in the morning and on my way to work, I was interrogated by a Sgt. Royal Marine and told to walk on the other side of the road to the Raleigh Gates, where it was confirmed that I was genuine and employed there. The Frenchmen were taken to a new gym shed where they were stripped down washed and instructed to lay down on the polished floor, the gym was completely surrounded by armed Royal Marines. I was one of the very few allowed into the building, twice everyday, to supply them with cigarettes and chocolate. It was four days before things got back to normal at the camp. One Frenchmen whose rank was one of the lowest in the French Navy, whilst in transit across the Channel, had found a French Naval Officers cap, and was wearing it when he entered through Raleigh Gates, so being recognised as an Officer was segregated from the rest of them and billeted in Officers Quarters until he was unmasked

ooOoo

Norman Beaver MBE. recalls:

It was not long before the French were causing problems, the Royal Navy boarded the *Surcouf* and there was loss of life on both sides. Down at the Laun's, where we played, French fishing boats were scuttled, to rest on the mud for the duration of the war. All the French Ships were crowded with troops, we had never seen so many ships in Devonport, and would never ever see so many gathered again. We boys were keen to pick up shrapnel after air raids. This consisted of pieces of anti-aircraft shells and bombs, much of it from the beaches at Torpoint. We did not realise the danger of this, the enemy also dropped Anti-Personnel bombs!

ooOoo

Thu. 4th Jul. **SOUTH WEST ENGLAND:**

A Heinkel 111 of 4KG54 was shot down by a Spitfire of 92 Squadron. Possibly the first kill to Group 10. Royal Air Force.

Fri. 5th Jul.

There was spasmodic bombing carried out over Devon and, at approx 1015 in the morning, one of the bombers flew over Plymouth, heading in the direction of the Oil Tanks at Thanckes Park. It dropped two bombs, exploding upon impact, the two bombs caused great craters in the field adjacent to the cricket field and Pavilion, the only damaged caused was dislodged telephone poles and lines, and knocking great holes in the surrounding dry stone walls.

[Authors Note: The following is a report made out by the Luftwaffe Pilot on that particular raid.English translation *with kind permission of Before and After the Battle.*]

SOMEWHERE IN GERMAN OCCUPIED FRANCE:

Command Division
Group Ic

5th Jul. 1940:
12.00

KR Telegram to L. M. S. Kurfurst, Sealion, Ic, and
Lfl. 5 over Ob. d. L.
Special information no. 9 of 5.7. 1940

A) Air Situation
2A
Preliminary report.

1. Junker 88 from III. /L. G. 1 (sarted 15.45 hours) for reconnaissance over : Falmouth
2. Junkers 88 from III./ L.G. 1 (started 13.00 hours) for attack on convoy over Falmouth

Results.

3. Junkers 88 from III./L. G. 1(started 13.20 hours), attack at 15.10 hours on the outskirts of .Falmouth. Good hits on warehouse. 1 hit on a transporter of 3000-4000 tons.

Bomb Pattern — 6 SC 500
Observation — Large convoy in area 50 11, westerly direction.
Weather — Low Cloud limit 1500m. 10/10 cover

4 Junkers 88 from III./L. G. 1(started 14.30 – 14.15)
1 Junker 88 attacked at 16.20 on a tank base in West Plymouth with 2 SC 500. One Oil Tank hit. Large column of smoke.
1Junker 88 attacked at 16.15 hours on Falmouth Harbour with 2 SC 500 . Direct hits on warehouses. good effect.
1 Junker 88 at 17.25, attack on 5000 ton transporter with 2 SC 500. Damage observed to the stern.
1.Junkers 88 at 17.20 hours, attack on 8,000 ton transporter from the Convoy in area 50 11 with 2 SC500. Effect not seen.

1 Do 17. from 2. / (F) 123 (started 16.50 hours) attack on 1 Warship and a Cargo ship 40 km. North of Cherbourg. Effect not observed.

Defence. — Light and heavy flak from the warshi

2b: — Fdl. fighter patrol on the convoy in the area 50 11 and 3138 (15- 20 aircraft)
Heavy flak defences at Plymouth from the cruiser's in the Harbour. Barrage Balloons were released as the aircraft flew in.

'unquote'.

Ref 2A. The reference to the damage caused by the bombs e.g. smoke from the hit tank?
2b. The heavy flak from the Cruiser Blyskawika. (see Charles Lowings report below).
[Authors Note: Five Torpoint residents recollect incident item 5 above]

Henry Banks recalls:

"I heard gun fire and looked up just in time to see a lone German bomber pop out of the clouds and saw two bombs leave the aircraft. Those two bombs hit and blocked the main road on the top bend of Thanckes Hill , they were the first bombs ever dropped on Torpoint.

[Authors Note: Slight correction the second two bombs dropped on Torpoint]

Charles E. Lowing recalls:

I was working for SWEB down at Wilcove, when we heard the sound of an aeroplane flying quite low, all of a sudden the guns on the two Polish ships the "Blyskawika" and the depot ship "Gydinia" moored over in the dockyard simultaneously started banging away. We spotted the plane as it flew over the oil tanks and saw two bombs being dropped from its belly, we watched them fall then there were two large explosions as they hit the ground out of sight. I remember saying "Crickey were being bombed". After we had finished work we went and saw the two bomb craters in the field opposite the Tanks.

Another gentleman named Mervyn Bersey from Millbrook relates, he was working in a field when he heard two dull thuds and flashes. Taking notice, saw plumes of smoke rising from the vicinity of Torpoint.
[Author's note: This Gentleman of Notability Mr. Mervyn Bersey, I refer to later in the chapter on 1941].

Another lady who wishes to remain anonymous, confirms this incident and remembers:

'That the bombs landed in the field above the cricket ground.'

Peter Rolfe recalls:

The Oil Tanks at Thanckes Park were always under constant threat of bombing, after an air-raid, the fields and roads in the surrounding area, would be full of potatoes and shrapnel, caused by the bombs which had missed the tanks and blown up in the potatoe fields.

ooOoo

Sat. 6th Jul. **PLYMOUTH:**

Alert sounded before noon, subsequently received its first real attack by enemy aircraft, bombs were dropped, 3 bombs landed in the area of Swilly Road Devonport, where houses were wrecked, there were casualties and deaths caused by the raid. Ack-Ack opened fire without any success.

Sun. 7th Jul.

Plymouth Alert sounded 15.40 during the afternoon when the second attack began, bombs were dropped causing casualties, one bomber was so low that a man on duty at the Laire Gasworks opened fire with a shot gun, the resulting raid caused much damage, killing 5 people, injuring four others. The bombers got away.

Mon. 8th Jul.

Between the hours of 0047-0500 Plymouth bombed, damage was caused to some private property and to Naval Gun Wharf outhouses. (no further details).

ooOoo

TORPOINT:

Norman Beavers MBE. recalls:

It was several months into the war before we had our first air raid. It was at night and to me at 12 years, it was very frightening not forgetting the rest of the family – my mother must have been petrified when dad was working night shift in the Dockyard and we were without house guidance. [Author's note June-July 1940]:

I also remember going to Maurice's Shop to buy a packet of Five Wild Woodbine cigarettes, the missus used to ask me If they were for my dad?' to which I replied 'yes' so she took my money and handed them to me, I took them up to the fields where me and some other lads smoked them. They were vile.

ooOoo

Tue. 9th Jul. **NORWEGIAN SEA:**

HM. Sub. *Salmon* was sunk in the Norwegian Sea when she entered a unknown German mine field, their were no survivors. Amongst those drowned was Torpoint Submariner:

P/M 39366. CERA. NORMAN JAMES HILL. D.S.M. Age 30.

CWG. PLYMOUTH NAVAL MEMORIAL Panel 39 Col. 2.

Wed. 10th Jul. **TORPOINT:**

Millbrook machine-gunned by low flying bombers, no casualties reported, but the bombers were overhead and the bombing of the South West had truly begun.

Mrs Lornia Dawson relates

I was on my milk round with little Freddie Finimore he was helping to carry the cans we were nearing the top of Anderton Hill when these bombers came around flying very low and began machine gunning along the top we both dropped the cans and dived into the hedge and watched in awe as these planes circled and began firing on the Millbrook quay side where there was a queue of workers waiting to get the ferry to work We found out later that Ron Davis was shot in the shoulder he said. 'If those buggers shoot me going to work I might as well join up. He did join up later. (No records available).

Thu. 11th Jul. **PLYMOUTH:**

Hurricane's of No.87 & 238 Squadron shot down 3 (three) Messerschmitt 109's.

Fri. 12th Jul. **TORPOINT:**

The first of three raids over Plymouth began with the 'Alert' siren sounding at midnight, that lasted for over an hour. Bombs fell in the west part of the city in the Keyham area, and across the water in Torpoint, where bombs fell on the foreshore close to the Torpoint Ferry, also hitting the Police Station that was severely damaged, fortunately without inflicting any casualties. However this event was part of Policeman 'Doug Mitchell's story, after he was posted from Liskeard to Torpoint as follows :

The time at Liskeard passed uneventfully, and the staff were being moved within reach of Plymouth. I was posted to Torpoint. Torpoint was in the firing line, and took some of the bombs that overshot Devonport. It was a ghost town, pounding the beat at night was eerie. Every night the ferry was full on each trip, bringing the residents of Plymouth over to join the trek out into the country. Prams were loaded with a few personal possessions, mainly blankets for the night's sleep in the fields.

The Police station was situated just in front of the Ferry Gates. On one occasion I was standing by the granite post at the entrance to the station yard, and three men were standing by the ferry gate, an air raid was in progress. I was suddenly aware that a bomb appeared to be heading perilously close. I flattened myself behind the post just in time to hear a massive explosion, and was aware of the smell of high explosive. The station had received a direct hit. I struggled to my feet, dislodged a load of slates that had landed on me, to find that one of the three men at the gate had been killed. Fortunately no one in the station had been injured, but the building was a write-off.

Un-named persons recalls:

My next experience was when I was taking the dog for a last walk up Fore Street, when I heard bombs being dropped, I dropped down on the ground by the Cornerstone Church sheltering the dog, I understand that the last bomb to fall, hit the ferry causing much damage. There were two fatalities caused by this incident?
[Authors note: Conflicting stories about the number maybe no one from Torpoint?]

Another excerpt from the Cornish Times dated 12th July 1940, refers to a Torpoint Council Meeting

'Quote'

TORPOINT URBAN COUNCIL

AIR-RAID SHELTER
DAMAGE IN PULIC PLACES
WATER SUPPLY PLENTIFUL

During the greater part of Torpoint Urban Council's meeting last Thursday, A.R.P. Organization was the subject of discussion.
The Chairman (Mr. D. B. Peacock) reviewed the work of the committee, over which he had presided during the past two years and referred to the provision of 364 Anderson Shelter's and the demand made during recent weeks for an additional supply. For those that turned down the offer of the Council Committee's to provide these shelters, provision of some form of protection was necessary, and well-appointed shelters had been erected in different parts of the town. In these 2,250 people could be accommodated and a further 250 people could take refuge in the school shelter which was in charge of Mr. E. Maddaford who was a Warden, after the children had left the school.
Mr. F. H. Roberts observed that community shelters were needed in the higher part of the town and the Western sector.
The Council decided to take steps to ensure protection for the staff at the Offices. Mrs. K Maddaford said there was need for first-aid attendants at the public shelters.
The Chairman expressed sympathy with Mr.J. E. Axon, a former Chairman of the Council, at the death of his wife who had been actively associated with various organisations of the town, also to **Mr. W. Roberts whose wife died in a shelter during a night raid.**
Damage at the Laun Recreation Ground and Bowling Green was reported, and members were assured that the police were dealing with the matter.
Mr. Roberts enquired whether the representative of the council on the Area Assessment Committee, was entitled to a payment of his Expenses, and the Clerk (Mr.A.N.F.Goodman) was instructed to give the matter consideration.
Mr. H.E. Jago for the Water Committee reported that Eglaroose and Crafthole reservoir contained over 4,000,000 gallons, and that the Fire reservoirs at Borough and Carbeale were full. This compared favorably with the same period in 1939 when 3,000,000 gallons were in storage.
Mr. Light, for the Finance and Rating Committee, said the County Valuation Committee did not approve of the Council's action, spreading the period for payment of arrears over three years.
The Surveyor (Mr. G. Rodley) reported that at the Laun Recreation Ground, the expenditure to July 4th amounted to £2316s 6d, and receipts £6.11s. The caretaker had resigned and it was decided that the necessary work should be done by the Council Staff, no successor to Mr. W. Roberts being appointed.
Mr. D.B. Peacock announced at the Council meeting that the Fund for providing comforts for local men serving in H.M Forces had been augmented by £9. 7s 3d given in collection boxes which had been placed in various parts.

'Unquote'.

[Authors note Mrs. **Annie Roberts** who was referred to within the meeting as stated above, by rights is a Casualty of the War. Having conferred with the Commonwealth War Graves Commission, who have advised that anyone who died as a result of an enemy attack would be considered to be a victim and added to the list of War Casualties. Enemy air attacks on Plymouth occurred from the 30th June 1940 on several occasions up until the 12th July 1940 (See above dates). The Newspaper article was published on the 13th July 1940. If a date and cause of death, can be established for Mrs. **Annie Roberts**, the evidence would be accepted by the CWGC. Thus she would become the first Torpoint Civilian Casualty of the War]

Sun. 14th Jul. **SOUTH WEST ENGLAND:**

Hurricanes of 238 Squadron Red Section, Pilots Flt/Lt. J.C. Kennedy,- F/O. C.T. Davis & Sgt. C. Parkinson shot down a Dornier 17P

On the same day in –

SCOTLAND - ROSYTHE:

Whilst HMS. *Furious* was under refit, a Torpoint sailor:
D/JX 136237. L/S. HORACE HENDER Aged 25 died, no other details.
CWG. TORPOINT HORSOM CEMETERY. Sec B grave 747.

Mon. 15th Jul. **PLYMOUTH:** Attacked, no other details.

Tue. 16th Jul. **MEDITERRANEAN SEA:**

HM. Sub. *Pheonix* was depth charged by the Italian torpedo boat *Albatros* off Sicily and sunk. All hands on board were drowned, amongst them was a Torpoint sailor:
D/MX52638. E.R.A. AUBREY GEORGE OLIVER. Aged 27
Torpoint's first submariner to be killed.
CWG. PLYMOUTH NAVAL MEMORIAL Panel 40 Col

On the same day in -

GERMANY - BERLIN:

Adolf Hitler issued a Directive and the following passage is of interest to those people living in Cornwall. *with kind permission of Before and After the Battle*

'Quote'

Since England, in spite of her hopeless military position, shows no signs of being ready to come to an understanding, I have decided to prepare a landing operation against England, and if necessary, to carry it out.

The aim of this operation will be to eliminate the English homeland as a base for the prosecution of the war against Germany and, if necessary, to occupy it completely.

I therefore order as follows.

The landing will be in the form of a surprise crossing on a wide front from Ramsgate to the area west of the Isle of Wight. Units of the Air Force will act as artillery, and units of the Navy as engineers.

The possible advantages of limited operations before the general crossings (e.g. the occupation of the Isle of Wight or of the County of Cornwall), are to be considered from the points of view of each branch of the Armed Forces and the results reported to me.

I reserve the decision to myself.

Preparations for the entire operation must be completed by the middle of August.

These preparations must also create such conditions as will make a landing in England possible, the English Air Force must be so reduced morally and physically, that it is unable to deliver any significant attack against the German crossing....

The Invasion will bear the cover name ' Seelowe '

ADOLF HITLER: DIRECTIVE No. 16. JULY 16 1940.

'Unquote'.

Fri. 19th Jul. **TORPOINT:**

During the hours of darkness mine-laying commenced in the Plymouth sound, minor number of bombs were dropped but there were no casualties.

Sat. 20th Jul.

A Junkers Ju. 88 Shot down by a Hurricane of 56 Squadron.

ooOoo

Released in the Press a Public Notice issued by the Ministry for Food. See copy below. (For clarification the wording states:)

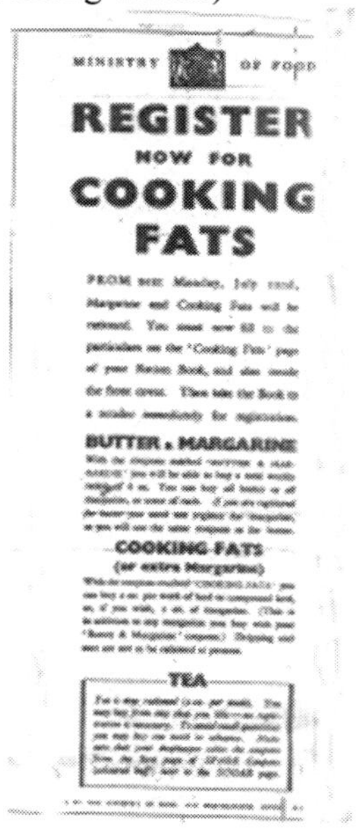

REGISTER
NOW FOR
COOKING FATS

From next Monday 22nd July, Margarine and Cooking Fats will be rationed. You must now fill in the particulars on the 'Cooking Fats' page of your Ration Book, and also inside the front cover. Then take the Book to a retailer.

BUTTER & MARGARINE

With the coupons marked 'BUTTER & MARGARINE' you will be able to buy a total weekly ration of 6oz. You can buy *all* butter or *all* margarine, or some of each. *If you are registered for butter* you need not register for margarine, as you will use the same coupons as the butter.

COOKING FATS

(or extra Margarine).

With the coupons marked 'COOKING FATS' you can buy 2oz. per week of lard or compound land, or, if you wish, 2oz. of margarine. (This is in addition to any margarine you buy with your 'BUTTER & MARGARINE ' coupons.) Dripping and suet are not to be rationed at present.

TEA

Tea is now rationed (2oz. per week). You may buy from any shop you like- no registration is necessary. To avoid small quantities you may buy one week in advance . Make sure that your shopkeeper takes the coupons from first page of SPARE Coupons (coloured buff) next to the sugar page immediately for registration

---

ooOoo

Sun. 21st Jul. **TORPOINT:**

Two HE bombs were dropped at Crafthole, no casualties. One Messerschmitt and one Dornier Do17, Shot down by Hurricanes of 238 Squadron. Another German reconnaissance bomber possibly on the same raid, took aerial photographs of Devonport and Torpoint. Thus obviously identifying future potential targets, and ships that were anchored or tied up in Devonport.

The list of ships and areas identified for future targets for bombing, were as follows:

1. French Courbet Battleship *Paris*:
2. French Cruiser *Surcouf:*
3. Probably Cairo Class anti-aircraft cruiser:
4. Netlayer *Guardian:*
5. Southampton Class light cruiser (probably HMS *Gloucester*):
6. French Fantasque Class flotilla leader:
7. Heavy cruiser *Hawkins* (probably under refit):
8. Escort vessel, apparently new type (perhaps *Woolwich*):
9. Ship, probably light cruiser in refit (perhaps Fiji in fact *HMS Trinidad):*
10. Light cruiser under repair, probably *Emerald*:
11. Light cruiser *Belfast* or, *Edinburgh*, (in fact HMS *Belfast*):
12. Heavy cruiser *Exeter:*
13. 2 French Bourasque class Destroyers:
14. British Ambuscade class Destroyer:
15. 5 British destroyers A-1 class:
16. Destroyer under repair (apparently Campbell class):
17. Accommodation Ship (old Warship), (in fact, Depot Ship HMS *Defiance*):
18. Tribal class Destroyer, (in fact, the Polish Destroyer ORP *Blyskowica*):
19. Floating dock in submerged condition:
20. Passenger Ship [Hospital Ship] 22-24000 BRT:

21. Passenger Ship [Channel Steamer, now an auxiliary cruiser] (in fact auxiliary anti air-craft Ship):
22. Supply ship:
23. Netlayer (HMS *Protector*):
'A State = (i.e. Naval Dockyard):
'B = Dockyard gasworks:
'C = Dockyard Power station:
'D = Oil Depot (Torpoint):
'E = Ammunition Depot:
24 Barrage Balloons:
25 Anti-aircraft Batteries:
26 Ferries (Torpoint ferryboats)

N.B: Item 20: This may well have been the Polish Liner Ship ORP *Gydinia,* that was moored in the Hamoaze just off of Torpoint.

[Authors Note: Unfortunately due to the size of the image the Classification by numbers cannot be seen].

With kind permission of the Imperial War Museum.

Mon. 22nd Jul. **SOUTH WEST ENGLAND:**

More Rationing introduced: Sugar, reduced to 8oz. Margarine, to 6oz, Cooking Fat, to 2oz. Tea allowance, reduced to 2oz, and Meat, down to 1/10p worth. All this per person per week.

TORPOINT:

On the same day during an air raid on Plymouth, a flight of mine-laying Ju 88 Bombers, dropped 25 bombs on Plymouth, many houses were wrecked. One of the Ju.88's flying low, opened fire with its machine guns on the civilians below. During the same raid, in a bizarre incident which happened above Plymouth, a Ju.88 Bomber trying to avoid a defence Barrage Balloon, stalled its engines and fell on top of it. Fortunately the propellers did not penetrate the Hydrogen gas bag. As the crew prepared to bale out, the aircraft slid off the balloon. The pilot regaining control of his aircraft, dropped his bombs before heading back out over the sea. Another bomber hit a balloon severing its cable. The balloon gently took to flight, with the cable trailing behind it. The runaway balloon landed on the top of roofs of the houses at the top end of Clarence Road, before once again taking flight over the open fields.

Edith Eady a resident of Wilcove remembers this incident.

The following morning, as I was riding my bike to work down the lane leading to Carbeile Mill Farm I was stopped by some soldiers, who ordered her 'Stop don't go any further'. She could plainly see why, the trailing cable of the runaway balloon had become entangled in the trees down near Carbeile Mill Farm (now part the Goad Avenue Estate).

Tue. 23rd Jul.

Torpoint was attacked, bombs were dropped, but it was more of a case of scare-mongering than anything else. In the raid 15 bombs were dropped and one magnetic mine landed near Kingsand.

[Author's note. The below story appears to fit in the with this incident]

John Peach recalls:

My first real scary moments came one summer's afternoon. I was with mum, who was pushing Marjorie in her pram, and Uncle Dick mum's brother, we were approaching HMS Raleigh when the droning sound of an aircraft could be heard. Looking up it didn't seem to be that far away. Next came the awful screaming sound of the bomb, mum pushed me into the hedge covering me with her body. There was an enormous explosion, I am not sure where it landed exactly, but too close for comfort. Needless to say the afternoons walk was quickly ended.

My school life started at the Infants School at Albion Road. One of the first things I can remember is seeing a metal meshed cage with a steel like top standing in the classroom, we were practicing sitting in it in case an air raid occurred. I cannot remember that happening, but we would be taken to the large concrete shelters at the bottom of the playground. One teacher Miss Mitchell, instructed us on how to put on our "Mickey Mouse" Gas Masks, they were called that because they were made to look like the face of "Mickey Mouse".

[Authors note: The metal case John Peach is referring to is called a Morrison Shelter, instigated by Mr.Herbert Morrison, MP as an alternative to the outdoor Anderson Shelter, was designed to be used as an indoor shelter of metal construction, approximately 6 feet x 3 feet, standing 3 feet in height and surrounded by wire caging, it could also be used as a bed area or a table].

Freda recalls:

As well as a Polish ship anchored in the Harbour, we had the Free French Ships in dock. One day some of the French sailors came across in a boat and were admiring our flowers in the garden. My mum said pick them a bunch of flowers', which I did, and handed them over to one of them. The next time they came across, they gave me a box of chocolates (a rare treat in those days), with a note which said, "For the beautiful flowers so gracefully given, Thank You". After that the Polish boys came across with a huge big bottle of wine in a wicker basket. We were sorry we could not invite them in for tea, with all our men away it wasn't the done thing in those days. What a difference it is nowadays. We never saw them again I do hope they got home safely. The sailor boys on the Polish ship many times saved us a lot, with all the Ack-Ack they put up.

Wed. 24th Jul. **SOUTH WEST ENGLAND:**

Junkers Ju. 88 shot down by Spitfire of 92 Squadron.

Thu. 25th Jul.

Stab StG/1 Dornier Do17m shot down by Spitfire of 152 Squadron.

Fri. 26th Jul.

1/KG4 Heinkel 111 shot down by Hurricane of 87 Squadron.

Tue. 30th Jul. **TORPOINT:**

Four bombs were dropped near Scarsdon Fort on the Antony Estate. An estate cottage was badly damaged. There was also one 250Kg UXB (Unexploded Bomb) found that landed at 23.15.
They were defused by the Bomb Disposal Squad.

Record Log No. 5187 incidents reported on Tuesday 30/7/40 - Incident 1:

23.15~ Torpoint.~ Explosions near Tregantle.
23.22~ Torpoint.~ bomb dropped in garden of Mr. Roger Wolson's house in Antony at 23.05, No Damage.
23.22~ Torpoint.~ Send Fire Engine at once fires near Tregantle fort.
23.55~ County A.R.P.~ Incident one. Incendiary bombs reported near Trevol Road Tregantle, Fort fires have been caused, Fire Engine has been sent.
23.35~ P.D.~ Incendiary bombs at Earth Hill north of Lyhner river. Dealt with by Saltash.

Record Log No. 5187 incidents reported Wednesday 31/7/40 - Incident 2:

00.05~Torpoint.~ Incident,One Torpoint Fire Engine sent.
00.16~to A.R.P.~ Officer Commanding Troops:
Tregantle believes bombs dropped at the top of Antony Hill, just off the road, causing search to be made by Officer Commanding Scarsdown Camp.
00.25~to County~ Following received from A.R.P officer commanding troops at Tregantle, believes 2 UXB's. have fallen just of the road at the top of Antony Hill, has commenced search as this is a military area, communicate direct with Scarsdown.
00.20~Torpoint.~ 2 UXB's have fallen near Tregantle, Scarsdown Fort. Fire engine returned, Captain of Fire Brigade refuses to send engine to Earth Hill, not in his district. No report yet from Trailer pump.
00.39~Torpoint.~ Trailer pump returns, reports no fires.
00.40~Torpoint.~ All sectors report casualties, damage to one cottage near Antony
Thursday 1st. August)
07.27~Liskeard Police~ About 11.30 p.m. last night 1 high explosive bomb was dropped 30yds Scarsdown Cottage, 1

Mile South West of Antony Police Station, in an open field Map Reference 144/625765. Windows of cottage blown out also windows in the... also damage. No casualties.
10.40~Liskeard Police~ Fresh craters found between Shorrow Point at High Tregantle, at a point 2 miles South of Antony. Between Contours 300/250, size crater 12 Feet by 4 feet. Bombs approx 24.00 hrs.

SOUTH WEST ENGLAND:

Thu. 8th Aug.

Hurricane of 238 Squadron shot down a Messerschmitt 110. Another Messerschmitt shot down by a Hurricane of 56 Squadron.

ooOoo

Fri. 9th Aug. **FRANCE:**

The Luftwaffe launched its initial air strike, by sending 300 aircraft in an attempt to bomb the Radar Stations dotted along the English South Coast including the one at Rame Head. Fortunately the Radar was doing its job, and fighter pilots of the RAF intercepted them. If they had succeeded, they would have the freedom of the skies. In preparation for the following massive air strike planned by the Luftwaffe known as 'The Day Of The Eagle' was to take place, these air strikes continued on the 11th and 12th. before the planned invasion on the 15th of September.

Sat. 10th Aug. **SOUTH WEST ENGLAND:**

Between the hours of 0005 and 0200 a.m, night-time raids were carried out over Devon and HE bombs were dropped, (no other details).

During the long hot summer of 1940. It became obvious that Plymouth, and the Royal Air Force base at St Eval, all having military establishments located within their boundaries, were to become the main bombing targets of the Luftwaffe, due to the constant raids and bombing of the Naval Dockyard at Devonport, Torpoint and Saltash were to suffer immeasurably. With the planes flight course set, the bomb aimers, having calculated the dropping zone, loosed their bomb-load on the intended target far below, unaware that many of the bombs would miss, and those bombs that did miss either fell into the river Hamoaze, St. Johns Lake or, landed on the other side at Torpoint and the surrounding area. Torpoint was to suffer badly from the rain of bombs that fell from the bombers above.

Sun. 11th Aug.

3/KG/54 Junkers Ju. 88 shot down by a Hurricane of 87, and a further two Junkers Ju. 88 of Stab II/KG 54 shot down by a Hurricane of 213 Squadrons.

Thu. 13th Aug. **'The Day of the Eagle':**

When 1,485 bomber planes of the Luftwaffe attacked the airfields, and aircraft factory's in Great Britain to destroy them. What the Germans intended to happen, they did not achieve. During the first four days of aerial battles, the Germans lost 164 Aircraft against 82 British aircraft.

The Battle of Britain had begun.

Fri. 14th Aug. **SOUTH WEST ENGLAND:**

8/KG27 Two Heinkel HE 111, shot down by Hurricanes of 213 Squadron 9/KG27. Three Heinkel He 111 shot down by Spitfires of 92 Squadron.

Sat. 15th Aug.

Messerschmitt 110 shot down by Spitfire of 234 Squadron, a further Messerschmitt was shot down by Hurricane of 213 Squadron.

Record Log No. 5187 incidents reported on Saturday 16/8/40 - Incident 3:

22.33~ Torpoint.~ No sirens, Three parachute bombs dropped, and one HE. bomb at Crafthole.
22.45~ Torpoint.~ High Explosive Bombs dropped Crafthole, four casualties, no damage to the roads, no roads blocked, windows and ceilings down. Follow up report later.

Sat. 15th Aug. **GERMANY - BERLIN:**

Rheichsmarshal Goring summed up the aerial battle so far

With kind permission of Before and after the Battle

'Quote':

The fighter escorts of our Stuka formations must be re-adjusted, as the enemy is concentrating his fighters against our Stuka operations. It appears necessary to allocate three fighter Gruppen to each Stuka Gruppe, one of these fighter Gruppen remains with the Stukas and dives with them in the attack, the second flies ahead over the target at medium altitude and engages the fighter, the third protects the whole attack from above. It will also be necessary to protect Stukas returning from the attack over the Channel.

2. **Night attacks on shipping targets is only fruitful when the night is so clear that careful aim can be taken.**
3. **More importance must be attached to co-operation between members of individual aircrews.**
4. **The incident of V/LGI on August 13th shows that certain unit commanders have not yet learnt the importance of clear orders.**
5. **I have repeatedly given orders that twin-engined fighters are only to be employed where the range of other fighters is inadequate, or where it is for the purpose of assisting our single-engined aircraft to break off combat. Our stocks of twin –engined aircraft are not great, and we must use them as economically as possible.**
6. **Until further orders, operations are to be directed exclusively against the enemy Air Force, including the targets of the enemy aircraft industry allocated to the different Luftflotten. Shipping targets, and particularly large Naval vessels, are only to be attacked where circumstances are especially propitious. For the moment, other targets should be ignored. We must concentrate our efforts on the destruction of the enemy Air Forces. Our night attacks are essentially dislocation raids, made so that the enemy's and population shall be allowed no respite. Even these however, should, where possible be directed against Air Force targets.**
7. **My orders regarding the carrying out of attacks by single aircraft under cover of cloud conditions have apparently not been correctly understood. Where on one afternoon 50 aircraft are dispatched without adequate preparation on individual missions, it is possible that the operation will be unsuccessful and very costly. I therefore repeat that such sorties are only to be undertaken only by specially selected volunteer crews, who have made a prolonged and intensive study of the target, the most suitable method of attack, and the particular navigational problems involved. By no means all our crews are qualified to undertake such tasks.**
8. **KGr 100 (Bombers) are also, in future, to operate against the enemy Air Force and aircraft industry.**

It is doubtful if there is any point in continuing the attacks on radar sites, in view of the fact that not one of those attacked has so far been put out of action.

9. **The systematic designation of alternative targets would appear frequently to lead to certain targets being attacked, which have absolutely no connection with our strategic aims. It must therefore be achieved, that even alternative targets are of importance in the battle against the enemy Air Force.**
10. **The Commanders–in Chief of the Luftflotten are to report to me on the question of the warnings to be given during enemy air penetrations over the Reich. At present the warnings are causing a loss of output, whose consequences are far graver than those caused by the actual bomb damage. In addition, the frequent air raid warnings are leading to nervousness and strain amongst the population of Western Germany. On the other hand, we must take into account the risk of heavy loss of life should an attack be launched before a warning has been given.**

REICHSMARSHALL HERMON GORING
KARINHALL. AUGUST 15th 1940.

'Unquote'.

ooOoo

Sat. 17th Aug. **TORPOINT:**

Record Log No. 5187 incidents reported on Saturday 17/8/40 - Incident 4:

0420~ Liskeard Police~ Sgt Johns of St. Germans reports 2 mines by enemy plane was dropped, first one approx. 20 yds south of New Inn Crafthole in a field, second approx 200 yds, south on golf course about centre of 8th Fairway. Crafthole Village in the Parish of Sheviock 2 miles south of Antony Police Station. Animals killed, about 30 to 40 fowls, and 1 dog. Damage to numerous houses in the village, doors, windows and roofs. Casualties several slightly cut by flying glass none serious. Craters found by the New Inn in a field, size 4 feet by 9 ft wide.

18.00~ Sub-controller~ Crafthole.

Miraculous stories are told of people and children have been taken from their beds, which had been covered in broke glass and plaster, with not even a scratch. Morale of people is very wonderful.

18/4/40 11.50~To A.R.P.O.~

Will you obtain from the surveyor, a percentage report of St. Germans damage and also periodical repair reports, based on percentage of original damage.

[Authors Note: Excerpts from this incident, were recorded in the Cornish Times during the following week, and can be read as a true reflection on the mood and understanding of the day, indeed at any happenings that were to occur, relating to further and later incidents, within the area of Torpoint's Urban District Council.]
The article was entitled as follows:

THIS ARTICLE REFERS TO THE Date 16/08/1940, WHEN THREE PARACHUTE MINES & ONE HE BOMB WERE DROPPED ALONG THE CLIFF TOPS LOCAL TO TREGANTLE FORT.
'Quote'

BOMB VAGARIES
AIR STORY OF EAST CORNWALL
CURIOSITIES OF THE COAST

A quiet coastal village in the South-West, which has been the happy hunting ground of tired visitors seeking a peaceful holiday, had the war in the air brought to its very doors on Friday night August 16th 1940, when two magnetic mines dropped between it and the sea, causing widespread destruction to property.

The blast was so terrific that 42 of the 49 houses were seriously damaged, several near the center of the village, being rendered un-inhabitable. Roofs were lifted, others crashed in, ceilings collapsed, forming heaps of broken plaster, walls cracked and bulged, doors were ripped from their hinges and thrown open, beds and nearly every window were smashed, thousands of glass fragments being hurled across rooms and embedded into the walls and furniture. Yet despite the cyclonic devastation, there were no casualties, with the exception of half a dozen people who received slight scratches

A.R.P. WARDENS STORY

A lone German raider, coming from inland, passed over the village about 10.30 p.m, just as many people were going to bed. A few minutes later, there were two deafening explosions which were heard miles away.

The occurrence was graphically described in "THE CORNISH TIMES" by Mr. E.J. Callaghan the Village ARP Warden. "I Heard a plane overhead he said", I went outdoors immediately, saw two parachutes floating down from the sky, and naturally thought that German troops were being landed. But within a minute of me leaving my house, there was an almighty bang, followed closely by a second, and then I knew they were magnetic mines. The force knocked me over. I have read of that happening, and never believed it, thinking it was a lot of bunkum, but I have altered my mind now. I then rushed to the phone, and put my message through".

Mr. Callaghan is of opinion that the plane, coming with a following wind, released the mines a few hundred yards from the sea in the expectation that the parachutes would drift over the cliffs, but instead they floated straight down.

The craters were very large, the biggest of the two was 16ft wide by 5ft deep, was there in the eighth fairway of the Golf Course, and the second falling at the rear of some cottages in the main street, demolished a hedge separating fields of Mr. A. Bersey and Mr. G. Hoskin. There was no stock in Mr. Bersey's, but Mr. Hoskin whose own cottage suffered badly, he lost 50 poultry when three fowl houses were destroyed, amongst them were nine prize Indian game birds, and the next day they were lying strewn about the field, which was littered with feathers and pieces of the houses and wire netting. "I was lying in bed at the time said Mr. Hoskin, and everything came right on top of us".

The only other fatality was "Billy" a terrier belonging to Mrs. A Bersey, Mr.

Hoskin's daughter Billy born in Jubilee Year, was lying in a chair in the front room of the cottage when he was blown through the window, and found later in the road, lifeless.

AND TERRY SLEPT

The Village Inn, The Chapel and the recreation club suffered with the rest, but the Village Inn was the most seriously damaged. The whole of the interior was littered with broken glass, doors were smashed, and even a heavy sideboard was blown from its place by the side of the wall to the middle of the dinning floor. I don't know what happened remarked Mr. W. H. Hearn", the Licensee, " I heard a plane and went outside, I did not think it was a German because it was flying so low, my wife however, called to me 'to come inside and shut the door'. I did so, went into the bar, and took up some glasses to give to my wife, all of a sudden I saw a vivid flash, and there was an explosion. The shutter came back and hit me on the head, and a bit of glass cut my nose".

Terrance Leather an evacuee aged eight, from Catford London, came with his sister Vera, to live with Mr. and Mrs. Hearn nine weeks ago, is such a sound sleeper that the explosion generally described as deafening, failed to rise him.

Parts of the ceiling of his bedroom fell in and ornaments from a mantle-piece were blown onto his bed, but he was uninjured when rescued by the Licensee's wife.

Mrs. Hearn said "I was in the parlour at the back of the bar counting the takings when the shutters on the window were blown half-way across the room. Fortunately I was out of their way, I rushed upstairs and called Terry, but there was no answer. We brought the little girl Vera downstairs in a wool blanket and then picked up Terry thinking he might be dead, but he was only asleep. In fact it was not until we got to the bottom of the stairs that he opened his eyes and asked my husband "what's the matter uncle".

BUSINESS AS USUAL

The cellar door was split in half, but not a bottle was broken. In an un-occupied bedroom masses of plaster from the ceiling fell on the bed, and in the bedroom of Mr and Mrs. Hearn, the wardrobe was flung across the empty bed

Next door to the Inn is a sweet shop owned by Mrs. Hearn, in which much of the stock was damaged and plate glass window's splintered.

Mrs. Hearn had only just finished making a quantity of plum jam, and the uncovered jars were dusted with powdered glass and plaster.

Owing to the immunity of the stock in the bar itself however, the Inn was able to open on Saturday for "business as usual".

Mrs. Wilfred Lee, Mrs. Hearn's married daughter, who was sleeping upstairs with her husband, said that a minute or two before the explosion occurred she was about to get out of bed and open the window, but her husband persuaded her not to. Had she been close to the window, she would have caught the full force of the broken glass and been struck by the ceiling which collapsed.

FARMHOUSE BATTERED

"St. Anne's", a modern farmhouse facing the sea, suffered the full force of the blast, and the interior damage is most in-conceivable. It is far the stoutest house in the village, but the roof lifted, ceilings collapsed, plaster came down in showers, doors were flung across rooms onto beds, and not only was glass blown out, but pieces of the window frames as well as crockery, pictures and a lucky black cat, were smashed, but strangely enough not a clock was damaged, or even stopped working.

The occupants are Mr. and Mrs. G.R. Hoskin, and the story of their dreadful experience was told by Mrs. Hoskin.

"My husband and I had gone to bed" she said, "when we heard the plane. No sooner had we heard it, than there was a terrific bang, and we thought a bomb had gone through our house, because our ceiling came down on top of us, and my husband had a mouthful of mortar. The glass from the window flew across the room, but did not hit either of us.

"We have a little evacuee boy, Billy with us, we rushed to his room and found the door lying across his bed, and heaps of broken glass and mortar all around him. We thought he was dead, we could not rouse him, but at last we succeeded. He was fast asleep, and absolutely unhurt

DIVED UNDER THE TABLE

"My daughter was in the kitchen, just getting ready for bed, she heard the explosion, and had the presence of mind to dive under the table, just before the glass from the window blew across the room.

"It was only providence that saved the lot of us", remarked Mrs. Hoskin feelingly. "When told Billy what had happened his only concern was that 'aunties' lovely house had been knocked about. We have been a long time getting this little home together, we have painted and distempered it this year, and now it is practically done in" she added sadly.

A Vicar and his wife from Southampton had spent a month's holiday at St Anne's and only left on Friday morning. In the evening, across the bed where they had slept, were pieces of window frame, with jagged bits of glass attached. Dairy and outbuildings so spick and span before, were littered with debris, but Mrs. Hoskin smiled bravely through it all and her last words to our representative were, good-bye and I hope you have better luck than we had.

HOME GUARDSMAN'S EXPERIENCE

Mr.E.R. Richards an Insurance Agent was one of two Home Guardsmen on the cliffs. He was accompanied by a 17 year old member Graham Lansellos.

"If we had not flung ourselves to the ground we should have both been blown over the cliffs", he told a press representative.

The Home Guard is very strong in the village, about 40 out of 50 eligible mates having joined. Another member, 17-year old Russell Greenaway was near the scene of the explosions. "I was ready to rush round and rally the fellows", he said.

Home Guard Headquarters, situated in a timber and corrugated iron-roofed building, formerly used by the Golf Club, received special attention from the "visitors". Here Home Guardsman Eric Grills was lying asleep when the explosions blew in one wall and brought half the ceiling down. A piece of timber fell away from the wall near his couch, but remained hinged over his head.

One curiosity of the explosion was that a window of the hut had three of the four panes blown clean out, the lower part of the frame coming away with them, while the fourth pane remained intact.

The Home Guards dartboard was blown through a window, and was found afterwards, picked up undamaged on the lawn outside.

CHILDS LUCKY ESCAPE

A little girl of four, who lives with her parents in a recently-completed bungalow facing the sea had a lucky escape, when the window of her bedroom blew in, it carried the blackout curtain with it. The curtain was flung over the child's face and protected her from injury, although the head of the oak bed in which she slept was pitted with broken glass.

Mr. Jack Triscott who has a little evacuee from London named Olive Neal staying with him, said the child received a cut on the hand. "If it had happened and hour earlier there would have been a lot of people killed, as there were plenty walking about" he said.

The occupants of a bungalow three-quarters of a mile away, said that the explosion threw her china dinner service out of the cupboard, and several articles were broken. A clock hanging on the wall was wrenched from its peg.

AMAZING FORTITUDE

The fortitude of the villager's was amazing. After the first shock, when many of them gathered at "St Anne's" for a welcome cup of tea prior to spending a sleepless night amongst their battered homes, they displayed all the characteristics of the British race. They felt that they were all in it together, helped one another and cheered one another up, and "one and all" agreed that "It might have been worse".

All day on Saturday workmen and villager's were sweeping away glass, patching up windows with galvanize and wood, and generally tidying up, so that the houses can be made reasonably habitable again. Whatever happens in the future, these hardy folk are determined to stay.

'Unquote.'

ooOoo

Sun. 18th Aug. **SOUTH WEST ENGLAND:**

Hurricanes of 56 Squadron shot down a Heinkel HE 111of 8/KG 53, a further four Messerschmitt 110 were shot down by Hurricanes of 56 Squadron.

Tue. 20th Aug. **LONDON:**

In the House of Commons, The Prime Minister Winston Churchill, made his famous speech, referring to the Fighter Pilots of the Royal Air Force

" Quote",

'Never in the field of human conflict was so much, owed by so many, to so few'.

Thu. 22nd Aug. **SOUTH WEST ENGLAND:**

Spitfires of 152 Squadron, shot down a Junkers Ju. 88. from 3 (F)/121 Killing the Pilot whilst 3 crew members baled out and were captured.

Sun. 25th Aug **PLYMOUTH:**

Night-time raids on Plymouth, when HE bombs and mines were dropped falling into the docks at Plymouth, no further information. Same night a Messerschmitt 109 was shot down by Spitfires of 152 Squadron. Another shot down by Hurricane of 87 Squadron.

Mon. 26th Aug.

Plymouth again night time raids, HE Bombs fell in the Keyham Area killing 5 people. Same night a Messerschmitt 109 was shot down by Hurricanes of 56 Squadron.

TORPOINT:

Tue. 27th Aug.

About 10 o'clock in the morning, a Dornier 17 from 3 (F)/31 on a photo-reconnaissance mission over Plymouth, was intercepted by two Hurricanes from 23 Squadron, who attacked and damaged the starboard engine, disabling the plane, which made a forced landed at Hardwick Farm near Tavistock, the German crew were captured unhurt. The aircraft was a write off. During the night-time the 'alert' was sounded as German bombers flew over Torpoint on their way to the north. They dropped some bombs and incendiaries, which landed at Downderry and Whitsand Bay, where an incendiary set alight a bungalow and destroyed it, no casualties reported.

Record Log No. 5187 incidents reported on Tuesday 27/8/40 - Incident 11:

01.40~ Millbrook.~ Five HE bombs at Millbrook believed to be dropped at the bottom of clay pit. No damage.
09.10~ Millbrook.~ 5 Craters at Inswork Farm Millbrook. 1 exploded, others doubtful, need expert opinion as soon as possible.

Record Log No. 5187 incidents reported on Tuesday 27/8/40 - Incident 12:

02.21~ Torpoint.~ Coastguards report that 3 HE, and about 50 incendiary's fell on the cliff side between Penlee and Rame, reported to have fallen at midnight.
04.00~ Millbrook.~ Incendiary bombs at Rame and three H.E's. Reports of windows broken, further report by daylight, believed to be one dud, which will be investigated.

Record Log No. 5187 incidents reported on Tuesday 27/8/40 - Incident 14:

06.00~ County A.R.P.~ Between Millbrook, Penlee Rame, Kingsands, Downderry, Fifty incendiaries and eleven H.E. bombs have fallen.
06.00~ Wilcove.~ One HE. bomb near Whitehall Farm, broken glass.
06.00~ County A.R.P.~ Incendiary bombs have now been reported to have reached 200 between Rame and Penlee
06.00~ Rame.~ Craters found in an open field on Rame Barton Farm. One is 20 feet by 15 feet the other one is 20 feet by 8 feet and is 15yds from Treshill Farmhouse which has windows blown in and is un-inhabitable.

Record Log No. 5187 incidents reported on Tuesday 27/8/40 - Incident 15:

04.43~ Torpoint.~ Reports one HE. bomb on the beach near Whitehall Farm. UXB believed to have fallen near Captain Barkers House.

Record Log No. 5187 incidents reported on Tuesday 27/8/40 - Incident 16:

10.38~ County A.R.P.~ Reports bombs fallen on Polhawn near Rame.
12.55~ Captain Barker.~ Two H.E. bombs and fifty incendiary bombs fell near Polhawn Farm, windows broken and ceilings down. No casualties.

PLYMOUTH:

Wed. 28th Aug.

Plymouth, another sharp raid. Six bombs and many incendiaries were dropped in the area of St. Budeaux and Crownhill, without any serious damage. Two Messerschmitt 109 were shot down by Hurricanes of 56 Squadron.

Thu. 29th Aug.

Plymouth Bombing raid. 1 5/KG 53 Heinkel He 111, plus 1 Messerschmitt 110 shot down by Hurricanes of 56 Squadron.

Fri. 30th Aug.

Plymouth Bombing raid, 1 5KG/53 Heinkel He 111 plus 1 Messerschmitt 109 shot down by Hurricane of 56 Squadron.

TORPOINT:

Sat. 31st Aug.

Bombing raids continued on Plymouth and surrounding areas.

Record Log No. 5187 incidents reported on Saturday 31/8/40 - Incident 23/24:

13.40~ St. Germans~ Sgt. Johns at St. Germans Police Station reported a UXB shell found in field at Polharin Farm Trerulefoot, in the parish of St Germans. The farm is situated by the junction of Misheard Torpoint/Saltash Road, hole is about 2 feet deep shape and diameter of a beer bottle.

Record Log No. 5187 incidents reported on Saturday 31/8/40 - Incident 25:

22.01~ Torpoint.~ From barrage balloon site, that a bomb was seen to be dropped just above Saltash Bridge.

Record Log No. 5187 incidents reported on Sunday 1/9/40 - Incident 26:

23.04~ Torpoint.~ Plane passed overhead going twelve o'clock, bombs reported over Mount Edgecumbe.

Record Log No. 5187 incidents reported on Sunday 3/9/40 - Incident 27:

23.37~ Torpoint.~ Torpoint 336 Balloon Barrage Site report,2 bombs dropped on Maker near balloon site.No casualties amongst the crew.

Thu. 5th Sept.

No direct attack on Plymouth, nevertheless, bombs did fall in the countryside in the Plymouth area of Wotter.

Fri. 6th Sept

During an air raid, Spitfires of 234 Squadron shot down two Messerschmitt 109's.

Sat. 7th Sept. **LONDON: Black Saturday.**

In preparation for the pending German Invasion, London takes the blunt of the bombing raids. Wave after wave of German bombers flew up over the Thames. Sufficient to action the Code Word "Cromwell", bringing the armed forces to a high state of readiness. Church bells were rung out all over the land as a pre- arranged signal that the invasion by the Germans was imminent.

Tue. 10th Sept. **GERMANY - BERLIN:**

Hitler postpones the invasion for three days.

Thu. 12th Sept. **PLYMOUTH:**

During a bombing raid on Plymouth, The Royal Marine Barracks at Stonehouse was hit, resulting in 13 people killed, including 8 civilians and many wounded.

Tue. 17th Sept. **BELGIUM – DUNKERQUE:**

During the night RAF bombers attacked the docks at Dunkerque. Sinking 84 invasion barges and causing serious damage to others. The results of this raid made Hitler postpone the Invasion of Britain in.

Wed. 18th Sept. **SOUTH WEST ENGLAND:**

Bombing attacks resumed over The South West, Spitfires of 92 Squadron shot down a Junkers Ju. 88 of 8/KG77.

Sun. 22nd Sept.

Spitfires of 234 Squadron,shot down four Junkers Ju. 88 Reconnaissance Planes.

Mon. 23rd Sept. **PLYMOUTH:**

Spitfires of 92 Squadron shot down two Messerschmitt 110. The Polish warship Gydinia was engaged firing heavy flak skywards.

Wed. 25th Sept.

Plymouth, 'Alerts' were sounded from 0845 a.m., through till 1055 p.m. at 1647p.m., 24 bombers with an escort of 12 Messerschmitt 110 crossed Star Point and attacked Plymouth. During the raids many bombs fell landing in and around Plymouth. At Goschen Street Keyham, a stick of bombs demolished 5 houses killing 10, injuring others. This was followed by a further attack the same day @ 2100-0100.

However, the RAF fighters had successes: 1/KG55 Heinkel He 111, 6/KG55 Heinkel He 111, 7/KG55 Heinkel He 111, 2/10-6 Dornier Do17. All shot down by Hurricanes of 238 Squadron. Spitfires of 152 Squadron shot down 1 Messerschmitt 110.

These daylight 'Dogfights' were very spectacular and had many people gazing up into the skies watching the planes weaving, diving and climbing, to avoid being shot down. The distant rattle from the machine guns overhead, added noise to the scenario taking place in the skies above Plymouth Sound. To add to the cacophony of noise, the ships anchored in the Hamoaze, sent up rounds and rounds of Ack -Ack and Bofors shells. The sky above was peppered with cotton wool burst from the exploding shells. It was a small wonder that the falling shrapnel caused no injury.

TORPOINT:

Record Log No. 5187 incidents reported on Wednesday 25/9/40 Incident 33

17.10~ Wilcove.~ Cove Lodge Wilcove is damaged, house still standing roof smashed no casualties. Fire engine sent as a precaution. To above report one person, slight concussion.

26/9.40
08.47~ Wilcove.~ Correction to yesterdays report one casualty slight concussion?

Thu. 26th Sept.

Dog fights between the RAF Spitfires, Hurricanes and the German Messerschmitt's above the skies over Plymouth, had everyone's eyes turned skywards. Two Messerschmitt 110 were shot down by Hurricane's of 238 Squadron.

Record Log No. 5187 incidents reported on Friday 27/9/40 - Incident 34:

21.10~ Torpoint.~ Heavy explosion in four o'clock direction, haystack fire at Rame Farm.
22.20~ Millbrook.~ Captain Barker reports that hayrick fire reported at 21.10 is incorrect. Incendiary bombs fell at Barton Farm, Rame Head but did no damage and were put out. I.B. fell at Antony Village in fields, and farmyards no damage. West of Antony Farm a number of I.B's fell at Penillard Farm, Rame Head, no damage, at about 21.00 hrs. Coastguard report 6 HE. bombs dropped on cliffs surrounding Rame head. Far as we know no damage or casualties.

Fri. 27th Sept. **SOUTH WEST ENGLAND:**
Spitfires of 152 Squadron shot down Junkers Ju. 88 reconnaissance bomber of 3 (F)/123, plus 1 Messerschmitt 109.

TORPOINT:

Record Log No. 5187 incidents reported on Saturday 28 /9/40 Incident 34:

22.45~ Millbrook.~ Captain Barker now reports that eight craters from HE. bombs have been found at Rame Head.

Sat. 28th Sept.

Sharp air raid at 2150 until 0314 hrs, 15 HE bombs and 11 Land Mines were dropped in the Cawsands, Spitfires of 92 Squadron shot down 1 Junkers Ju. 88 of 3/KG77.

Sun. 29th Sept. **PLYMOUTH:**

Bombers flying over Plymouth headed for South Wales and Bristol. Spitfires of 92 Squadron shot down Four Messerschmitt 109 One Messerschmitt by Hurricane of 238 Squadron.

Mon. 30th Sept. **LONDON:**

The Blitz on London began in earnest, wave after wave of bombers attacked the city. Buckingham Palace was hit and also the British Museum and 10 Downing Street.

'IT WAS JUST THE BEGINNING'.

Mon. 7th Oct. **SOUTH WEST ENGLAND:**

Hurricane of 238 Squadron shot down a Junkers Ju. 88 of 5/KG51. Another Messerschmitt by Spitfires of 152 Squadron.

Thu. 10th Oct.

15 reconnaissance planes were spotted flying over the south west area, bombs did fall on the Peverell area of Plymouth causing two deaths and damage to housing.

TORPOINT:

Record Log No. 5187 incidents reported on Thursday 10/10/40 Incidents 36 37.

20.18~ Torpoint.~ There is a plane overhead that has been signalling by flashlight and we have heard nothing about the IB. at Trevole, but are still enquiring.

Fri. 11th Oct. **PLYMOUTH:**

Another quick raid on Plymouth, an air-raid shelter at 'Tor House for the Blind' was hit, as it was under water and not fit to be used, fortunately the Matron had kept them all inside the home.

Sat. 12th Oct. **TORPOINT:**

At Shillingham near Torpoint a 250Kg bomb landed at 2045 that failed to explode (UXB), another 250kg UXB landed in Torpoint, both were defused by the army BDS (Bomb Disposal Squad). Spitfires of 92 Squadron shot down Two Messerschmitt 109's.

Sun. 13th Oct. **SOUTH WEST ENGLAND:**

Spitfires of 92 Squadron shot down a Messerschmitt 109.

PLYMOUTH/TORPOINT:

Tue. 15th until the 17th Oct.,

The 'Alerts' constantly sounded in Plymouth.

Record Log No. 5187 incidents reported on Tuesday 15/10/40 - Incident 38/39

22.25~ Torpoint.~ barrage balloon site, 11 reports of IB's on the Saltash side of the River Lyner due north of Antony Estate.

Wed. 16th Oct.

Late in the evening Incendiary bombs were dropped on Trevol Camp (HMS *Raleigh*) Torpoint, that caused many fires, but they were all put out by the shore establishment fire party.

Thu. 17th Oct.

15 bombers attacked, dropping bombs in the Pennycomequick area. Severe damage was caused over a wide area but little or no casualties. However a mini-blitz took place at Landrake and St German's, causing little damage.

[Authors Note no report available on this raid, possibly due to it being in the Saltash ARP. Area].

Sun. 20th Oct.

Another raid, incendiaries landed on the outskirts of Torpoint towards the Antony area. Spitfires of 92 squadron shot down 1 Messerschmitt 110.

Record Log No. 5187 incidents reported on Monday 21/10/40 - Incident 40/41:

23.10~ P.D.~ Reports IB's at Antony.

23.15~ P.D.~ Reports large fire to west of Naval Barracks.

23.21~ Antony.~ Police report no fires in their area, butfire in the direction of St. German.

Tue. 22nd Oct.

A lone aircraft was splotted off the Devon coast at 0550, a parachute landmine on its way down, exploded just off of Rame Head.

Record Log No. 5187 incidents reported on Tuesday 22/10/40 - Incident 42:

23.50~ Torpoint.~ Report from Kingsands. A mine fell in the sea and exploded, broken glass only. Investigation reveals that the mine exploded in the air about 50 feet out to sea, also broken glass.

Wed 23rd Oct.

A single German bomber swooped low over Victoria Park with a sharp burst of machine gun fire, carried on flying south of St. Budeaux dropping 4 HE. bombs on the way, flying straight over the Hamoaze, towards Wilcove then open fired with its machine guns before veering left towards the Rame Peninsular and the sea.

Bill Eady recollects this incident.

He was leaving his cottage Glendale at the top end of Wilcove, when a German plane came roaring up towards Maryfield. Its front gunner, plainly visible to see, opened fire, machine gun bullets hit the road right past his doorway, he had to dive back inside for cover.

Freda recalls the same incident:

I along with Mr. & Mrs. Webber, saw a German aircraft bearing down at low level with its front gunner firing his machine guns, they had to dive into the shelter to escape the bullets.

ooOoo

Sat. 26th Oct. **PLYMOUTH /TORPOINT:**

Another raid over Plymouth, Spitfires of 92 Squadron shot down 1 Messerschmitt 109.

Sun. 27th Oct.

Another hit and run raid, 1: 250Kg UXB bomb landed in Torpoint. defused by the (BDS) Bomb Disposal Squad..

Wed. 31st Oct. **GERMANY - BERLIN:**

Hitler abandons his plans for the invasion of Great Britain and turns his attention towards the Russian Eastern Front. By abandoning his plans to invade Great Britain it ended the Battle of Britain. In the previous three months of intense aerial bombardment, 2,433 German airplanes had been shot down over Great Britain with a loss of 1,519 German airplanes destroyed during the Battle of Britain against 956 British Fighters. But the Aerial Raids were still to continue.

ooOoo

Wed. 31st Oct. **TORPOINT:**

T/229664. DRV. HERBERT JOHN HOSKING ROWE. was conscripted as a driver into the Royal Army Service Corps. Herbert was a member of the Torpoint St. John Ambulance Service and served in the Western Desert, Italy, and other countries. During his period of service in the Western Desert, Drv. Rowe did not forget Torpoint. On the front of his lorry he painted the words "**TORPOINT FERRY**" (See photograph below.) He was to serve in East Africa, Egypt, North Africa and Italy, (see his progressive yearly Christmas Greetings). Eventually he returned back to Torpoint in 1946. (See last chapter and read his invitation to a dinner held by Torpoint Urban District Council, to honor the return of Torpoint's servicemen & women).

ooOoo

Norman Beaver MBE. recalls:

There is a picture of H.J. Rowe in a wartime copy of the Western Evening Herald standing in front to his truck in the desert. The front of his truck was painted in white words

"TORPOINT FERRY"

Torpoint

Somewhere in North Africa

Sat. 2nd Nov. **PLYMOUTH:**

Plymouth: During an 'Alert' night time observers were able to watch a spectacle, when searchlights held a German bomber in its concentrated beam for several minutes, before the Ack Ack guns responded, firing rounds of ammunition into the sky until the raider dived down towards the Millbrook area, but apparently got away. However, Spitfire's of 92 Squadron shot down 3 Messerschmitt 109's.

Tue. 5th Nov.

Another Messerschmitt 109 was shot down by Spitfires of 92 Squadron.

Thu. 7th Nov.

Plymouth: After six 'Alerts' during the day, Plymouth was caught unawares, when during the night German bombers were clearly heard flying low over the city. Bombs were dropped before the 'Alert' was sounded. Damage was caused over a wide area, killing several people. The nearest bomb to Torpoint was at Kings Street Devonport, where two people were killed.

Sat. 9th Nov.

Bombers flying north over Plymouth on their way to Liverpool, were attacked by Spitfires of 92 Squadron. A Junkers Ju. 88 of 1/KG77 was shot down and a Dornier Do17 of 1/606 was hit and crashed at Bonnoc Woods Liskeard.

Mon. 18th Nov.

Another air raid on Plymouth by 2 Dornier 17 of KGr606, began about 03.30 a.m. dropping bombs and incendiaries, which killed 9 people, the incendiaries did little damage.

Mon. 25th Nov.**TORPOINT:**

After a big raid on Bristol, on their return flight Aufk1.Gr.Ob. d.l. Dornier Do17 Dl215 was shot down by Spitfires of 234 Squadron and crashed into the sea, a mile off Kynance. Another Dornier 17 of 1/ Kurstenflugergruppe, after becoming lost by British 'Meacon' counter measures, whilst flying back over Plymouth, flew into balloon barrage site 64/11 hitting a barrage balloon cable, which crippled the aircraft. All four crew members managed to bale out. Lt. Zur See Martin Saueracker, Obergefr. A. Hoferichter, Uffz. H. Weiss, and Uffz. K. Eiselt. One was fished out of the sea at Cawsands. Three others landed in the vicinity of Millbrook and were captured. The plane crashed and burnt out at Penlee point 10.40. p.m.

Record Log No. 5187 incidents reported on Sunday 24/11/40 - Incident 47:

22.45~ Torpoint.~ Enemy aircraft hit a balloon cable in the Sound and crashed into the sea, reported by Captain Barker. Torpoint fire engine sent to scene of crashed plane and identified it as German plane. Plane was thought to be returning from bombing raid in Wales and was loosing height before crashing into the cable, and is further thought to be a Dornier Aircraft. Crash was at Rame Head a mile and quarter south of Kingsands.

[Authors note] There are a number of stories about this incident, all are basically factual, all have been voiced verbally in conversations with the Author, nevertheless, one such record is described in books written by Betty Keller, 'Trouble at Amen Corner' also 'Trouble in the Tea Cups'. Far too long to be inserted, but can be obtained in the local Library. Two very interesting books about the war years in Millbrook and Torpoint, however, the Author was invited by Mrs. Iris Bush [local Pet Groomer] to visit her father, Mr. Mervyn Bersey, a resident at Greenview Nursing Home in Torpoint, who could relate a few stories about the war years. I met Iris and was introduced to her father, nevertheless during my meeting, I was fortunate enough to meet another regular visitor a Mr. Norman Beaver MBE.

When introduced to Mr. Mervyn Bersey, I had a very pleasant surprise to discover he was 101 years old. Although in a wheelchair, I could see from his stature he was a big man, his hands dwarfed mine. He had limited sight, hard of hearing, unable to walk, but was in full control of his memory. Iris had already mentioned to me that during the war, he lived in Millbrook so, that is when I asked him the question about the above incident. To my surprise Mr. Bersey related the facts about the incident with clarity, he was the very man I had heard about. Although he had volunteered to join up, he had been rejected, due to a gammy leg, instead he became a Special Constable with the rank of Sergeant at Millbrook Police Station.

Sgt. M. Bersey, was the very man who had taken custody of the four German airmen in question, although understandably, he did not know their names, he related the facts of where they did come down and land, including one airman who came down in the mud in the lake and fired off his pistol to attract attention. He also stated about the airman who parachuted into the sea. He was fished out by two fishermen from Cawsands who in their haste, forgot to put the spike back into the bottom of the boat, subsequently as they rowed out, the boat began to fill with water, they eventually dragged the airman out and into the boat, which was nearly full of seawater. Somehow they made it back to shore beaching the boat in shallow water, where he was handed over to the police, to join his other three comrades already in the safety of Sgt. Bersey's cells. They were picked up later by the army and driven off. A story as they say 'direct from the horses mouth'. Nevertheless, Mr. Bersey related more incidents about he war, which will be scribed in the appropriate events, as they took place. Mr. Norman Beaver, having listened to the tale became very interested in the fact I was researching the War Years of Torpoint, and was happy to relate his stories about his experiences during the war, which as appropriate are recorded within the text. However on another visit by Norman to Mervyn, he related a

further addition to his above story.
Norman Beaver MBE. recalls:

Mervyn related again the tale of the pilots, when one a Lt. Zur See M. Saueracker's, demanded Mervyn to clean his boots, he was the one who landed in the mud in Millbrook Lake, quite close to Silver Terrace at Southdown, where a resident (name unknown) covered the recovery of the pilot with his shot gun, which he held through his bedroom window. Mervyn reported this demand to Chief Inspector White of the Special Constabulary, who was a retired army officer who had a newsagents in Millbrook, C.I. White produced the police fire bucket and a sandbag and advised the prisoner to "get on with it". All the crew of the bomber were all sure they would be shot and were amazed at the treatment they were afforded during their stay in Millbrook Police Station.

Another addition to the incident was submitted by Nicola Dunbar a Personnel Assistant at HMS. *Raleigh* who relates a tale told by her great-aunt Mrs. Elaine Hickman (nee Jeffrey).

Members of the Home Guard or equivalent, went out to find the Germans, taking with them broom handles as their weapons. They arrested the men and brought them back to a house in Millbrook. The owner told everybody, 'that she had brought every scrap of food she had in the house and placed it on her kitchen table. When the men were brought in she said to them, ' See were not starving'.
[Authors note: I believe that the German propaganda war machine advised the Germans that the English were starving.]

ooOoo

:

PLYMOUTH:

Wed. 27th Nov.

The first major attack on Plymouth began at 1830 hrs., 112 Luftwaffe bombers attacked Devonport. The Concentration Point (hereafter CP) was the city center and the Devonport Docks. Five of the attacking bombers aborted. The number of bombs dropped from the remaining 107 aircraft were 109,45 tonnes of HE and incendiary comprising: 1 - SD 1400. 9 - SC1000. 9 - SC500, 1 - LZZ250, 5 - Flam 500, 466 - SC50, & 170 - BSK bombs. The German crews reported that the bombs dropped, had caused many large fires, especially in the north and north west part of the city. A large jet of flame followed an explosion in the south part in the Devonport Dock area. On the same night incendiaries were dropped at Southdown Torpoint, and in many other rural areas, where fires and other damage was caused. The attack lasted 7 hrs 40 mins the participating aircraft were:

Gruppe	Aircraft	Time
KGr606	8 Do. 17	1830 – 1856
III KG27	13 He 111	1850 – 1925
KG1	15 He.111	1930 - 2210
KG1	8 Ju. 88	1930 – 2210
KGr806	6 Ju. 88	1945 – 2020
III/KG26	7 He.111	2120 – 2200
I/KG54	7 Ju. 88	2123 – 2220
II/KG54	5 Ju. 88	2222 –2345
II/IIIKG1	13 Ju. 88	2233 – 0032

KG77	9 Ju. 88	0055 – 0210
KGr 606	8 Do. 17	1830 – 1856
III KG27	13 He.111	1850 – 1925
KG1	15 He.111	1930 - 2210
KG1	8 Ju. 88	1930 – 2210
KGr806	6 Ju. 88	1945 – 2020
III/KG26	7 He.111	2120 – 2200
I/KG54	7 Ju. 88	2123 – 2220
II/KG54	5 Ju. 88	2222 –2345
II/IIIKG1	13 Ju. 88	2233 – 0032
KG77	9 Ju. 88	0055 – 0210

The shriek and crash of bombs exploding, together with the banging of anti-aircraft guns and searchlights criss-crossing and waving about the sky, must have been horrendous yet fascinating for those in action. There were no reports of any enemy aircraft shot down either by ground Ack-Ack or by the squadrons on night patrols. The Germans got away with this first major attack on Plymouth.

TORPOINT:

Mr. Bersey remembers the night he was in Newton Abbot, having driven a local Millbrook family there to get away from the bombing. He started his return journey, about 10.00 p.m. at night and with all the bombing going on in the Plymouth area, he was not prepared to risk driving back through Plymouth. He decided to take the northern route back to across the moors, heading for Tavistock, Gunnislake, then towards Polbathic. It was pitch black until suddenly, a great flash of light would erupt, caused possibly by a bomb or the anti-aircraft gunners, firing their guns. As he drove along getting closer to Plymouth, he saw the Devonport Dockyard ablaze, somehow he made it to Polbathic the last leg of his journey, when suddenly near Wolston, the car dived into a bomb crater, unable to drive it out, he left it and walked the rest of the way back to Millbrook.

Frank Bolton recalls:

We lived in Clarence Road, and I remember looking out of the window and seeing the Dockyard ablaze from one end to the other. Even at my age, I remember thinking " How can anything survive in that"?

Thu. 28th Nov.**PLYMOUTH:**

Fortunately, the Luftwaffe did not press home their previous attack on Plymouth, and sent only one aircraft to bomb the city, a Junkers 88 from 11KG 51 between 0050-0208, a lucky, but direct hit on the oil tanks at Mount Batten RAF Sea Plane Installation, and set that alight, its intensity soon ignited others. A Sunderland sea plane at its moorings was set alight. The smoke and fires attracted more bombers which plastered the surrounding area with incendiaries, setting alight Staddon Heights, which appeared as a world of fairyland lights. The inferno caused by the tanks, blazed away and for many days, clouds of dense black smoke from the burning fuel tanks drifted upwards into the sky, and with the prevailing winds changed direction several times.

ooOoo

December. 1940.

Because of the success of the moonlight raids in November's moon pattern, 4 days either side of the full moon phase, the raids reduced in their intensity, however the Ack-Ack guns were always in action, whenever enemy aircraft were present in the night skies above, with the noise of the guns constantly banging away gave little or no time for people to sleep.

Sun. 1st Dec.

The target that night was Southampton with bombers over the sea, whilst at Plymouth, bombers dropped mines along the Sound.

Mon. 2nd Dec. A repeat of the previous nights activity

Wed. 4th Dec.

Same activity again however, a Dornier Do17 of 3(F)3.1 was shot down by Spitfires of 234 Squadron Group 10's, first kill for days.

Thu. 12th Dec.

At 0042. 1 Dornier 17 of KGr606. flew over Plymouth, possibly on reconnaissance?

Sun. 15th Dec.

10 bombers from the Brest airfields, flying in between Plymouth and Star Point, on their way to a bombing raid on Sheffield. Only one attacked Plymouth dropping some bombs (no further information). After this there appears to have been little attention placed on Plymouth as a target. Most of the bombing raids from that night on, were concentrated on London, Birmingham, and Liverpool, however there was breathing space over the Christmas period, when the Luftwaffe ceased activity.

Wed. 25th Dec. **SOUTH ATLANTIC:**

Christmas Day the *S.S.Jumna* a Merchant Ship, having left Liverpool bound for Calcutta with 62 crew members, 2 gunners and 48 passengers, was the target for the reported German ship the *Admiral Hippen,* which opened fire on the *Jumna* and sank her, approx 200 miles North of the Azores. There were no survivors. On board was a Torpoint sailor:

D/Z 38626. YC/S. T. A. WAYE. RN. Age 49

ex *HMS President III/ Jumna*

CWG. PLYMOUTH NAVAL MEMORIAL Panel 39 Col 2.

Fri. 27th Dec. **LONDON: The first of the many waves of bombings began**

Sun. 29th Dec. **PLYMOUTH:**

The Luftwaffe turned its attention to Plymouth which was attacked by 21 bombers. Their CP was the city. 17 tones of HE bombs comprising: 1 - SC1800, 12 SC1000. 1- SC 500, 347 - BSK, 12,492 - IB's were dropped. Houses, shops and 2 Hospitals were hit and set on fire, but no damage occurred to Military Installations. The brief attack started at 1837 until 1915 hrs approx.The aircraft taken part are listed below as follows

Gruppe	Aircraft	Time
KGr100	9 He 111	1837 –1927 (3 Aborted)
IIKG55	9 He 111	1850- 1915
IIIKG26	3 He 111	1841 –1853

ooOoo

TORPOINT:

Fred Timms recalls:

The year of 1940 came to an end with a few reconnaissance raids that took place about 1 p.m. The aircraft would fly in low over Fourlandsend School and over Raleigh Parade Ground, scattering the sailors here there and everywhere. (At that time no air-raid shelters had been built).

LONDON:

. The bombing raids continued upto the end of the year creating a Firestorm to hit London, the bombing carried out practically destroyed the City, which became an inferno. Marking it as the last bombing attack by the Luftwaffe to take place in Great Britain during 1940.

ooOoo

1941
YEAR TWO

Wed. 1st Jan. **NORTH AFRICA - LIBYA:**

British and Australian troops advanced towards Tobruk. By the 5th they had captured the Fortress of Bardia and with it, the capture of 35,000 Italian soldiers. They continued with their onward advance towards Tobruk.

Sat. 4th Jan. **SOUTH WEST ENGLA ND:**

A Wekusta 26 Dornier Do17 Shot down by Spitfires of 152 Squadron. Group 10's, first kill of the year.

Mon. 6th Jan. **MEDITERRANEAN SEA:**

Under the code name 'Operation Excess' 3 (three) Merchant Ships with an escort of 5 (five) Royal Navy Warships, amongst them were, HMS. *Southampton* & the Aircraft Carrier *Illustrious,* left Gibraltar bound for Athens. As the convoy approached Malta on the 10th January 1941, German bombers based in Sicily attacked the convoy. During the seven hours of intermittent bombing, two Merchant ships were sunk. HMS. *Southampton* was so badly damaged her crew sank her.
HMS. *Illustrious* was also severely damaged, 160 crew members were killed amongst those was a Torpoint sailor:
D/M 40211. P.O. THOMAS WILLIAM CROCKER. Age 31
CWG. PLYMOUTH WAR MEMORIAL Panel 56 Col 1.

Fri. 10th Jan. **PLYMOUTH:**

A single aircraft attacked Plymouth 1 (one) large bomb was dropped, intended for The Dockyard, landed short near the top of Devonport Park, opposite Portland Place killing two people and damaging many houses.

Sat. 11th Jan.

A huge un-exploded bomb, which had been dropped during the raids on the 28th December, that landed at Woolston Place Plymouth, was finally defused and removed. It was 9-0 long with and extra 2'-0" of tail fins and weighed 1 ton 1 cwt. (1,000kgs. A very definite example of what could be dropped from the skies above.

Sun. 12th Jan.

Mine-laying off Plymouth by IX Fluiergerke continued. One bomber was reported shot down over the sea. The crew did bale out, but no trace was found.

Mon. 13th Jan.

Devonport attacked by 49 bombers, dropping 21 tonnes of HE bombs comprising: 1-SC1000, - 2 -SC500, 4 - LZZ 250, 23 - SC250, 236 - SC50, 749 - BSK, & 25,954 - I.B's. Explosions and fires were in the docks and the south east part of the city, where in other parts of the city fires raged. The Gas and Electricity Power Plants at Cattedown were ablaze. One aircraft on anti-shipping patrol in the Bristol Channel, finding no ships on its way back, decided to drop its bombs on Plymouth. The raid lasted 4 hrs & 7 mins. The aircraft taking part are as listed below.

Gruppe	Aircraft	Time
Kgr100	11 He 111	1843 – 1907
III/KG27	10 He 111	1900 - 2015.
I/KG27	16 He 111	1908 – 2025
Kgr606	12 Do. 17	2028 – 2050

TORPOINT:

This is a copy of a letter submitted by an **un-named person** of their personal accounts during that period:

My first experience of bombs on Plymouth, was when they bombed the petrol tanks at Cattedown. The next was later on when we were just about to cross on the ferry, which had stopped, and we all had to stay in the waiting room on the Devonport side. When the ferryman came up and told us that they were going to make a special journey across and he would take us, providing we stood on the end of the ferry, as they couldn't allow us onto the central car part as they had four army trucks to take over, which we later found out were all fully loaded with ammunition. If the ferry had been hit, that would have been that?

Freda recalls:

It was a very early morning start when we would catch the 06.30 ferry across to Devonport. The so called lounge areas of the ferry was crowded with men and women, the air was blue from the smoking, enough to choke anyone never mind one's self. Starting work at 07 00, with an hour and half for lunch then worked until 17 00 hours in the evening, a very long day. One evening we were caught up in an air raid and stayed in the Devonport Ferry waiting room until ten o'clock. That was the night the Laire Oil Depot was bombed and caught alight. The ferry always stopped running during raids unless there were ammunition trucks to be carried across the river. Much of time we caught those ferry's and kept our fingers crossed until we safely reached the Torpoint side. On one such night as we crossed, a sailor boy began to sing the song 'How still is the night', above the racket of guns and planes overhead all we could hear was this sailor boy's beautiful voice.

I was home very late that evening but I was up the next morning to catch the half past six ferry. We were young and full of go in those days!

ooOoo

Thu. 16th Jan. **PLYMOUTH:**

Another short sharp air raid on Plymouth, lasting just over two hours duration from 2156-2300. 6 Heinkel HE 111 from III/KG55 carried out the bombing mine-laying off shore.

Fri. 17th Jan. **BRISTOL:**

During an air raid on Avonmouth, the first Royal Air Force servicemapoint killed was:

865245. A/C 1ST/Cl. CYRIL HENRY WATERS. Age 35
Royal Air Force (Aux) 927 Balloon Sqd.
CWG. TORPOINT HORSOM CEMETARY Row 7 Grave 469.

Sat. 18th Jan. **PLYMOUTH:**

Bombs were dropped by several aircraft, (possibly the same as the 16th raid), including dropping mines in the sea off Plymouth. The bad weather over the next few weeks saw little or no German air-raids.

ooOoo

TORPOINT:

Norman Beaver MBE. recalls:

Another memory is the destruction of Mount Edgecumbe House, and here my family were involved. The Earl asked my Uncle George Skinner, to be present when his safe at Mount Edgecumbe was blown open, and to take him and his personal belongings to Cotehele House. The removal to Cotehele was by a Bedford 17-seater bus (registration number OD 4473). By the time all had been loaded up ready to take to Cotehele, It was not possible to return to Millbrook the same day as wartime restrictions forbade the return journey at night. Uncle George and a Jack Hancock therefore, stopped off at Millbrook on their way to Cotehele and I remember we all had a clandestine peep at his Lordship in the front seat of the coach, the coach was packed full to the roof with contents from the house and I remember the Earl was wearing a fur coat and Homburg Hat and he looked very much like Flanagan and Allan)! My uncle's widow is still living in Millbrook and at the time of his demise, was in service with her sister at Mount Edgecumbe). The outcome of this story is that both George and Jack were offered a bed at Cotehele, "a four–poster", my uncle reckons he never slept a wink!! I often think about this when I visit Cotehele and view the sleeping accommodation and understand two in one those beds was not the ideal way to rest after a hard day.

[Authors note possibly Feb. 1941. It should be noted that the Earl's Chauffeur Jimmy Burgess, his wife Ruth, daughter Joan and son Tony, moved with the Earl to Cotehele House. The family lived in a cottage on the estate where Joan & Tony were born. The fate of Tony is referred to later].

ooOoo

Wed. 19th Feb. **PLYMOUTH:**

A strong force of German bombers on their way to attack South Wales dropped a string of bombs, which landed from Stonehouse to Stoke.
(no further details).

Tue. 25th Feb. **TORPOINT:**

1 un-exploded Ack Ack shell landed at Foss Farm Millbrook, it appears that not only bombs were a danger?, but on the rare occasion, Artillery Ack Ack shells.

Tue. 4th Mar. **PLYMOUTH/TORPOINT:**

1 Bomber attacked Plymouth, (no further details).

Wed. 12th Mar.

1 Bomber attacked Plymouth, (no further details).

Sat. 15th Mar.

11 Aircraft attacked Plymouth/Roborough and bombed the city between 2115-2310. Damage was caused to many house's across the city. Five deaths were reported, bombs also fell at Saltash and Torpoint, (no further details). The raid lasted 1hr - 55 mins, during the raid the Plymouth AA defences were in action. The aircraft taken part are as listed below.

Gruppe	Aircraft	Time
1 /KG27	5 He.111	2115-2145
1/KG 51	1 Ju. 88	2125
IIIKG26	1 He 111	2128-2200
III/KG 51	1 Ju. 88	2207
III/KG55	1 He.111	2240
II/KG55	2 He.111	2240 – 2310

Mon. 17th Mar. Rationing: Preserves 8oz per month.

Thur. 20th Mar. **PLYMOUTH:**

During the day Their Majesty's King George the VI and Queen Elizabeth visited Plymouth, toured the Royal Devonport Dockyard, meeting the workers and Naval Personnel, before they left by train on their homeward journey. It was not many hours later, when Plymouth was on the receiving end again. At 1900 hrs-152, aircraft began their raid dropping 159 tonnes of bombs on a Consentration Point at the mouth of the Hamoaze, and at the dock installations, east end of the Great Western Dock. The HE bomb loads comprised of: 17 - SC 1000, 63 - S 500, 248 - SC 250, 36 - LZZ 250, 633 - SC50, 153 - SD50 & 31,716 I. Bs. The weather forecast reported fog to be closing in later that night. Accurately placed incendiaries in the target area, greatly aided the bombers around Sutton Harbour and the city, causing numerous fires to develop. Close to north west of the Great Western Dock, a very large fire ignited and blazed out of control. Considerable damage was done in the city, including the Millbay Dock area. All public utility services were badly disorganized, including both road and railway transport. Railway stations were damaged and two trains burnt out. The raid lasted 6 hrs. and 20 mins, during and throughout the raid, the Plymouth AA Guns were in action firing 2,793 rounds of shells at the invaders, which were from the following.

Gruppe	Aircraft	Time
II/KG27	15 He.111	1900- 2212
KGr100	16 He.111	2041- 2103
III/KG27	8 He.111	2051- 2150
I/KG54	13 Ju. 88	2055- 2135
Kgr806	7 Ju. 88	2103- 2112
II/KG55	15 He.111	2115- 2225
III/KG55	15 He.111	2115- 2240
III/KG 51	12 Ju. 88	2116- 2158
I/KG55	13 He.111	2128- 2150

StabKG55	3 He.111	2148- 2200
II/KG54	10 Ju. 88	2158- 2235
II/KG51	9 Ju. 88	2200- 2225
I/KG27	16 He.111	2220-2320

TORPOINT:

Record Log No. 5187 incidents reported on Thursday 20/3/41-Incident 51:

20.50~ Torpoint.~ Inc. bombs dropped at four o' clock. Fires in Plymouth also at four o'clock heavy gunfire heard.
21.02~ Torpoint.~ There is a fire at Staddon Heights time 4.30 still heavy gun fire heard.
21.10~ Torpoint.~ High Explosive bombs dropped at 21.00.
21.15~ Torpoint.~ Kingsands reports two parachute mines dropped somewhere near Wilcove could be delayed action.

Fri. 21st Mar. **PLYMOUTH:**

The second major attack in two nights, Plymouth and Devonport suffered its worst attack so far. The docks at Plymouth were the C. P. for 162 bombers. Once again the weather forecast reported heavy fog later. The bombers began their attack at 20.43 during the following 4 hours, they dropped 187 tonnes HE bombs comprising: 19 - SC1000, 83 - SC500, 331 - SC250, 44 - 1ZZ250. 645 - SC50, - 36,108 I.B's. The target area was the south part of the docks, between the mouth of the Hamoaze and Sutton Pool. Despite the difficulty in seeing the target area below, large fires in the vicinity of Devonport Docks, assisted the air crews in dropping their bombs on the target area. Extensive damage was caused to the municipal and commercial centre of the city, which was largely destroyed by fire. With the fire fighters unable to maintain steady jets of water, mainly caused by damaged water mains from the previous nights bombing. Another factor was that of the many fire brigades called upon to assist, could not couple up their hoses to the city's fire appliances, they being of different size and type of coupling. Eight churches, one being St. Giles in the centre of the city, (now the sole reminder of the war) and six schools were hit. Hotels were hit and destroyed among them was The Royal, Westminster, Hackers, Waverley, and Farley. It was at the Westminster Hotel, that a certain young Torpoint lady by the name of:

POPPY EMMA CURWOOD Age 19, met a sudden death.

Poppy resided at St Leonards Carbeile Road with her mother and father, Mr. William E. and Mrs. Hilda. H. Curwood. **Poppy** was possibly to become the first civilian casualty from Torpoint.

PLYMOUTH COUNTY BOROUGH CEMETERY.

Damage was also caused at the Devonport Docks and the 303 tons trawler HMS *Asuma* anchored in the Sound was hit and sunk, 10 of her crew were reported missing. Other incidents were reported at Towell Park, Deer Park, St. Demonic, Mount Edgecumbe, Stoclisland, Carbeile Mill, Torpoint, Picklecombe Fort, Weade Quat Halt, Antony and St. John's Lake. At Mount Edgecumbe, incendiaries hit and burnt the place down and gutted the house. As one eye witness reported 'The whole of Mount Edgecumbe, right along the top of the Rame Peninsular where incendiaries had rained down, were well alight and burning, just like a firework display'. Amongst the noise and mayhem that was ongoing on the Plymouth side, and the constant drone of aircraft overhead, Torpoint was receiving all the misplaced bombs, which landed as follows:

1- 50Kg HE UXB landed at 2245 was located at the ferry gates and later defused by the BDS.

7- 50Kg UXB bombs landed at Borough Farm Torpoint, (time unknown) these were defused by the BDS.

1- 50Kg UXB bomb landed in St. Johns Lake at 0100 hrs this was defused by the BDS.

1- 50Kg UXB bomb landed at Penmildow House Antony, (time unkown) this was defused by the BDS.

The air raid lasted 3hrs. The time each aircraft was over the target area, averaged two minutes, dropping 1.27 t./bms./min. The aircraft taking part in the raid were:

Gruppe	Aircraft	Time
II/KG76	16 Ju. 88	2043 – 2210
KGr 100	9 He 111	2050 – 2110
I/KG51	14 Ju. 88	2108 – 2232
Stab KG55	3 He 111	2110 – 2133
I/KG55	11 He 111	2115 – 2205
II/KG55	8 He 111	2115 – 2147
I/KG77	9 Ju. 88	2117 – 2319
III/KG55	16 He 111	2120 – 2135
I/KG 27	14 He 111	2125 – 2225
III/KG51	12 Ju. 88	2132 – 2148
III/KG26	10 He 111	2140 – 2340
III/KG77	11 Ju. 88	2146 – 2243
II/KG 27	12 He 111	2105 – 2153
II/KG51	9 Ju. 88	2155 – 2225
II/KG77	11 Ju. 88	2155 – 2259

The following is an Excerpt from a German aircrew man's diary.

By kind permission of Before and After the Battle.

'Quote'

"Bombs were indiscriminately dropped due to dense cloud over the target area. Ten fighters appeared just before we viewed the south coast of England. But where were we to drop our bombs? From the Isle of Wight onwards there were dense clouds. In the cockpit, the pilot and observer were becoming increasingly agitated, 'what was to be done'? I heard the words. 'back to base with the bombs, much to dangerous landing with all the bombs'. Then the pilot said where is the town? it's high time we saw it now. Everything was dropped and they hurtled down into the blanket of clouds below. But onto what. That was painful".

'Unquote'

TORPOINT:

Mr. Mervyn Bursey recalls:

That same bombing raid with incendiaries, caused serious damage to Mount Edgecumbe House, so much so the house was gutted. Sgt. Bursey was already in the vicinity, and stated that a day before the house was destroyed, 1 HE bomb landed in front of the main entrance. The eruption it caused, threw mounds of earth upwards which landed on the roof. The same day the grounds-men clearing away the debris cleared all the soil off of the roof, leaving it clean. On the second night during the air raid, it was in the second wave of bombing when the damage occurred. Only one incendiary landed on the roof, which ignited and caught the roof alight. Sgt. Bersey was in the house and rushed from room to room, gathering all the bed linen and other linen, placed them in a linen basket, before removing them from the house to get them away from the fire. In the mean time the grounds-men, using the house fire hoses, were trying to extinguish the fire on the roof, unfortunately, the previous explosion had damaged the water mains, so there was insufficient water pressure to reach the roof. Consequently the incendiary burnt through the roof, fell to the lower floor, where the fire quickly spread towards the East Wing, it was not long before the house was a total blaze. There was nothing anyone could do to save it before it burnt down. The following day they went around the grounds removing dud incendiaries from the grass areas surrounding the house.

Henry Banks recalls:

When one of the big 'Blitz's was on, the whole of Torpoint was emptied (evacuated) some people were even out as far as Crafthole, people were everywhere, sleeping in hedges, gateways, fields and in the road. Plymouth was getting hammered and fire bombed. When we got back I remember standing in front of the Queen's Pub and looking across at the Dockyard, it was on fire from the Coal Heap all the way down South Yard and further. It was a terrible sight and we all had mixed feelings.

Freda recalls:

How we hated moonlight nights, in those days sometimes we were up half the night, but I laid down on the bed and got a little bit of sleep before I had to get up. But most times my friend Dorry who lived next door in the semi-detached, would stand outside the shelter and watch what was going on. We thought it was great fun until the 'Blitz' of dear old Plymouth, we both stood there and saw the whole of Plymouth alight, it was dreadful, and we were crying thinking of the poor people, our friends and workmates. The next day Dorry asked me if I would go to Plymton to see if her married sister and family were all right, I agreed and I will never forget the sights. We caught the ferry and walked to Plymouth, the houses were burning, one fireman tuned his head in out direction and I saw the side of his face was scorched red raw from the heat of the fires it was terrible, but all the people were cheerful, as they pulled out pieces of their possessions from their bombed homes, which I found doing myself at a later date. When we arrived at her sister's we were happy to find that they were well, we stayed for a cup of tea before making our way back through the rubble that was once Plymouth, we hardly knew it, whole streets had destroyed..

ooOoo

Record Log No.5187 incident reported on Friday 21/3/41-Incident 52:

17.25~ Torpoint.~ Bombs fell in area 6 HE's in the field at Burough Farm, one HE. in the field near the main road under R. Merrifield 06" map. One HE. in Mount Edgecumbe near the balloon site, 41 above Hoe Lake Cottage.

ooOoo

John Vigus remembers his mother telling him.

'They (his mother & father)' were called away from their greengrocers shop in Fore Street, (which later was the laundry shop) to return back to their farm house at Maryfield, (now privately owned) the bomb exploded close to the Antony Road in the field called Merrifield (the old name), where their horse grazed. When they got there, their horse was dead, shrapnel from the exploding bomb had cut right through the throat of their brilliant white horse.

Henry Banks recalls:

One evening my dad and I were going over to see my Aunty Polly at St Leverns Road, when we were caught up in an air raid whilst walking up Pottery Road. There was an almighty BANG and the pair of us were blown back about 100 yards. When I picked myself up I could not see dad as he had caught the full force of the blast and was a good fifty yards further back than me. It had been an aerial Parachute bomb, which had landed at the bottom of Devonport Park. That was the first time I had been blown up and we were both badly shaken. It took a while for us to recover enough to carry on and while we were walking past some houses that had collapsed, we could hear faint cries for 'HELP.' So my dad poked his head into a black space where the door had been, he turned to me and said, 'It's coming from in here', as he stepped inside he just disappeared, he had fallen into the basement, but he did find a man and a woman who were not hurt, so he helped them up to me and off they went somewhere. By this time the bombs were going off everywhere, and dad said to me 'I think we had better go home boy so we did', I never did get to see my Aunt Polly. When we arrived back in Torpoint, dad went straight up to the ARP Headquarters because he was the Transport Officer. I went home to tell mum what had happened, then went up to the Head quarters, I still remember that as I walked past St. James Church there were dozens of Incendiary bombs burning in St. James Road, of course lots of people were trying to cover them with sandbags to put out the fires, but I reported in first and was told to take my ambulance out of Torpoint and wait for the 'All Clear'. So I drove it out just past the Antony House entrance and parked opposite the old filter bed. In the field opposite were four anti-aircraft guns, after a few minutes of standing and listening to all the noise that was going on, all four guns fired together and I literally jumped a foot of the ground. (Gosh what a fright that was). When the 'All Clear' went I drove my ambulance back towards Torpoint and the road by the Thanckes oil drums, where the tar had caught alight, the flames were about four inches high and as I drove through it, of course the tar stuck to my tires and when I got back to the H.Q. several people told me that my ambulance was alight, but I knew of course that it was only the hot tar stuck to the wheels, some sand and water soon put out the smoldering tires.Then I was sent down to the ferry to collect casualties, there were four bodies that were loaded into the back of the ambulance and in those days a canvas curtain that served as doors was fastened tight. It was not a nice job, especially when the ambulance was on a slight slope, blood was running out and dripping onto the road. war is a dreadful business and SO cruel.

Unnamed person recalls:

During the March Blitz, I was on duty at the fire station on one of the phones, when the sirens went off sounding the all clear. We all went outside and stood watching the sight of Plymouth burning. I was later told that the oil tanks at Thankes Park had been hit and were on fire, but only three were burning, the smoke pouring out of them blocked the main Antony Road.

[Authors note: The following story submitted by Pat Ravensdale (nee Gliddon) sister of Peter Gliddon, (The Family Butchers in Fore Street), who was 10 years old at the time, sent in her story. (Although Pat could not place the dates of these following exerts, as she stated she was only 10 years old, however, I believe her first entry was referring to this particular night time raid].

The night Plymouth caught fire I was only about 10 years old. My father came into the air raid shelter we were in and told my mother and aunt they must come out and see the sight of Plymouth on fire. I asked to go outside too, and stood at the top of the hill, leading down to the ferry.

The whole of the sky and area across the river was an orange glow.

We also had our caravan moved to Downderry where we went every night during the blitz. One morning on returning home there was an un-exploded bomb at the end of Macey Street and the roof of my parent's bedroom had disappeared.

A couple of nights after my brother Peter was born, we were all down stairs sitting under the dining room table because there was a raid on. We were very concerned that my mother and new baby brother were still upstairs in bed, I remember my father carrying them downstairs. She also remembers that on a certain night they were in the shelter down at Torpoint School during an air raid, after the bombing had finished they returned home to find a un-exploded bomb had dropped through the roof and was suspended about a foot above baby Peters cot. They made a hasty retreat.

ooOoo

Sun. 23rd Mar.

1 50Kg UXB bomb landed at Home Farm, another 50Kg UXB landed at Entacoombe Farm at Mount Edgecumbe, both was defused by the BDS.

Mon. 24th Mar.

At 1845 3-250Kg UXB'S landed close to South Down Cottage Millbrook, another 50Kg UXB landed at Home Farm and a further 50KG UXB landed at the Brickworks.

Record Log No. 5187 incidents reported on Sunday 23/3/41 - Incident 54/55/56:

18.37~ Torpoint.~ Six bombs dropped at St. John's Lake approx 18.25.
18.48~ Torpoint.~ Three HE. bombs dropped in the creek south side of Site 7, near Trevol Range.
19.15~ Torpoint.~ From R.A.F. H.Q. Wolston. 1 UXB fell in the vicinity of site, 2 fell about 18.45. One is 60 yds from site, and the other is at Cremyll, the first one is definitely endangering site 2. Three more UXB's in Southdown Village. Both sets of bombs have been identified by RAF officers.

Sat. 29th Mar.

Torpoint air-raid: Single bomber dropped 2-50Kg bombs, one landed at Stone Farm Millbrook, the other at Blerrick Farm Antony, both failed to explode. UXB's were defused by the BDS.

Sun. 31st Mar. **SOUTH WEST ENGLAND:**

Rationing: Allowance reduced to 1s. 0d.

During the following 10 days or so, due to bad weather, there were few air attacks during the night-time. But that was soon to change in April.

Wed. 2nd Apr. **TORPOINT:**

Another single bomber dropped 1 50Kg bomb that landed at the Searchlight Site Triangle, but failed to explode. UXB was defused by the BDS.

Mon. 7th Apr. **PLYMOUTH:**

Attacks carried out on shipping outside Plymouth. Night attack on Devonport Dockyard little damage caused. One Heinkel He 111 of Stab 9/KG26 shot down by Hurricane of 87 Squadron.

Wed. 9th Apr. **TORPOINT:**

Torpoint air attack, more harassing than anything else. Several firebombs fell on Torpoint plus 3 HE bombs. Damaged was caused to private property and there were four casualties, not serious.

Record Log No. 5187 incidents reported on Wednesday 9/4/41 - Incident 57:

23.37~ Torpoint.~ Inc.bombs just fallen by the workhouse at Cambridge Fields, now many are falling all over town inform Fire Brigade to stand by.
23.39~ Saltash.~ Post G.1. reports enormous fire at Torpoint.
23.40~ Torpoint.~ We need urgent help in putting out fires.
23.47~ Saltash.~ Fires no longer visible.
23.55~ County ARP ~ Col. Gillespie sending HMS Raleigh's men to help out should be able to cope.

On the same day-

CORNWALL:

Torpoint airman serving at 4 Wing Technical Training RAF HALTON, died from illness.

541487. F/SGT. EDWIN CHARLES BROAD. Age 45.

Royal Air Force

CWG. HALTON St. MICHAEL CHURYARD. Plot L Row U grave 107.

Thu. 10th Apr. **PLYMOUTH:**

Air attack on Plymouth (no further details):

Fri. 11th Apr.

Plymouth attacked again (no other details):

Sat. 12th Apr.

Harassing attack on Plymouth (no other details):

Mon. 14th Apr.

Spitfires of 152 Squadron, shot down1 Heinkel He 111 of Stab Wekusta 51.

Tue. 15th Apr.

Plymouth attacked by 6 bombers of Luftwaffe Stab 3 (no other details):

Tue. 22nd Apr.

Devonport was the target for 120 aircraft at 2139 hrs, the first wave dropped numerous fire flares to illuminate the C. P. below. Within the dockyard many fires were started on the east bank side of the Hamoaze. The following waves dropped 139 tons of HE bombs comprising: 31 - SC1000, 49 - SC500, 224 - SC250, 38 - LZZ 250, 361 - SC50, & 35,996 I.Bs.

PLYMOUTH / TORPOINT:

At Sutton Pool, six bombs landed causing very large explosions along with others, within the Dockyard on HMS. *Drake?* The Tower of Boscawen was set alight before being hit by another bomb, which exploded in the basement (being used as a shelter for Navy personnel), claiming the lives of 96 sailors. When Keyham Gasworks was hit, one enormous blast erupted, subsequently the fire blazed away.
Bombs landed near the Torpoint South Ferry, damaging it so much, that it was put out of service until repairs were completed one month later on the 22nd May. When the bomb exploded a civilian Torpoint Ferryman was killed.
JEREMIAH MAHONEY **Age 54.** 3, Park Road Torpoint.
PLYMOUTH COUNTY BOROUGH CEMETERY.
Torpoint also came under extensive bombing by the Luftwaffe, much damage was caused to houses in the town and, the following list of civilians were killed:
SAMUEL EMERY BROWN. M.M. **Age 50.** Firewatcher of Standard Inn, Fore Street.

HENRY ROBBINS. **Age 31.** Firewatcher of Clarence Road.

Both killed on duty at the Octagon Plymouth.
PLYMOUTH COUNTY BOROUGH CEMETERY.

ERIC EVERINGTON. **Age 42.** Home Guard of Ferry Street.

***WILLIAM HENRY LEACH.** **Age 59.** 2nd Officer Torpoint Fire Brigade. 39, Fore Street.

***WILLIAM THOMAS PEACH.** **Age 57**. Torpoint Fire Brigade 36, Fore Street.

EUNETA CLARICE WESTLAKE. **Age 37**. 14, Carew Terrace.

DAVID WESTLAKE. **Age 10.** 14, Carew Terrace.

COLIN WESTLAKE. **Age 5**. 14, Carew Terrace.

The following three were killed at 14, Carew Terrace.

CHARLES PUCKEY. **Age 65.** 13, Macey Street.

MABEL PUCKEY. **Age 55**. 13, Macey Street.

LILIAN MABEL NORTHCOTT. **Age 33.** 13, Macey Street.
ALL ABOVE TORPOINT HORSOM CEMETERY.

LEONARD WYBORN. **Age 39.** Address unknown

- Fire Watchers **W.H. Peach. and T.W. Leach.** were out on duty when a bomb landed in Fore Street.

- ** **P.O. G.W. WHITE. Age 47**. Stationed @ HMS *Raleigh* **P.O. White** was possibly visiting friends in Torpoint.

The raid lasted 4 hours. Aircraft 2.15 minutes over the target, 1.87 tonnes of Bombs were being dropped every minute. During the bombing raid the German aircraft taking part were:

Gruppe	Aircraft	Time
KGr100	9 He 111	2139-2155
I/KG27	10 He 111	2145-2318
III/KG27	10 He 111	2146- 2230
II/KG55	8 He 111	2200-2220
I/KG 55	18 He 111	2200-2245
Stab/KG55	1 He 111	2215
III/KG55	17 He 111	2230-2250
III/KG26	8 He 111	2239-2326
II/KG1	13 Ju. 88	2345-0027
KG77	14 Ju. 88	0025-0140
III/KG1	12 Ju. 88	0042-0140

Record Log No. 5187 incidents reported on Monday 21/22/4/41 -Incident 60:

21.32~ Torpoint.~ All communications broke down during early part of the air raid, have to rely on military directive. Report of damage from military 23.30. Oil tanks at Thanckes Fuel Depot on fire. Torpoint fire engine in attendance Inc. bombs in Wilcove, military sending help, also Inc. bombed schoolyard. Torpoint farms were on fire at Mount Edgecumbe and six HE. bomb craters were found in the mud near Torpoint. At 10.55. A.R.P.O. Torpoint arrives at Control and gave the following report. Many HE. bombs in the water. One HE. bomb on the shore near the Gas Works, a general fall of Inc. bombs some penetrating houses.

ooOoo

Frank Bolton recalls:

The bombs that went off in the mud flats, landed just off shore, when they exploded they sent showers of mud up, which splattering the houses in the town with lumps of mud. It was only after the rain came, which streaked the outside of the house and eventually in time, they were washed away.

John Peach recalls:

1941 saw the start of an intense bombing period, which was called the Blitz. Plymouth being a Naval Port was an obvious target. Night after night the bombers would come, and Torpoint being so close had many houses destroyed and sadly the loss of civilian lives. It was April the 23rd that Granddad Peach was killed. He had just stepped outside of 36, Fore Street when a bomb exploded directly opposite, destroying the stable building (now Abercrombie Flats). The blast killed him immediately.

[Author's note: I believe the following extract refers to the above bombing raid].

Henry Banks recalls:

During one night-time raid I came home from work late, it was dark and almost immediately the warning sounded, so I started to walk up to the H.Q. On rounding Grangers Corner there was a terrific bang, the next thing I knew was when I woke up inside of Mr. Grangers passage feeling very unwell. In the half -light I could see where the front door had been, so I crawled out back into the street but could not stand up. Someone came along and said 'Are you hurt'? to which I replied 'Where am I'? I was then picked up, it was quite a shock to be able to stand up. Although a bit shaky, somehow I got to the H.Q, where my dad said to me 'Do you know that our house has been hit, and a bomb has been dropped on the bake-house'. Actually it just missed the bake-house and that was the one that nearly got me. I asked dad if I could go home and see how things were. 'Yes lad you do that and report back to me'. The scene was not good, a bomb had struck the deviding wall between number 39 and 40, so the top floor of both houses was gone plus all the doors and windows. I shouted out loud and my mother shouted back. 'We are all alright, is your dad o.k'? to which I replied, 'We were, and could I leave them for the time being'? then mum shouted back 'Come home when it is daylight'. I then returned back to H.Q. to report back to dad. That raid lasted until four-o'clock in the morning, and then dad and I went back home and dug our way into our family. Dad being a shipwright had made a very strong shelter under the stairs and it stood the test of time but of course if the house had caught fire it would have been another story, because the shelter was all made of wood. From then on it was a case of saving all that we could. All the large furniture was taken along with other peoples to be stored in the Antony House Stables for war storage, even the beds; we all transferred up to my sisters flat in Shamballly Terrace now a part of the renamed Antony Road. Eleven of us slept the first night on the kitchen floor. On top of that, my brother who was training at Blerrick Camp in the Royal Marine Commandoes, had broken his leg in two places and was sent home on sick leave, of course he could not climb the stairs with his leg in plaster, so he had the front room and shared it with five other people, who slept on the floor. Everyone in our family was still living there when I got called to the colours. Mum had to find another shop in which to sell her rationed goods from and that was not easy. In the end I think she found one in Harvey Street where the flats are now just behind Fourbouys the newsagents opposite Redding's the ironmonger.

Fred Timms recalls:

1941 arrived and proved to be my luckiest year. The four main air raids during March and April saw me climbing out of the rubble two nights running, the house was damaged by bombs and we had to move out. The last house was number 1, Hooper Street (Clinic car-park) directly opposite the now Torpoint Library. It took about twenty minutes before the dust settled down, the overhead electric cables outside the Wheelers was laying on the ground, sparks flying everywhere. To get to my dad who was in Wellington Street, to inform him that mum, sister Winnie Farrell and her daughter Patricia were all o'k, I had to make my way down to and around the King's Arms to get to Elliot Square. In the process I stumbled over what I thought was a bulk of timber, but was in fact the body of Mr. Leach who had taken Downings Horse (Empress) over to Hoskins field, now Hamoaze Road. He had returned to fire-watch the stables at Abercrombie House. Next night the 24th April, the oil tanks were well alight, all those that had transport were told to go to Polbathic, out of the way of danger and were settled down into a wooden hut. That wooden hut is still there today, where so many people slept during that night, half if not more, standing upright. The next day when we got back to Torpoint, living space in the house was at a premium, so at night time we had to sleep in the Anderson Shelter in the back garden. From then on I spent every night in that shelter until the end of September. The air raids continued but not on such a large scale. Now when I walk down the back lane I stop and try to visualize what it was like then.

Wed. 23rd Apr. **PLYMOUTH / TORPOINT:**

Devonport under attack again. Barely had the citizens of Plymouth recovered from the previous nights attack, when they were subjected to another 5 hours of intense devastation. between the hours of 21.45 p.m. to 01.58 a.m. The main C. P. area was the southern part of the dockyard where 125 aircraft dropped 146 tonnes of HE bombs comprising: 1- SC1800, 28 - SC1000, 42 - SC 500, 242 - SC250, 31 -

LZZ250, 2 - SD250, 529 - SC50, and 35,796 I.B.s, these bombs hit the Power Station, Gas Works and Food Offices, causing large fires, which blazed out of control. At approx. 22.30, one large explosion was heard and seen, by various people. 8,000 tons of Petrol and 3,000 tons of Diesel Oil were ignited, the inferno blazed away for days.

TORPOINT:

Torpoint did not escape the bombing, bombs rained down on the town devastating Coryton Terrace, Fore Street, Ferry Street, and Carew Terrace. The oil tanks at Thanckes Farm were set on fire with the loss of 10,500 tons of oil, causing black columns of smoke to drift over Torpoint or, when the wind changed direction, blew it the opposite way. Bombs landed on either side of the South Ferry, still under repair from the previous bombing incident, sustaining more damage, leaving Torpoint almost isolated, with only one ferry in service for essential traffic only, until August 8th. The overall repair took sixteen weeks (16 weeks). During the bombing two ferry employees lost their life, when an anti-personnel bomb blew up. One man un-identified, (it is assumed from elsewhere else) the other a Torpoint Civilian.
Ferryman. ARTHUR ERNEST O'GORMAN. Aged 56 4. Ferry Street.
TORPOINT HORSOM CEMETERY.

[Authors note; It has also been suggested that he was killed by a raiders machine gun bullets, whilst driving the 7 o'clock ferry across to Devonport. This is doubtful as the raid finished at 01.58 hrs]
Other Torpoint civilians killed that night were:
HERBERT ARTHUR EVANS. **Age 56.** 8, Ferry Street.

ALBERT BENJAMIN HOAR. Age & Address unknown

ALBERT ALFRED JOHN PARKER. **Age 34.** 43, Fore Street
TORPOINT HORSOM CEMETERY.

Air raid lasted 5 hours 25 minutes. Throughout the raid, Plymouth's AA s were in action, firing 2,645 shells at the aircraft overhead. Each aircraft spent approx 2.52min over the target, releasing 3.5 tonnes of bombs a minute. The German aircraft taking part were:

Gruppe	Aircraft	Time
I/KG27	8 He 111	2145-2217
III/KG27	8 He 111	2145-2240
KGr100	9 He 111	2150-2219
III/KG55	19 He 111	2200-2320
I/KG55	17 He 111	2210-2305
Stab kg55	1 He 111	2224-2325
II/KG55	11 He 111	2230-2255
III/KG 26	8 He 111	2235-2350
I/KG77	12 Ju. 88	2239-0158
III/KG1	7 Ju. 88	0005-0055
II/KG77	11 Ju. 88	0010-0050
II/KG1	10 Ju. 88	0025-0100

Record Log No. 5187 incidents reported on Tuesday 22/23/4/41 -Incident 61:

21.40~ Torpoint.~ The raid lasted until 03.25. 23/4/40. Message received from Torpoint that several HE. bombs had fallen requesting First Aid and Rescue parties. A further message timed at 23.11 and received at midnight asking for two ambulances. Rescue and First Aid parties sent to Torpoint. At 04.20 Torpoint reported that HE. bombs has fallen all along the riverside from the Institution to the ferry. Casualties were estimated as 12 dead and 7 minor injuries, the Police Station House was damaged. UXB at the ferry stopped aid reaching Torpoint, but will be cleared by the afternoon and the ferry can resume service. Two HE bombs killed two people in Cremyll the result of a direct hit on a bomb shelter, 10 houses damaged as a result of the blast. 1 HE. bomb on Cremyll Road, 1 HE. bomb on Cremyll Arms.

ooOoo

Mr. Mervyn Bursey recalls:

I was called away from Millbrook, to attend to the attack at Cremyll where the bombs had dropped, Mr. Bersey helped in the rescue of the stricken. Three people were dead, and they were:

Mr. Crowther.

Mr. Lewis Howard. of the Cremyll Ferry

Mr. Tucker.

Record Log No.5187 incident reported on Wednesday 23/4/41 -Incident 62:

21.48~ Torpoint.~ Another air raid lasted till 01.45. oil tanks at Thancke's Fuel Depot on fire. Direct hit on three houses in York Road, fires broke out. Final report from Torpoint sums up as follows, HE at York Road and fires. Casualties four dead from direct hit on shelters, 19 Injured, five serious.

The devastation in Coryton Terrace caused by bombs brought havoc and mayhem, along with death and other casualties, specifically to one family as follows:

ARTHUR CONNING.	**Age 32.**	15, Coryton Terrace
RUTH CONNING.	**Age 30.**	15, Coryton Terrace
BARBARA CONNING.	**Age 2.**	15, Coryton Terrace
BRIAN CONNING.	**Age 2 MONTHS**	15, Coryton Terrace
UN-IDENTIFIED REMAINS.	Age Unknown	15, Coryton Terrace

ALL ABOVE: TORPOINT HORSOM CEMETERY.

Also during the raid.

ARTHUR AUGUSTUS DEVONSHIRE living at 15,Tremayne Terrace, received severe injuries, was rescued and taken to the Medical Reception Centre.

The tragedy of the Conning family, happened when a bomb hit the Anderson Shelter they were in, destroying it and the surrounding area including demolishing houses, the devastation caused by the bomb must have been by a big bomb, possibly an SC1000, that is something that will never be known. Rescue Workers (RW) was soon at the scene, and by some sort of a miracle at the beginning of his research in 1998, the Author and Mr. Mike Pigeon Warden of St. James Church, were reviewing the book containing Torpoint's Roll of Honour for its War Dead. Mr. Pigeon pointed out that 'an unnamed rescue worker dug out 3-year-old Jean Conning alive'. This statement intrigued the Author, somehow I was going to find out what had happened to a Jean Conning after the war. Two separate versions of this incident have since been voiced, one stated, a rescue worker digging his spade into the rubble, saw the back of a body, the second account referred to the rescue worker as swinging his pick-axe into the rubble, pierced the back of a child, luckily it just scratched the surface of the skin. It was not until 2005 when by chance, I mentioned my interest in finding out about the Conning family to Carol Stevens, then the owner of Trecaro Greengrocers, and was surprised when she told me that it was her mother. Carol mentioned that her mother would be very reluctant to talk about the incident. However, Carol arranged for me to meet her mother Jean, who invited me to her home where she did relate the true story. After some encouragement, Jean did agree to write her story down for me, which is the true account of what happened. Read the story written by:

Mrs.**Jean Peach (nee Conning)** who was the child in question. However, it is not known whether the **ATS** stated above, whose remains were found at the same scene, was a friend visiting the Conning family at the time. To this day her identity remains un-disclosed. Her remains are buried in Horsom Cemetery Plot 657.
[Authors note: Read Henry Banks account of the incident].

Police Constable Doug Mitchell recalls:

Disaster I was to find, brings out the best in some people. During the raids, a number of people were killed in Torpoint, there was a Mortuary set up in a tin shed on the rivers edge, and on a regular basis two W.V.S. ladies, would report to the Police Station (now installed in the previous Ferry Offices), to collect the keys of the mortuary. If this happened when I was on duty, I would offer to go with them (to give moral support). The shed had a 6' x 6' porch, and when entering they would say "lets have a fag " and I would join them. The cigarette smoke in that confined place did a little to alleviate the smell coming from the building. Fags finished, they would say "let's get on with it". There was no surprise as to what they were to find on entering the building. They set about their task with objectivity. Bodies were wrapped in blankets, ensuring that they were appropriately labelled. In some cases bits of whole families were put into a sandbag. Job done, we would lock up. I took the key back to the Station. They went their way – to return following the next raid to repeat the process. Who these ladies were I never knew, but the guts they had, filled me with admiration for the true bulldog determination of some people in the face of disaster.

Henry Banks recalls:

I remember another night when I was sent to where a bomb had landed in York Road, The private Anderson Shelter had been hit and the whole family killed. Whilst climbing over the rubble in the semi-darkness, I fell and put my hands out to save myself and felt something slimy. It upset me to find out it was a squashed head (this is an awful memory).

[Author's note: Henry Bank's disturbing account relating to the incident in Coryton Terrace, which is now York Road.]

[Author's note: **RECORDS at TRURO** refers to all names of the identified casualties in Coryton Terrace. There was only One (1) un-identified, whose remains were buried separately in Horsom Cemetery, that was no doubt the ATS girl.
In conversation with another lady I met, Mrs. Florence (Phil) Woolcock, a survivor of that bombing raid, remembered that night very well, she related the following]

I was living at number 27, Tremayne Terrace opposite Coryton Terrace, with my daughter Cecilia, now married and living in Torpoint (Mrs. Cecilia Shrewing). After the previous couple of raids, the town was not in a very good shape, with all the devastation along the foreshore and up into the town. We understood there had been casualties but not the numbers. This latest raid was the third night in succession they had come over. We had heard the wailing sound of the Alert over in Plymouth, I cannot remember the exact time but it was the same as other nights round about 9.o'clock. I suppose as our normal practice, from the start of an air raid, we took shelter in the front room, cowering under the table, as a protection against the bombs. The air raid had already begun over in Devonport, the noise of airplanes flying overhead was incessant, it seemed to go on and on forever, along with the exploding bombs over in the Dockyard and other explosions,was dreadful, and it certainly frightened the life out of us. We heard bombs dropping closer and closer they must have been down in the town? Right close to us, a couple of large explosions went off, one after the other, I immediately grabbed Cecilia, I thought we were goners, the house shook, window glass was flying everywhere, my hearing was effected and my heart was pounding, Cynthia was clinging to me sobbing, terrified we hugged each other close, the ringing in my ears did not help, I was in a daze and not sure what had happened, I said my prayers. Then there was silence before the shouting began. In the glow of fire, I saw through the open space, which had been the front window, rescue workers running past, and still the planes droned on overhead and the bombing continued. Guns were firing, there appeared to be no respite, until the last planes droned out of hearing, and I vaguely heard the 'All Clear' sound. It wasn't until daylight when we ventured out, that we saw the destruction opposite in Coryton Terrace. But ours like others in Tremayne Terrace had caught the blast. Most of our neighbour's houses were badly damaged. What a lucky escape for us, unfortunately our house was not fit to live in. The wardens said we should pack our bags and get out. The house was quickly boarded up and Cynthia and I were

evacuated to Polreath along with all our furniture. She also related another story, which she said happened before that night. During the start of an air raid, the local Air Raid Warden whilst on patrol, had noticed a chink of light was showing through her black-out curtains, attracting her attention, he shouted out to her.
"Mrs. PUT THOSE LIGHTS OUT NOW, JERRY WILL SEE THEM" Mrs. Woolcock hearing the ferocity in the ARW's warning, became extremely indignant, stormed out of her front door and shouted back at him.
'NEVER MIND MY BLACKOUT PROBLEM YOU GO AND PUT OUT THE FIRE'S IN THE TANKS. THAT'S A MUCH GREATER ATTRACTION THAN MINE'.
[Authors note: This must have been when the tanks were first hit a few weeks before. Mrs. Woolcock's husband, a regular serving in the Navy, was away on board HMS *Guardian,* engaged in laying anti-submarine nets in various ports around the coastline].

A further interesting story submitted by Lt. Com. (Rtd.) Gordon Crocker R.N., who was born in 1938, was 4 years old at the time of the incident, his wartime memories are as follows

We lived in Coryton Terrace (now York Road) at No. 21, My parents had bought the house as new build. My father who was in the Navy, and my mother were both Torpointer's and both sets of grandparents lived in Torpoint, my paternal grandparents in Carew Terrace, and my maternal grandparents had the shop on the corner of Beatrice Terrace.

Early in the war because he was in business, Granddad Eustace still retained the use of his car. In 1941, as the night-time air raids became more frequent and heavier, he used to drive us out into the country to sleep in the car returning in the morning. Strangely Grandma Eustace never went with us preferring to spend the nights in the cupboard under the stairs.

On this particular night we spent the night in the gateway of a field just as you go up the hill to Sheviock (it's still there). On returning to Torpoint in the morning, there was a ladder across the road by the Council Chambers and our house and others in the road were no more. We were later told that the bomb that had done for our house had gone through the ceiling of my bedroom into next door before doing its worst, but even more tragic was a direct hit on the shelter of No 15. Where the only survivor was baby Jean.

After the bombing we were homeless, so we went to live with my grandparents at No. 3 Beatrice Terrace, it was a bit cramped as my aunt Megan who was in the WRNS. at HMS *Raleigh* and married to my uncle Jim Wilkinson a submariner was also living in the house. There was no hot water system, no bathroom and one outside toilet, nevertheless we did have a tin bath, which was placed in front of the dining room fire and filled with hot water, heated in the copper stove in the out-house wash room. But we survived. We went to live at Beatrice Terrace for a while before my father moved us to Torquay, as he thought it would be safer, before he went off to sea never to return, he was killed in HMS *Trinidad.* After his death we moved back to Beatrice Terrace, until our house was rebuilt after the war.

My paternal grandparents Win and George Crocker, were also bombed out of Carew Terrace and went to live in Sydney Road, with a lovely view of the Fuel Storage Depot.

GJC. Dec. 2007..

Norman Beavers MBE. recalls:

The night our house was damaged, dad was with us and we must thank God for that. Some of our neighbours were killed, including children – a very gruesome and frightening time for us all. The time had come to evacuate Torpoint and of course the school closed. To me at this time, although I was never that keen on school, there seemed to be a vacuum.

At this point I must say that although I was never conscripted into the armed services, my family and I were in the front line when the Blitz of Plymouth was going on. Dad was lucky, on the night the Dockyard was under heavy attack, he was at home with us. On his return to work the following day, the sail loft, (he was a sail maker) had been destroyed and those working there had been killed. He also had the gruesome task of identifying his brother-in–law, my uncle Leslie, [Authors note: Resident of Kingsand], who had been a victim of the almost total destruction of South Yard. There were no medals for the heroes of this battlefield.

We were fortunate that my grandfather had a haulage business in Millbrook (F.J. Skinner & Sons), and was able to provide us with a lorry to load what we could from Torpoint and take with us to Millbrook. Now another challenge, a new school to attend! Fourlanesend School was situated between Millbrook and Kingsands, a mile walk for me. The Headmaster was a Mr. Whale and by nature he was very tall and big. When he visited my class, he always carried his cane with him. Discipline in those days very much to the fore. My first teacher was a Mr. Cardew whom I did not care for, but it was not long before he was called up and an older man, a Mr. Eastman took over, we got on better.

At Fourlanesend I met up with another boy who had been evacuated from Torpoint. His name was Bernard Stone and he was staying with his uncle at nearby Wiggle Farm. Later in life Bernard joined the Devon Constabulary and we lost touch with each other, however, during my time at Fourlanesend, I tagged onto Bernard and after school I helped on the farm. I really liked what I was doing – food production was a priority and I loved doing something for the war effort.

We were still not far from the front line, Plymouth was still being bombed the Dockyard and Warships being targeted by German bombers. At Wiggle we had a searchlight manned by the Army and a Balloon Barrage Site manned by the RAF, so we had constant reminders of the dangers of war. However, well after my school days I still spent many happy hours at Wiggle Farm and I shall always remember the late Mr. and Mrs. Passmore, they had a great influence on my life and my mind, and helped me face the future.

Mrs. Eddy who lived at 85, Clarence Road remembers the tanks being blown up, and at one stage after the raid, the dense thick oily smoke was so bad, that the Navy came along to evacuate the residents. Her father Mr. George Waldron a member of the Home Guard and a veteran of the First World War, refused point blank saying.

'We are staying put in our own house'.

Fortunately the wind changed direction diverting the smoke out across open countryside towards Antony. She also recollects that during one of the raids, her father who was on duty at the Laun, when some German bombers heading for the tanks began to aim and drop Incendiaries at the Oil Tanks. Having missed them, set the Laun grass ablaze, Mr. Waldron armed with a rifle took aim fired with several shots at the attacking bombers. **"So Dad's Army did retaliate"!**

Frank Bolton recalls:

After another raid I looked out of the window and saw the Laun like fairyland, with what must have been hundreds of Incendiaries bombs, one had hit the Laun, which had to be put out.

Mrs.Wendy Plant (nee Patton) recalls:

Miss Wendy Patton then aged eight, a survivor of the Devonport raids remembers her school teacher drove her in her car out to Crafthole, where she was to stay with aunts. The journey took the car past the blazing Oil Tanks. Wendy remembers the heat and those they had to drive through thick palls of oily black choking smoke drifting across Antony Road. Her mother had to walk all the way.

Pat Ravensdale recalls:

The night the Oil Tanks caught fire, the whole family had gone out into the country where we had a caravan. Next morning when we returned to Torpoint, the air and everywhere was covered in black smoke from the tanks.

ooOoo

FRANCE VILLAROCHE:

An exert from a German crew-member reads as follows.

With Kind permiision of Before and After the Battle

'Quote'

22nd/23rd Apr.

Take off Villaroche 21.20. Hrs.
The objective for my 30th Operational flight is Plymouth, that sorely tried city. Well-aimed bomb drops are possible. But then we are shown aerial photographs for the first time, and see that the cty is in fact destroyed down to its foundations. Have the inhabitants been evacuated? Surely We also convince ourselves that the Londoner's have undoubtedly been evacuated. Anything else would indeed be un-imaginable.

But Plymouth, the Seaport in the south, has in fact been attacked more than all the other towns. Did that really have to be so?

Unquote'.

ooOoo

Wed. 23rd Apr. **MALTA G.C. :**

On the that same day in Malta a **Torpoint civilian**, whilst attached to Royal Navy Dockyard Malta, died (cause unknown**).**

RAYMOND ROBERT CREWS Age 21 Formerly of 7, Beatrice Terrace**.**
CWGC. Malta G.C.

Thu. 24th Apr **PLYMOUTH / TORPOINT:**

Another major attack started at 2146 hrs. The Luftwaffe returned for the fourth successive night. Plymouth was stretched to its limits, food reserves had been destroyed and the mains water supply was inadequate. During the daytime hours, people still queued for what limited food was available, until the bombing began again. 109 aircraft targeting Plymouth and Devonport. The air raids, came in two waves, the first lasted about two hours, quickly followed by the second, lasting just over three hours. Dropping 118 tones of HE bombs comprising: 7 - Sc 1000, 72 - SC500, 232 - SC250, 30 - LZZ250, 196 - SD/Sc50 and 18,484, IB's. This time the C.P.was the Dockyard and Port installations. Two large fires from the previous night in the south west part of the city, were still burning. Very quickly these were soon

joined by more in and around the Dockyard, providing evidence that it was one big oil fire, producing volumes of dense black smoke. Records state that at 23.20 the German aircrews reported seeing a particular big explosion, followed by succession of smaller ones. In one of the docks, a ship was seen to be on fire. The attack was less severe than the previous two nights, and lasted 3 hrs. The Plymouth AA was again in action and fired 2,183 shells.
Casualties were again serious. Over the period of the three raids over 400 people had been killed and 256 seriously injured. The aircraft taking part were;

Gruppe	Aircraft	Time
Kgr100	9 He 111	2146- 2230
III/KG1	9 Ju. 88	2205- 2236
II/KG1	14 Ju. 88	2206- 2302
III/KG54	12 Ju. 88	2239- 0020
I/KG77	11 Ju. 88	2242- 2313
III/KG26	7 He 111	2245- 2330
II/KG54	11 Ju. 88	2300- 0005
II/KG54	15 Ju. 88	2305- 0005
III/KG27	12 He 111	2315- 0000
I/KG27	9 He 111	2350- 0051

ooOoo

During that raid the oil tanks at THANCKE'S PARK were hit and set on fire, they were to burn for four whole days and nights before they were finally extinguished. The below Aerial Photo illustrates the pattern of clouds almost enveloping the area:

With kind permission of Before and after the Battle

APRIL 1941

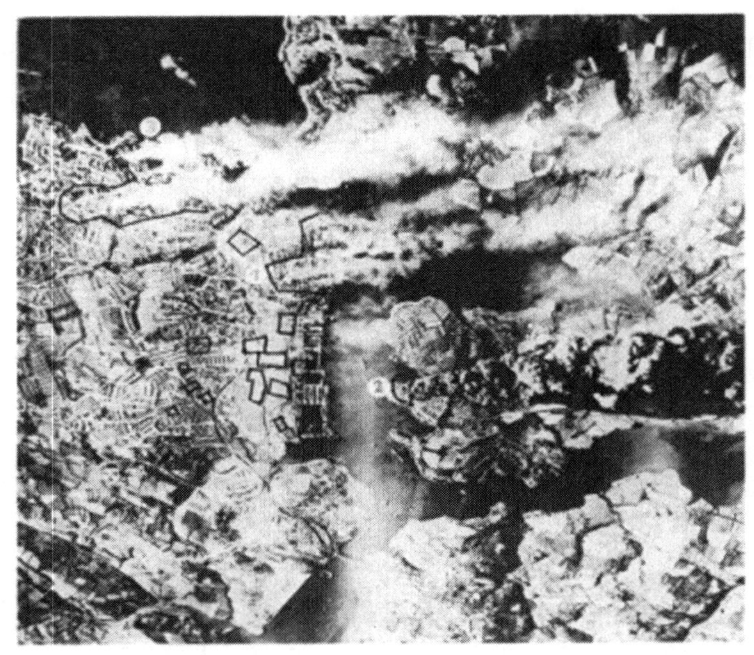

Just how much could one take? After an all-too-short respite to lick its many wounds, that other great south coast naval city, grievously bleeding from the previous week's attacks, now came in for more punishment. Ministry of Home Security April 30: 'Plymouth is an accessible target to the G.A.F., who may hope by these heavy attacks to further Germany's success in the battle of the Atlantic. The enemy may have been led by the reports of these heavy raids to suppose that he could get the population "on the run" and deprive the dockyards of labour. If he is changing his strategy, and intends to try to put single towns out of commission one by one by repeated bombardment, urgent consideration will have to be given to the arrangements for maintaining the community's life and work in the face of such attack. A valuable respite will be secured for the development of these arrangements by the increased hours of daylight, but the problems nevertheless are many and pressing. It should not be forgotten that the need for a change of tactics on the enemy's part is in itself an encouraging sign, and the courage and resolution of Plymouth have been finely maintained through these heavy attacks.'

ooOoo

Freda recalls:

The night they bombed the oil tanks and set one on fire, It was an awful night, we spent all the night in the shelter, and we were fortunate, as the wind was blowing in the opposite direction, but the smell of burning oil was everywhere. But the wardens came and told us that we couldn't stay there the night, so we went and stayed at Mrs. Powell's Devick, and was up very early to catch the 6.30 ferry, I soon got fed up of that and returned back home. The tank burnt for some time until it burnt itself out, luckily it was only one tank. The air raids still kept going on, but we all stayed cheerful' "Keeping the home fire burning' as they say.

Unnamed person recalls:

During the April Blitz we were staying in the caravan at night and returning home in the early hours next morning. We noticed my mother's bed and some of the furniture were left lying in the street. We had had firebombs lodged in the roof that had been put out by the local Fire Brigade. On the second night the German's dropped many bombs on Torpoint, and one had gone into the Institute, which was later discovered to be a time bomb, after being shifted by the bomb disposal squad, it later exploded about 8 o'clock in the morning. When we retuned back home to 23 Fore Street, where we found that the roof had been blown off and all the local shop windows were smashed to smithereens with the woodwork hanging out. Fore Street was not a pretty sight to behold, but there again under the circumstances it was normal.

[Author's note: with the above stated shop number in Fore Street, a member of the Vinter Family, who owned a green grocers shop? could well have submitted this story].

Below photograph with kind permission of the Imperial War Museum.

TORPOINT'S BLITZ
APRIL 21/22 1941

A LARGE PALL OF SMOKE FROM THE BURNING OIL HANGS OVER TORPOINT AFTER THE OIL TANKS AT THANCKES PARK HAD BEEN HIT BY BOMBS

ooOoo

Henry Banks recalls:

While working at Plymstock, I had to cycle six miles each way every day including weekends, and after I had finished that job, I got one as a Drayman in the Brewery which was just off the Ferry Beach at Devonport, of course all this time we were burdened with many heavy air raids. I remember once before my brother Arthur got called up we were both asleep in the back bedroom when our mother came into the room shouting 'wake up wake up we are having an air raid'. We did wake up to find the whole window blown in and the ceiling covering our bed. A stick of bombs had landed at the bottom end of Carew Terrace. All the windows in the back of our house had been blown in, after he had repaired them, dad had a full time job putting them all back in. He was good at that sort of thing.

PLYMOUTH:

Mon. 28th Apr.

After a brief respite, once again Plymouth and Devonport were attacked. 123 aircraft arrived at 2205, dropping 159 tonnes of HE bombs comprising: 2 - SC1800(Satan), 31 - SC 1000, 38 - SC500, 295 - SC250, 43 - LZZ 250, 336 - SC50, 76 - SD50, and 29,500 I.B.s. Again the Dockyard suffered badly. *HMS Drake* still under repair, received a direct hit. Fires raged in the City as well as Devonport. In the north west area the Gasworks were hit, many small fires developed into one large fire, too difficult to contain. Many bombs missed the Dockyard and fell into the river across onto Torpoint. One 50Kg landed at the Searchlight Site at Tregantle, fortunately it did not explode a UXB, which was defused by the BDS in HMS *Raleigh*. One HE Bomb was a direct hit on an air raid shelter, with devastating consequences, killing 42 Royal Navy and 24 Royal Engineer's servicemen those names are as follows:

ROYAL NAVY PERSONEL KILLED

ACKERING. E.	47	PO
ANNETTS. R. J.	19	O.S.M
BARKER. L.	Unknown	O.S.M.
BRIMBLE. R. D.	29	O.S.M.
BROADHEAD. F. K.	19	O.S.M.
BROOM. J.L.	Unknown	O.S.M.
BUTTLE. A.	18	O.S.M.
BYERS. J.	27	O.S.M.
COCKBURN. T.	Unknown	O.S.M.
CRANSTON. A. MC.G.	20	O.S.M.
CURTIS. T. H.	26	O.S.M.
DUFFY. T.G.	28	O.S.M.
FINDLEY. A. M.	27	O.S.M.
FISHER. W. K.	Unknown	O.S.M.
FITZPATRICK. J.	Unknown	O.S.M.
FORTH. S.	Unknown	O.S.M.

FOSTER. W.H.	Unknown	O.S.M.
GILLESPIE. H. W.	27	O.S.M.
GOODMAN. H.	Unknown	O.S.M.
GRATTON. W.	Unknown	O.S.M.
HIGGINS. F.	Unknown	O.S.M.
HODGES. W. R.	19	O.S.M
HOLMES. J.C.	19	O.S.M
LANGRIDGE. R. A.	20	O.S.M.
MEAD. A. T.	Unknown	C/PO.
PICKERING. K.	47	P.O..
RANDY. G.	Unknown	O.S.M.
READING. T.	18	O.S.M.
SCHOLFIELD. J.	20	O.S.M.
SELLICK. W. W. J.	28	O.S.M.
SLOMAN. M.	19	O.S.M.
SOMERS. W.A.	25	O.S.M.
SYKES. R.	18	O.S.M.
TORDOFF. J. H.	18	O.S.M.
TUNNAH. J.	54	C/P.O.
WALKER. J. C.	26	O.S.M.
WHEELER. A. E. F.	27	O.S.M.
WHITE. E. J.	26	O.S.M.
WHITNALL. D.	18	O.S.M.
WILLIAMS. F. J.	16	O.S.M.
WOODHAM. T. J.	Unknown	O.S.M.
YEARNSHIRE.W. R.	26	O.S.M.
YOUNG. J. H.	27	O.S.M.

ROYAL ENGINEER'S PERSONNEL KILLED

BROGDEN. J.	21	SPR.
BRYAN. J.	30	DRV
CARTER. G. H.	31	DRV.
CLARKE. H. C.	22	SPR.
COULTER. J.L.	25	SPR.
EGAN. P. J.	22	SPR.
EMERY. S.	Unknown	SPR.
GILES. J. F.	29	DRV.
GROTH. W.H.	Unknown	SPR
GYPPS. W. H.	Unknown	SPR.
HARVEY. E. A.	24	L/CPL.
HORNE. R.	18	SPR
HUGHES. W. E.	Unknown	SPR.
LISTER. R.F.	21	SPR
MAR.SHALL. A.V.	21	SPR.
MCK. CHAPMAN. D.	20	SPR.
PARNELL. K. E.	32	DRV.

PATERSON. J.D.	26	CPL.
PINCHIN. W. S.	21	SPR.
SHARRATT. R.	21	SPR.
SHOWBRIDGE. K. R	Unknown	SPR.
THOMAS. H.	25	SPR.
WATSON. A.	20	SPR.
WEARING. R. W.	Unknown	SPR.

During the raid, an **AFS Torpoint Fireman Patrol Officer** was seriously injured. The raid lasted 5hrs. 46 mins. During that time Plymouth's AA defences were in action and fired 2,783 shells during the period 2150-0138. Four enemy aircraft were claimed as shot down and others damaged. The following aircraft took part:

Gruppe	Aircraft	Time
KGr100	7 He 111	2201 – 2216
II/KG1	14 Ju. 88	2205 – 2243
II/KG27	9 He 111	2210 –2255
KG77	20 Ju. 88	2211 – 2315
III/KG27	6 He 111	2212 – 2236
I/KG55	18 He 111	2215 – 2345
III/KG26	10 He 111	2230 – 0012
III/KG55	17 He 111	2230 – 2300
StabKG55	2 He 111	2240 – 2255
II/KG55	8 He 111	2240 – 2327
III/KG1	7 Ju. 88	2243 – 2309
KGr100	3 He 111	2340 – 0047
StabKG55	1 He 111	0035 – 0055
III/KG27	2 He 111	0138 – 0210

ooOoo.

SOMEWHERE IN FRANCE:

Excerpt's from the diary of a member of a German aircrew:

With kind permission of Before and After the Battle

'Quote'

28th Apr.

The target again is Plymouth. Does it make sense to drop so much on the South Coast just because it lies nearest to us?

'Unquote'

ooOoo

TORPOINT:

Record Log No. 5187 incidents reported on Monday 28/4/41 - Incident 63:

21.55~ Torpoint.~ Raid started at 21.55 and ended 01.15.

29/4/40.
23.55~ Torpoint.~ Bomb damage 160 houses. Casualties 10 injured 6 serious,4 slight. Gas and water mains wrecked. Reports 06.10 arrival of Bomb Disposal Squad commence all clear, Ferry resumes service.

Tue. 29th Apr. **PLYMOUTH:**

The fifth night of heavy bombing and the heaviest raid on Plymouth and Devonport, 120 aircraft took part in the bombing of Devonport, 210 tons of HE bombs were dropped comprising: 58 - SC1000, 100 - SC500, 295 - SC250, 29 - LZZ250, 4 - Flam250, 422 - SC50, and 19,124 I.B's. The main weight of the attack fell on Devonport North Yard, Keyham, Camels Head, Bull Point, St. Budeaux and across the river in Torpoint and Saltash. Residential and shopping areas in Plymouth suffered again. Very early in the raid 20 fires were burning in Devonport and Torpoint, the Oil Tanks were hit again. In Devonport Dockyard which had been severely hit, two large explosions were recorded. Five enemy aircraft were claimed shot down and more damaged. The following aircraft took part:

Gruppe	Aircraft	Time
KGr100	7 He 111	2154-2215
I/KG27	10 He 111	2210- 2250
III/KG27	5 He 111	2213- 2220
II/KG1	14 Ju. 88	2215- 2348
KG77	22 Ju. 88	2215-2310
IIIKG26	8 He 111	2220- 2330
IIIKG/54	13 Ju. 88	2240- 0015
IIIKG1	12 Ju. 88	2253- 0038
IIKG54	16 Ju 88	2320- 0010
IIIKG54	13 Ju. 88	2340- 0015

Wed. 30th Apr.

One Torpoint civilian was killed:

WILLIAM GILBERT BISHOP. Age 44. 8, Quarry Street died in the Royal Naval Hospital Devonport, it is assumed that he was a dockyard worker and was killed in the dockyard during the heavy bombing in the early hours of the morning of the 30th. PLYMOUTH COUNTY BOROUGH CEMETERY.

TORPOINT:

In the early hours of Wednesday, At 0200 hrs 1 - Parachute mine landed at the South Lodge, Mount Edgecumbe but failed to explode. The UXB was defused by the BDS. At Antony House, 2 - 500Kg bombs landed in the grounds those too failed to explode and were defused on the 6th May by the BDS.

The latest intense attack, the fifth over a period of nine days, left the morale of the people stretched to the limit. Some 40,000 people were left homeless. Food distribution became a problem, as did accommodation for the unfortunate. Nearly 600 people had been killed and 450 seriously injured. Little remained of the City Center and shopping area, and 20,000 houses had been damaged. Fortunately for the people and the Royal Navy, this big raid by the Luftwaffe, was to be the last of the Blitz on Plymouth. The Luftwaffe finally turned their attention away from the besieged city.

Record Log No. 5187 incidents reported on Tuesday 29/4/41 - Incident 64:

? Torpoint.~ Air raid lasted two days, Tanks on fire again, Land Mine at Cremyll. Ferry was closed, houses in the village evacuated.

Freda recalls:

Then it was our turn This night Torpoint and Saltash had the full Blast a Boat was hit off Bull Point it was full of ammunition with the bangs and crackers that went off everywhere, we thought that there was a landing going on. Then a plane came overhead and dropped incendiaries which caught the grass alight in Whitehall Farm, no one put them out, so when another bomber came over they dropped a bomb that landed right In our garden on top of the summer house, we had a piano, sawing machine chairs etc, but there was nothing left but a big hole in the ground and the house was pitted with shrapnel. But the Blast was the worst; it went inside the house up the stairs everywhere was blown to bits. It was a blessing that Mr. And Mrs. Webber had taken refuge in the shelter that night as they usually stayed in doors. I went and pulled a few things out, t was all broken up But I found a Union Jack Flag and a Photo of our dear King and Queen, that I got hold of and scrambled across the room to the gap where the window had been and hung out the Union Jack and placed the photo on the ledge, Just to show Hitler and Co. that we were not downhearted. When the Wardens came to see what damage had been done. The shell of the house still stood firm but inside was shattered, they certainly knew how to build houses in the old days. We took what was left and usable down to Antony House for storage, but unfortunately some things got stolen. Mum and I went to stay with friends in Cawsands for a while but I found the journey to work very tiring so we returned back to Wilcove. My sister who rented one of the wooden bungalows from the First World War use to let people stay with her when they were visiting their husbands stationed in and around the district, at that time she already had one little boy and was pregnant. So someone she knew, when they heard of the Blitz had invited her to go to Wales and stay with them, so she took her young son and went to stay in Wales, where her second son was born during her stay in Wales. It was fortunate for mum and me as we moved into her bungalow called "Shambles" whilst she was away, the raid still continued and my sister invited us to go and stay with her in Wales, but of course I could not give up my war work. And mum hated the thought of leaving me alone, but to get her to go I said I would go down to Torpoint and stay with my Aunt Bass during the week and return on the week-ends to Wilcove that she agreed too and went off to Wales she stayed for six months, which did her the world of good after all the raids and we had been bombed ourselves. And the toil of bringing up four of us without a husband. She was a wonderful mother and there is not a day that goes by I give thanks to her.

Freda's Photo of 5 Pato Point with picture of
King George VI & Queen Mary

John Peach recalls:

Not long after we were evacuated to Calstock, we went to live in a very large house called North Park, situated just outside Calstock itself. It was in a very large field with a long driveway approach. A woman called Miss Maud Culhum (who lived there with her two cousins, as well as our own family), owned it. Our part of the house was also home to Granny Hambly, aunt Violet (mum's sister) and our cousin Betty. Dad would travel to and from the Dockyard by train, but when he was on nightshift, he would stay with his aunt Hetty who lived in Arthur Terrace. My brother Geoff went to the local school, which was half a mile away. Miss Culhum ran a private school for children of my age in her house, so all I had to do was open the door of our living room and I was in my classroom. I think there were six or eight pupils apart from me. They were evacuees from the London area. The only one I can remember was a little girl called Valerie Bull. The fees were a shilling a week, so I suppose I could boast and say I once attended a fee paying private school.

Sat. 3rd May **PLYMOUTH:**

Plymouth bombed again (no further details).

Sun. 4th May. **TORPOINT:**

Attacked, (no further details).- One Torpoint civilian injured.

VIDA DOWNING. Aged 27. 7, Chapel Road Torpoint.
Taken to Bodmin Hospital where she died from her injuries.
BODMIN MUNICIPAL BOROUGH CEMETERY.

Mon. 5th May. **PLYMOUTH:**

15 aircraft attacked Devonport, 12 of the German aircrews were in-experienced. They dropped 16 tonnes of HE bombs (no full details of bomb sizes available) but 1,296 I.B's. The bombing started at 1200-0215, 2 - SC250Kg UXB landed. One in Armada Road Cawsands @ 23:33 another at the refuse tip in Torpoint.
At 23:35. a further SC50kg bomb landed in Vicarage Road, that failed to explode. The UXB's were defused by the BDS.

Mon. 5th May **SOUTH WEST ENGLAND:**
Rationing: Cheese reduced to 1oz. per person.

TORPOINT:

Keith Lilyman's recalls:

To supplement the meat ration, dad used to buy the Rabbiting Rights to Scaresdon Farm – not that there was that many rabbits left in those days. The Marines at Blerrick were accomplished catchers, dad used to put down the snares on Saturday a.m. to give us more time ferreting out.

ooOoo

Tue. 6th May. **PLYMOUTH:**

Plymouth: 30 aircraft bombed the Docks and Devonport at 2326-0400. No other details available.

Wed. 7th May.

Plymouth fires started by Incendiary bombs 1 - SC250Kg landed at Penhill Farm Millbrook, but failed to explode it was defused by the BDS.

Thu. 8th May.

Bombers attacked Plymouth, three bombs and one Parachute Mine was dropped, which landed in Central Park causing damage and creating a wide-open space. One Sc250Kg landed at Tregantle Road, Torpoint but failed to explode, was defused by the BDS. However, Plymstock received a few bombs killing two civilians and injuring three. The two people killed were residents of **Torpoint**.

EDITH MARY CAREY Aged 43. 2, Hillsborough Torpoint died at -
3, Hareston Cottages Brixton.
PLYMTON ST. MARY RURAL DISCTRICT CEMETERY.

Also on the same day-

Her son, a member of the Home Guard, sustained injuries whilst on duty at
3, Horston Cottages Yealmpton.-
Died at Greenbank Hospital on -

Fri. 9th May.

ARTHUR JAMES CAREY. Age 17. 2, Hillsborough Torpoint.
PLYMOUTH MUNICIPAL BOROUGH CEMETERY.
[Authors Note: Why both were there in the vicinity of Plymstock, it can only be assumed that they were staying there avoiding the ongoing blitz in Torpoint].

Sat. 10th May.

2 aircraft attacked Plymouth Docks [Zerstrangriffe's] and dropped bombs. No further information. On the same day in the Cottage Hospital, a firemen from Torpoint who was injured on Apr. 28th in Torpoint, died from his injuries.

AFS WILLIAM HYND. Age 30. address unknown.
LOOE URBAN DISTRICT CEMETERY.

Sun. 11th May. **LONDON:**

Hitler's Luftwaffe turned their attention away from Plymouth, instead they bombed London, one of the heaviest air attacks began in the evening. During the intense bombing raid the Houses of Parliament, Westminster Hall, Big Ben (although it still kept time) the British Museum and four Main Line terminal stations were among the places hit, a night to remember by all Londoner's.

Mon. 12th May. **PLYMOUTH:**

As a reminder, a single aircraft attacked Devonport and hit an Oil Tank at Keyham, no further information.

Tue. 13th May.

Plymouth attacked by three aircraft. Bombs were dropped, no further information.

Thu. 15th May.

Plymouth attacked and bombed, no further information.

Thu. 22nd May. **MEDITERANEAN - CRETE :**

In the defence of Crete, having secured Maleme one of the main airfields, the Germans flew in reinforcements to swell their numbers. Although being shelled from the sea by Navy Ships, there to assist and support the defending Allied Forces, they were unable to stop the German advance. During the battle, many ships were damaged, among them the battleship HMS.*Valliant,* serving on board was a certain sailor Lt. Prince Philip of Greece.

Fri. 23rd May.

Lord Louis Mountbatten's ship HMS.*Kelly* was sunk. Lord Louis was able to swim clear. Cruisers HMS.*Fiji & Gloucester,* were dive-bombed and subsequently sunk by the Germans. Several of the survivors from the *Gloucester*, whilst clinging to wreckage, had been machine-gunned by the German Stuka Bombers.
725 crew members of both ships died or, drowned. Amongst those killed on HMS.*Gloucester* were three sailors and one Royal Marine from Torpoint.
D/KX 55359. STO. EDWARD HENRY DRAKE. Age 41.
Panel. 52 Col.3.
#. unknown. Com/Grn. ERNEST EDWARD HOUSEHOLD. Age 38.
Panel 45 Col.1
D/J65439. S/M. FREDRICK ALEXANDER WHITING. Age 41.
Panel 50. Col.1
PLY/X 952. R.M. SGT. JOHN CRISPIN ROBERTS. Age 25.
Panel 59 Col. 1
ALL THE ABOVE CWG. PLYMOUTH NAVAL MEMORIAL.

ooOoo

MEDITERANEAN SEA:

Arthur Corbidge aboard *Renown recalls:*

We used to escort the "*Ark Royal "Furious", &"Argus*" into the narrows to fly Hurricanes into Malta.

The *Argus & Furious* used to ship the aircraft to Gibraltar, where they use to assemble them then roll them over to the *Ark Royal,* assembling the remainder and then we would go to the Narrows and fly them off to Malta. This used to give Malta at least 30 Hurricanes each time. It used to be hell at times as the enemy aircraft use to come over to bomb us when we were on our way back, but we were very lucky, I think I would be right in saying we only had one misfortune in all that time, thanks to the efficiency of a excellent Skipper, yet we use to call him Soap Box Mc Gregor. He was that small he had to have a box to stand on to see the compass, but with all his difficulties he was the finest Captain a sailor could have wished for. He did finish up as Admiral of the Fleet, the highest rank you could achieve in the Navy.

When HMS.*Hood* was sunk with all hands, we were ordered to steam north and cut off the *Bismark & Prince Eugene* from entering Brest. So up went the whole of Force H, consisting of us, *Ark Royal,* one Cruiser and the two Flotillas of Destroyers, I quite agree a nice size force. We steamed north and saw the *Prince Eugene* spotter plane, the *Bismark* turned and was making for the north, thinking the British Fleet were ahead of her, but the *Ark Royal's* planes were not going to let that happen, so they went in with torpedo bombers and one made a direct hit on the *Ark Royal's* rudder, and she started going around in circles, but the *Prince Eugene* made good her escape to a Northern Port, but the main one we had. I was looking at her all night through my gun telescope, our Admiral Commander in Chief of the Home Fleet, Admiral Tovey said keep look out until we get there. Our Admiral took off his hat and threw it over the side and said 'I might as well be an ordinary seaman'. Next morning down came the Home Fleet consisting of the *K.G.5. Rodney,* & Norfolk, YES two 1919 boats, they went in and fired a couple of torpedoes into her and down she went.
[Authors Note: Date 27th May]

ooOoo

Tue. 27th May.**PLYMOUTH:**

Air raid attack, 1 - 50Kg UXB landed at Top Pennel Wood Kingsand. Defused by the BDS.

Wed. 28th May.**TORPOINT:**

Air raid attack, 3 - 50Kg bombs landed at Freathy Farm Tregantle, but failed to explode, UXB's defused by the BDS.

Record Log No. 5187 incidents reported onWednesday 28/5/41 - # ?:

00.03~ St. Johns. ~ One HE. bomb in front of Freathy Farm St. Johns House, cottage damaged, Telephone wires damaged, no casualties. Several Inc. bombs in the river between Devonport and Torpoint. 3 UBX's as follows:
1 In marshy ground 30yds from Freathy Farm, farmhouse evacuated. 2 in the field near Tregantle Farm. 3 in a ploughed field near Tregantle Searchlight Site.

ooOoo

Keith Lilyman recalls:
[Author's note: believe this one relates to the above incident]:

By the time the concentrated heavy "Blitz's" of earlier raids had petered out, and raids had become more sporadic, sometimes the alarms would sound and nothing would come, so eventually we tended to become a bit blasé about it all. My dad had to be at work by seven o'clock and I had to leave for school at Saltash at 7.30. This particular night when the alarm sounded, my mum and sister went out to the shelter in the corner of the garden, dad and I stayed in bed, then were heard the drone of the aircraft and the guns opened up. Dad shouted 'shelter' and we got as far as the porch when we heard the piecing whistle of an approaching bomb there was a enormous bang and we thought it was a lot closer than Syd's about 300 yards up across the field.

Thu. 29th May.

Air raid attack, 2 -50 Kg bombs landed, 1 at the Balloon Site Cremyll another at Field Home Farm, both failed to explode were defused by the BDS.

Sun. 18th Jun **LOOE :**

The Torpoint civilian who was injured during the Torpoint air raid on April 23rd, whilst convalescing in Looe, died from the injuries he received.

ARTHUR AUGUSTUS DEVONSHIRE. Age 65. 15, Tremayne Terrace
LOOE URBAN DISTRICT CEMETERY.

Mon. 30th Jun. **SOUTH WEST ENGLAND**:

Rationing: Cheese increase from 1oz, to 2ozs per person.

Sat. 5th Jul. **TORPOINT:**

Snap air-raid at 0105, 1 - 500Kg bomb landed at the RAF Balloon Site Cremyll failed to explode, UXB defused by BDS.

Sun. 6th Jul.

Snap air raid on Torpoint, 2 bombs fell on Mount Edgecumbe failed to explode, UXB's defused by the BDS.

Record Log No. 5187 incidents reported on Saturday 6/7/41 - Incident 69:

00.59~ Mt Edgecumbe.~ Two HE. bombs landed near Balloon Site, 1 UXB at Mount Edgecumbe Park.

Mon. 7th Jul. Meat Ration increased from 1s.0p to 1s. 2p. per person.

Wed. 9th Jul.

Plymouth attacked, 3 bombs fell near Antony House causing damage to a nearby cottage.

Record Log No. 5187 incidents reported on Wednesday 9/7/41 - Incident 70:

00.05~ Antony.~ Three HE bombs dropped near Antony House, roof of cottage in the park damaged.

ooOoo

Freda Hawken recalls:

On one of the air raids a bomb landed down the drive of Antony House, it destroyed a house called the "Kennels" where the Scawn Family (Mr. R.G. Courtier) lived but no one was hurt.

[Author's note: An interesting subject was found out regarding Mr. Courtier, the then occupier of the cottage in question. Whilst talking about the first bombs to be dropped on Torpoint, his son Ralph Courtier mentioned that his mother and father lived at the Kennels and were evacuated after the bombing incident, he also mentioned that his father had designed an invention for floatation purposes used on submarines, these letters he produced for me to read, which I did and could see by the letters that his invention was looked at seriously and was forwarded to the Admiralty in the March. His invention was not taken up by the Admiralty, but did receive a commendation on his theory and the work done.]

Sun. 13th Jul.

German aircraft reported flying over Plymouth area possibly on recognisance.

Mon. 14th Jul. **RED SEA:**

Having left Aden bound for Suez, The *S.S. Georgic* came under attack by either, German or Italian unidentified aircraft? She was set on fire and eventually beached, somewhere on the coast which is not known. During the attack 26 crew members were killed, amongst them was a Torpoint sailor.

D/JX 152229. A/B. JOHN ORR. Age 21.

CWG. PLYMOUTH NAVAL MEMORIAL Panel 48 Col 1.

Fri. 18th Jul. **PLYMOUTH:**

German aircraft reported flying over Plymouth possibly on reconaissance.

ooOoo

CANADA:

Arthur Corbidge *recalls:*

Just after this (sinking of The *Bismarck*) in August, we were ordered to Halifax in Nova Scotia Canada, to pick up The Prime Minister Sir Winston Churchill and his staff who had been attending a conference with Roosevelt in America. We brought him back to Greenock where we stayed for a few days, then went back to Scarpa. On the 20th October I was sent home to meet my doom. Yes I tied the knot with my tongue that I could not undo with my teeth on the 22nd. I returned on the 3rd of November, when we sailed for Rosythe where we had a refit and those who had not had leave while we were in Scarpa, were each sent on a 2 weeks leave.

ooOoo

Sun. 17th Aug. **PLYMOUTH:**

A Junkers Ju. 88 A-5 shot down by Plymouth Ack Ack fire, crashed and disintegrated at Gorton Wood near Tavistock at 11.02 pm. All four crew members, Lt. E.O Wentzler-Gefr. A. Reimann, Gefr. R-S. Von Heimann, and Gefr. H. Pusch were killed

TORPOINT:

[Author's note: I believe the following story by John Peach refers to the above incident].

John Peach recalls:

My brother Geoff and I certainly enjoyed our time at North Park. There was plenty of space, large lawned gardens, trees to climb and even cows to chase, sometimes we would look out of our window and we would see the orange glow in the night sky, this was of course Plymouth ablaze again after more bombing. One night while we were watching, an aircraft came into view. It was a German bomber which had been hit by gunfire, smoke and flames were visible as it came closer. It eventually crashed into wooded area about half a mile away. We never did find out whether the crew survived.

ooOoo

Sun. 28th Sept.

Two bombs hit Trevol Camp (HMS. *Raleigh), n*o further details.

Record Log No. 5187 incidents reported on Tuesday 28/9/41 - Incident 71:

21.57~ Torpoint.~ One HE. bomb landed near and 1 UXB in Trevol House gardens.

ooOoo

SCOTLAND - SCARPA FLOW:

Fred Timms recalls:

Late in 1941 I left and went to join HMS. *Prince of Wales a new Battleship, the problem was I was in Torpoint and the ship was in Scarpa Flow (Orkney Isles). Luck was once again on my side, my train journey should have taken twenty-three hours but due to hold ups on the way, it took fifty hours. When I eventually arrived at Scarpa Flow, the ship had already left to her final destruction in the South China Sea. Luck was again on my side, when a canteen assistant on* HMS. *Kent died suddenly, and as I being readily available was ordered to join the ship. Our detailed operation was escort duty on Artic Convoys to Russia. Just before Christmas we went ashore in Russia, the place name I cannot remember but it was about twenty miles away from Murmansk. Nobody on the ship had checked out the place, the ships lookout had reported seeing through his binoculars four mounds of snow with smoke coming from one of the protruding chimneys. Anyway to cut a long story short, I along with thirty seamen went ashore and made our way to these mounds, which we discovered was a camp for political prisoners, the trouble was they were all women! We were to spend two and a half hours amongst these women. The pure smell of the hut was that of a piggry. There was no way we could contact the ship, we had to wait until four thirty, by that time we were all nearly frozen stiff, during which time the women kept on touching us, one woman that I had to keep brushing away from me, was about thirty two years of age, she spoke reasonably good English and she told me she was a Law Student and had spent twelve summers in the camp doing hard labour, judging by her face and hands, that had been exposed to the extreme elements during that period of time, were just too horrific to see. (No hand and face cream available), I often wondered how she and her fellow prisoners survived the rest of the war. The cold in that hut was so intense, that one of the Petty Officer's in our party dropped down and died from the cold, hypothermia as its called today. The Russian guards insisted we take him back with us to the ship. Easier said than done! The next day, we gave him a Military Funeral, over the back of the ship sewn in his hammock.*

ooOoo

Sat. 12th Oct. **TORPOINT:**

Sharp air raid over Rame Penisular. 4 bombs dropped at Crafthole causing damage to water mains and blocked the road to Rame.

Record Log No. 5187 incidents reported on Saturday 12/10/41 -Incident 72:

02.30~ Crafthole. ~ Four HE. bombs, 1.1/4 Miles southwest of Crafthole in Whitsand Bay, road,and water mains burst, and telephone wires down,road blocked, no casualties. One UXB 50 yds. In the field near the road at Tregantle. Tregantle Road to Crafthole blocked, bomb marked category 'B.'

Record Log No. 5187 incidents reported on Saturday 12/10/41 -Incident 73:

19.33~ Torpoint.~ 1 HE. bomb dropped east side of Blerrick Camp 4 miles west of Torpoint.

ooOoo

Keith Lalyman recalls:

On another occasion they dropped a stick of bombs across a meadow beside the Tregantle Road opposite what was then the Marines Camp at Blerrick. I was on half term break and heard Fred Lakeman, our milkman telling our neighbour that these bombs had been dropped 'Down the bottom of Trelay Hill' I was out of bed, on the bike, and first there about 8.30 for the plum share of shrapnel.

There were three large craters, but after a few minutes exploration I found a smaller hole so I did an "emergency exit" and went down to warn our local Bobby PC. Keast that I thought there was an unexploded bomb there. He strolled across the field after telling me. 'Not to be so bloody daft', took one look and turned and ran. It was defused a couple of days later.

ooOoo

Sun. 24th Oct.

Torpoint sailor killed at HMS *Raleigh.* No other details

D/KX113119. STO. GEORGE BOWMAN Age 19.

CWG. TORPOINT HORSOM CEMETERY ROW 7 GRAVE 932.

Mon. 25th. Oct. **NORTH AFRICA- Possible EYGPT.**

Drv. Bert Rowe sent this Christmas Greetings in time

ooOoo

TORPOINT:

John Peach recalls:

In November 1941 we returned to Torpoint, back to Victoria Street number 15 this time. Granny Hambly also came to live in Victoria Street, right opposite in number 17. The raids continued and as we did not have a shelter, we used the large one situated in the barrage balloon field, the RAF manned it. The Queens Park Council Estate now covers this area. As the alarm sounded we would tumble out of bed, put on our Siren Suits [Authors Note :refer back to Jean Peach Story.] and trek across the field, accompanied by Granny Hambly, clutching her black bag. which contained her important papers and policies.

ooOoo

MEDITERRANEAN SEA :

The events for Force 'K' based out of Malta, were not going too well and they were suffering severely. HMS. *Ark Royal* was sunk on the 13th November, followed by two further ships being sunk on the 25th. November. The Battleship HMS. *Banham,* was hit by three torpedoes before one of her main magazines blew up and she sank.

ooOoo

Mon. 17th Nov.**TORPOINT:**

Torpoint sailor killed at HMS. *Raleigh.* No other details.

LT. COM. THOMAS CECIL HOLT. Age unknown

TORPOINT HORSOM CEMETERY GRAVE 1000.

Mon. 24th Nov. **PLYMOUTH:**

There was a thrilling sight when an unknown bomber was shot down by a Polish night fighter, a flicker of flame which quickly turned into a roaring streak. The crew members baled out before the bomber crashed near Roborough.

Mon. 1st Dec. More rationing: sugar increased back to 12oz: meat increased to 1/2p: cheese increased to 3oz. Preserves increased to 1.lb (per month): Points Rationing 16 points per month. Basically it was to remain like this for the rest of the war. Furthermore rationing of other various foods and commodities, allowed per person per week, fluctuated in quantity throughout the rest of the war and beyond, until it finally ceased in 1954 when rationing finally came to an end.

Sat. 6th Dec. **TORPOINT:**

Two separate alerts were sounded in Plymouth. Although each lasted several minutes, the first was more exciting, one bomber was engaged by Spitfires over Whitsand Bay, was hit and crashed into the sea. No further details of the its crew.

THE WAR IN THE FAR EAST:

The war in Europe had at that time, not reached the Far East. Whilst the war was being fought on the battlefields of Europe and the North African Coast, only a fraction of our Forces were deployed in India, Ceylon and the Crown Colonies of Singapore and Hong Kong. With the Far East Fleet, based at Colombo and Singapore, were the Battleship HMS. *Prince of Wales* and the Aircraft Carrier HMS. *Repulse.* Both of these ships bore a large presence of the might of the British Navy in Far East waters. Although the Japanese were at loggerheads with the Chinese, something which had been ongoing since the early thirties, before it finely erupted, into the Sino-Japanese War in 1936-37. Its outcome had never been settled, subsequently as early as July 1941, the Japanese had occupied French Indo-China, in turn Hitler was urging the Japanese Empire to join forces with the Axis powers, and attack Russia from the eastern side. This was never to be fulfilled.

Fri. 5th Dec. **SINGAPORE:**

British Service personnel although at war, were enjoying luxuries not available in war torn Britain. War did not erupt in the Far East until December 1941. It was never envisaged that the Japanese, already with a strong foothold in China and Indo-China, would even contemplate either to bomb or attack Singapore. Nevertheless, just as a precaution, prior to the outbreak of any possible hostilities, Evacuation Forms were issued to all service and resident civilian families, which had to be completed and returned to the authorities, providing details of the immediate family, including a first and second choice, as to where they wanted to be evacuated to. On the same day, Force 'Z' consisting of the two battleships HMS. *Prince of Wales & Repulse* together with four Destroyers HMS. *Electra, Express, Tenedos &* HMAS. *Vampire, s*et sail from Singapore bound for Port Darwin Australia. However, unknown to the British, the Japanese had assembled a Japanese Invasion Force in the South China Sea, in preparation for the invasion of several Colonies under the rule of the British, French and Dutch Governments. The Japanese plan was also to attack the mighty American Pacific Fleet at anchor in Pearl Harbour, who at that point were not at war.

Sat. 6th Dec.

Information was received in Admiralty HQ. Singapore stating: 'In the Gulf of Siam the Japanese had assembled a large concentration of Japanese Force's.' This information was immediately signalled to 'Force Z' to change course, head North for the Gulf of Siam, to counter attack any intended invasion.

Sun. 7th Dec. **PACIFIC Island OAHU:**

366 Japanese Air-Force bombers took off from their aircraft carriers in the Pacific Ocean, to attack the American Fleet in Pearl Harbour, including the American

dominated Islands of Guam, Wake & Midway where their airfields were based. The success of the Japanese bombing had dealt a mighty blow to the American Pacific Fleet. Their Air Force had gained air superiority and practically control, of all of the Pacific and Far Eastern Seas, leaving the seaways undefended and open, for the invading Japanese Forces to be shipped in large numbers across the Pacific.
The Americans immediately **Declared War on Japan**. Possibly, something Churchill had previously strived to achieve, to persuade the Americans to enter the war.

HONG KONG:
At 12 noon the Japanese in China attacked the British Colony of Hong Kong.

Mon. 8th Dec. **LONDON:**
The Prime Minister of the United Kingdom Winston Churchill declares:
War against Japan.

Tue. 9th Dec. **SOUTH CHINA SEA:**
Meanwhile 'Force Z' was steaming North, making good progress through heavy mist and rain, under the impression that their progress had been undetected, yet unbeknown by them, a Japanese Submarine had sighted 'Force Z' and informed its Head Quarters. Unfortunately three Japanese recognisance planes spotted the Force after the rain and mist had cleared, to present a blue cloudless sky. 'Force Z' having already been sighted, with the element of surprise gone, turned towards Malaya heading for Kota Bahru, in an effort to avert the intended invasion. Furthermore, it was necessary for HMS. *Tenedos,* being low on fuel to turn back and head for Singapore to refuel.
The Japanese invasion plans: to invade Siam, advance west across Burma into India, at the same time invade Malaya, advanced south towards Singapore and the Dutch East Indies. On the east coast of Siam they landed at Singora and Patani. Whilst further south, they landed in Malaya at Kota Bahru.

Wed. 10th Dec.
A large force of 84 Japanese air planes, carrying torpedoes, found 'Force Z' steaming towards Kota Bahru. Immediately they attacked the two Battleships, sinking both, with substantial losses. 840 men were either killed or, drowned.
On board HMS. *Repulse* were two Torpoint sailors, assumed drowned.
D/KX80192. P.O. WILLIAM THOMAS BOLTON. Age 31.
Panel 51. Col. 3.
&
 # ? C.S.O. JAMES WILLIAM HENRY ATKEY. MBE. Age 47.
Panel 45 Col 2.
BOTH AT CWG. PLYMOUTH NAVAL MEMORIAL.
1,258 survivors, were picked up from the sea, by the escorting ships.
One survivor on board . *Prince of Wales* was Torpoint Royal Marine.
PLY/X1131. R.M. VICTOR HAROLD SMART. Age 24.
(fate to be referred to later).

Thu. 11th Dec. **GERMANY - BERLIN:**
Hitler rather pleased with the developments in the Far East, declared war on the United States. Whilst the Netherlands declared war against the Japanese.

Fri. 12th Dec. **SIAM/ MALAYA**

With the sinking of our only two major warships. One being an Aircraft Carrier which including losing all its fighter aircraft, compounded the situation, losing control of the seaways and with the skies above almost devoid of Allied aircraft, both being dominated by the Japanese Forces. The Japanese Army, pressed home their advantage, splitting their forces into two, those landing at Singora, taking a northerly route through Siam to Burma, the second, landing at Patani in Siam and a smaller force at Kota Bahru in Malaya. Both advanced in a southwest direction across Siam over the Siam/Malay borders, into the State of Kedah & Perak, reaching Alor Star the Capital of Kedah on the 12th.

Sun. 15th Dec. **MALAYA:**

With little resistance, the Japanese reached the border town of Kroh in Perak on the 15th their objective, to secure the single line railway link, the only vital means of transportation from Rangoon to Singapore, that travelled south along the west coast of Malaya. An additional advantage they had secured was, having landed in Kota Bahru on the east coast, the Japanese advanced west and south, into the Highlands of Malaya sweeping all before them. Although there was great resistance from the British Forces, they were no matches for the thousands of advancing Japanese troops.

On the same day-

MEDITERRANEAN SEA:

On her way back, returning from an unsuccessful search for an Axis Convoy, the cruiser HMS. *Galatea* sailing thirty miles west of Alexandria, whilst charting through a mine swept channel, was hit by two torpedoes, fired by a U boat No. *U-557.* Very quickly HMS. *Galatea* rolled over and sank, with a heavy loss of 470 members of her crew. On board were two sailors from Torpoint either killed, or drowned. Circumstances unknown.

D/KX 86961. L/STO. LEONARD ALBERT PIDGEN Age 24.
Panel 52 Col 2.

&

D/MX 53925. E.R.A. 5th/Cl. ARTHUR RONALD WALTER CARR. Age 21.
Panel 51. Col. 1.
BOTH AT CWG. PLYMOUTH NAVAL MEMORIAL.
[Authors Note: HMS. *Griffin & Hotspur* picked up the 144 survivors].

Tue. 16th Dec. **TORPOINT:**

Four bombs fell on Blerrick Camp, demolishing the Armoury Guardroom and Officers Mess, one serviceman injured.

On the same day-

MALAYA -PENANG ISLAND:

The evacuation by the British had been completed. The Japanese, meeting very little resistance from the British Forces, the support from the depleted Royal Air Force was insufficient to fight off the Japanese air superiority, and they eventually took the Island. The British Army, although putting up stiff resistance, fought a rear guard action back towards Singapore. As the Japanese relentlessly made their way south, the speed of the advancing Army was devastating.

On the same day-

BAY OF BISCAY:

A Merchant convoy, left Gibraltar bound for Britain, her escorts included HMS. *Audacity, Blankney, Exmoor, Penstermon, Stanley & Stork.* On the 17th *U-131* was sunk north east of Madeira. On the 18th U- 434 was sunk north of Madeira, both by depth charges dropped by *Blankney & Stanley.*

Thu 18th Dec.**HONG KONG:**

However, a similar advance by the Japanese was taking place on the mainland of China opposite Hong Kong. A mistake was made by the British Military, thinking that the Japanese with their troops already committed against the Chinese forces, suspected the Japanese would favor a sea invasion of Hong Kong, having deployed practically all its troops to the seaward side of the Island. Instead, the Japanese turned their attention towards Hong Kong from Mainland China, keeping up a steady heavy bombardment of Hong Kong's shore defences, including bombing raids, which soon put out of action heavy shore-located batteries. The Artillery positions of Fort Collinson and D'Aguilar, after the destruction of their heavy guns, were forced to withdraw back to Hong Kong, providing little resistance to the Japanese who landed on the northeast section of the Island and steadily advanced inland.

Fri. 19th Dec. **BAY OF BISCAY:**

The Escort Ship HMS. *Stanley* part of the merchant convoy which left Gibraltar three days before, was stationed at the rear of the convoy, unaware she was being tracked by another U. Boat. *U 574,* discharging her torpedoes scored a direct hit on *Stanley,* which exploded and sank. On board was a Torpoint sailor:

D/KX 77705. P/O. Stk. ANDREW HALL WAGGOT. Age 33.
CWG. PLYMOUTH NAVAL MONUMENT Panel 52. Col 1.

On the same day-

HONG KONG:

In the afternoon, a British counter attack against the Japanese proved unsuccessful.

On the same day-

MEDITERRANEAN SEA:

The Royal Navy Force 'K', sailing 20 miles east of Tripoli, ran into a mine field. HMS. *Aurora & Penelope* both struck mines, unfortunately HMS. *Neptune* struck two mines. To provide assistance, HMS. *Kandahar* entered the mine field, she too struck a mine, which blew off her stern. HMS *Aurora* was badly damaged, turned and headed back to Malta. When *Neptune* struck a third mine, HMS. *Penelope* went to her assistance. Finally *Neptune* struck a fourth mine and sank. Either killed or drowned, on board was two Torpoint sailors:

D/MX 57479. P.O. GEORGE WILLIAM RICHARD LOWINGS. Age 29.
Panel 56 Col.1.

&

D/L 14721. P.O. Ck. CHARLES WILLLIAM LANCHBURY. Age 39.
Panel 55 Col. 1.
CWG. PLYMOUTH NAVAL MEMORIAL.
[Authors Note: There was only one survivor from the *Neptune* who was picked up by the Italians on the 26th December.]

Sun. 21st Dec.**ATLANTIC OCEAN:**

Convoy 'HG 76' of thirty-two Merchant vessels with escorts, one Carrier, three Destroyers, four Sloops and ten Corvettes, was in a running battle with 'U' Boats. Two escorts vessels were separated from the convoy, one being HMS. *Audacity, a*pproximately 500 miles west of Cape Finisterre *w*as located by U- Boat *'U' 571,* who fired its torpedoes hitting the *Audacity.* Killed on board was a Torpoint sailor:
D/JX 137307. L/Tel. FRANK. FISHER. Age 25.
CWG. PLYMOUTH NAVAL MEMORIAL Panel 50 Col. 2.
[Authors Note: In the follow up, HMS. *Audacity* along with the other ship (unknown) located *'U'-567.* Attacking with depth charge successfully sunk her.]

Mon. 22nd Dec.

Unfortunately, after one of the toughest battles of the Atlantic the escort carrier HMS. *Audacity* sank. On board was another Torpoint sailor:
#? Grn. HAROLD STRICKLAND. Age 41. assumed drowned.
CWG. PLYMOUTH NAVAL MEMORIAL Panel 45 Col. 1.

On the same day-

HONG KONG:

The Japanese landed more troops on the north east coast of Hong Kong. By then the Island had been split into three parts, with an isolated force inland. Further small British pockets to the west, holding out at isolated positions. The Japanese, unceasingly attacking the east of the Gap at Tai Tam Bay. Intensive bombing from the air, together with artillery mortars and artillery, kept up incessant attacks. The water and food situation became desperate, but still the British forces held out.

Tue. 25th Dec.

The British finally surrendered. It was the first British Colony to do so. 11,000 service personnel were taken prisoner, amongst them were two servicemen from Torpoint:
1415795. S/Sgt. GERALD GOLLEDGE. Age 40.
Hong Kong and Singapore Royal Artillery Regiment.

Also

From the shore based HMS. *Tamar,* abandoned on Fri. 12th. Dec. 1941, was a Torpoint sailor:
D/MX 46040. C.E.R.A. LESLIE GEORGE PERKINS. Age 32.
[Authors Note:The fate of these 2 Torpoint servicemen to be referred to later].

Wed. 26th Dec.**MALAYA:**

The fighting continued, by which time the Japanese had reached Taiping, but history has shown us that it was only going to be a matter of time, before the Japanese took over the Malayan Peninsular. The British, Australian, Indian, and Gurkha troops putting up a stiff opposition against the Japanese as they retreated, giving themselves more time to get to Singapore, they blew up bridges and roads, in an attempt to stem the advancing Japanese.

Tue. 30th Dec.**SINGAPORE:**

The evacuation of approx 5,500 civilians, mainly families, women and children, had been ongoing since the beginning of December.

ooOoo

The following is a transcription of **JEAN PEACH'S** story from her original.

Memories of Long Ago
Written by Jean Peach

My parents, Ruth and Arthur Conning were married on 1st August 1936 at Looe Church (St. Martin's) as my mother who was called Ruth A'Lee came from Polperro and later Looe. My father was brought up and educated at Torpoint, where they went to live after their Wedding.

Dad found them a flat in Victoria Street, so this is where they started their married life. I was born on 29th August 1937, in 1938 we moved to a newly built house in Coryton Terrace known as York Road. The following year my sister Barbara was born. She was baptized on 21st May 1939 at St. James Church.

I can't even begin to imagine what life must have been for my mum and dad, they had a lovely new home two lovely little girls and a lifetime of happiness stretching before them, then suddenly their country is at war!

However, life does go on and in February 1941 my baby brother Brian was born. Life could not have been easy, my dad worked in H.M. Dockyard and every night there was always the fear of the air raid siren going off. When this happened, you had to quickly bundle your children down to the air raid shelter, which was invariably at the bottom of the garden. Children tended to wear 'all in one suits'. These were made out of warm material and covered their feet, legs, body and arms and usually had a hood. The garments were buttoned up the front and were called 'SIREN SUITS', simply because when the siren sounded, you put them on.

My dad was getting increasingly anxious about mum and us children, so he persuaded her to try and find accommodation with her family in Looe. Looe was far enough away from the hostilities to be considered safe. The plan was dad would stay in Torpoint during the week and go to Looe on Friday afternoon's after work and travel back to the dockyard on Monday mornings.

On 22nd April 1941 my mother left my sister and me at my Paternal Grandmother's home, and traveled to Looe with baby Brian with the idea of arranging accommodation for her family. She managed to do this and was going to stay in the safety of Looe until the end of hostilities, whenever that might be! She returned home again that same afternoon and collected her girls from Grandma. She then went home to get the family's tea. Dad was thrilled with her news when he came home from work, as she had arranged to go back to Looe the following day with all her children. I am sure that night after packing up clothes and toys for their journey, they went to bed with light hearts.

In the early hours of next morning 23rd April, the sirens went off and they proceeded down the garden to their air raid shelter.

German bombs had dropped on Plymouth and H.M. Dockyard causing great destruction. Our little humble house was on the flight path of the returning German planes, they always jettisoned any armament out of their planes before going home. Unfortunately for us a bomb landed almost directly on our house. All that was left of our house was the two end walls, even our air raid shelter was raised to the ground.

After the all clear sounded many volunteers left their homes, not sure of what they would find, but willing to help their fellow man in his hour of need. Billeted in the Council Chambers were some young sailors from HMS Defiance who were on 'Fire Watch'. Their job was to assist the air raid wardens and any other volunteers, to put out fires and look for anybody who might be homeless and distressed.

One young man who was on duty that night, was A.B. 'Robbie' Robinson who had only been in the Royal Navy a few short months, When the all-clear sounded Robbie left the Council Chambers and proceeded down the back lane of Coryton Terrace to see if he could find or indeed help any survivors. The devastation was over-whelming, he had never in his young life seen anything like it. As he neared the end of the first half of the Terrace he saw in the beam of his flashlight what looked like a doll's hand protruding out of the rubble, he immediately thought where there is a doll there could be a child! so he approached the object and started calling out, but when he touched it he realized in was in fact a child's hand. He frantically cleared away the bricks and rubble with his bare hands and there on the ground lay a young child in a blue siren suit.

He lifted the child very carefully and laid it in his arms hoping the warmth of his body might revive him, in his mind this was a dead young boy. He had never experienced anything like this before! Suddenly he heard voices and people were coming with spades, shovels, anything they could dig with to find the rest of the family. The child suddenly opened his green eyes and smiled at Robbie, he bent down and kissed the child and he never forgot the feeling of awe and relief that he felt, he would always remember it for the rest of his life.

The child was passed to an Air Raid Warden, Robbie then joined in the search for bodies. The child was taken to a First Aid Post, where she was identified by a dear lady, always known as Nurse Eddy. After a quick check she was finally taken to her Grandma's house in Gawen Terrace. Her Grandmother Mrs. M.C.A. Conning took her in and brought her up. Later that same dreadful night the Police came to inform her that the broken bodies of her son, daughter-in-law, grandson and granddaughter had been recovered from the rubble.

How she coped with all that grief I will never know, but she did. I pay tribute to a remarkably strong loving lady, my Grandma Mary Caroline Ann Conning.

This story does not end here. Many years later probably 17 years ago, Robbie Robinson came stay at a Plymouth Hotel for a Naval Re-union. After a few beers the 'old boy's' started telling their old war stores.

These stories had probably been repeated over and over again, but the 'old comrades' always derived great pleasure from their telling.

Robbie told his story. A story about a small boy he had dug out of the rubble with his bare hands, and whose eyes and smile had stayed with him all of his life. Was the boy still alive? Where did he live now? He always referred to the child as male because he wore a blue Siren Suit.

One of the men challenged him to go to Torpoint the next day, which was a Sunday and make some enquiries to see if he could find answers to these questions. He went back to his friend's house where he had a restless night. The following morning he was determined to cross the Tamar and look for answers.
He drove over to Torpoint and found his way back to the Council Chambers. He parked his car and started to walk down York Road, where a man was approaching him, on a whim he stopped him and politely enquired if he was a local man? He said he was, Robbie then recalled his wartime story.

The man smiled and asked him to accompany him to his home. On the way he explained that the child was in fact a girl, one Jean Conning who had married a local man John Peach, they lived in Torpoint and had three children. Whoever he was (we never found out), he knew all this but not where they lived, this is why he took Robbie to his home to look me up in the telephone directory, we lived in Lamorna Park. This wonderful man gave Robbie directions and sent him on his way.

One Sunday morning my husband and I had come home from church and I was in the kitchen making coffee, it was our normal Sunday routine. What happened next was to change my life immediately. A man appeared on our doorstep and asked to speak to me, my husband naturally asked him who he was and he explained briefly the story. He was welcomed into our home and he told me the wonderful story, which I have just related.

Robbie was a lovely man and we became great friends. He met all my children and grandchildren, and he even brought his wife to meet us the following summer. Unfortunately he lived a long way from Torpoint in the Wirral, so I did not see as much of him and I would have wished. My son, who at that time was a Lieut. Commander in the Royal Navy took him on board one of H.M. Ships. He was given a full tour of the ship and had lunch in the wardroom. Sometime after, I received a lovely letter from him saying that as he was an ex- Navy man, my son Graham's 'trip out' for him was one of the highlights of his life. This for Robbie was unbelievably wonderful. Unfortunately Robbie died a few years ago, but I treasure his letters and a photograph of him taken at Lamora Park, and believe it or not I actually have a photograph of him when he first joined the Navy. The image in the photograph is the face I would have seen when I opened my eyes in his arms all those years ago.
JEAN PEACH 25TH May 2005

"Robbie" Robinson taken July 1944. 3 years. 3 months after The 'BLITZ' on Coryton Terrace.

Mrs. Jean Peach- Robbie- Mr. John Peach Taken at Lamorna Place November. 1988 47 years 7 months after the 'BLITZ' on CorytonTerrace.

No. 15 CORYTON TERRACE

Photos with kind permission of Mrs Jean Peach.

Rear View CORYTON TERRACE

Date : 24th. APRIL 1941

n.b. Just visible near centre of picture is Next Doors neibours ‘Anderson Shelter.’

1942.
YEAR THREE

Tue. 6th Jan **CORNWALL:**

A Torpoint airman whilst serving at the *Royal Navy Air Station St. Merryn,* Died cause unknown.

364366. F/SGT. SAMUEL DERRY WILTSHIRE. Age unknown

Royal Air Force.

CWG. St. MERRYN CHURCHYARD Grave 6.

SOUTH WEST ENGLAND:

Notes from Western Morning News:

[Authors note: All the following Western Morning News snippettes were submitted by Mrs.Betty Kellar, Author of two books on Torpoint and Millbrook.]

Monday. January 5th. Salvage Drive:- £50 worth of paper salvage sold in Liskeard.

"Invasion off" practice over the weekend, Civilian population responded splendidly. Landings by sea and air. Twenty four hour exercise. Loud-Hailer vans telling people to stay in their homes. Tear gas used (gas masks). Enemy were supposed to be forming a bridge-head from which to attack the rest of England, cutting the Cornish peninsula off. Boy Scouts used as "casualties" One Town "captured" by Commandoes. Sunday dinners disturbed by people going to their doors and seeing "enemy" creeping down the streets. Lesson learned? - the futility of the "stay put" advise to civilians. Mock bombs dropped, fires, Civil co-operated with the military hiding behind garden hedges. Thousands of Red Cross workers at post, to deal with too few casualties.

Wed. 7th Jan. **MALAYA:**

The battle of Slim River, possibly the last defensive position held by the British Army in Malaya, half way between Ipoh and Kuala Lumpur the bleagured English, Australian and Gurkha 28th Brigade dug-in in an attempt to stem the rapidly advance of the then superior Japanese Army. Bitter fighting occurred, but the Brigade were reduced to a third of its strength many taken prisoners or slaughtered, those that did reteat south were in a state of 'fight and reteat'. The resulting battle at Slim River provided the Japanese open control over Central Malaya.

SOUTH WEST ENGLAND:

Western Morning News reports

Friday January 9th:

Still talk of "scorched earth" policy to be undertaken by civil services. Questions asked in The House of Commons but no answer given in the public interest.

Ministry of Food advertising for large quantity of potatoes for canning. Specified which sort.

Sun. 11th Jan. **MALAYA:**

Four days after the Battle at Slim River The Japanese captured the Malayan Capital Kuala Lumpur. The Japanese were half way to Singapore.

SOUTH WEST ENGLAND :

Western Morning News reports

Monday January 12th

Cheese to be reduced from 3 ounces to 2 ounces,in February.

Friday January 16th:

Plymouth women fined £1 for blackout offence. Policeman had to break her window to put the light out.

Monday January 19th:

Isolated raids over South West but little damage (Saturday) a plane grazed a tree on a farm after flying low over the roof, then flew out to sea.

ooOoo

LONDON:

Copy of letter regarding The Home Guard.

'Quote'

Circular 2564

Ministry of Health

Whitehall, London S.W.1.

Sir,

THE HOME GUARD:

I am directed by the Minister of Health to refer to statements recently published in the newspapers on the subject of the Home Guard.

It has been decided to divide members of the Home Guard into classes(I) and (II):

Class (I) members will, on the mustering of the Home Guard in an emergency, be required to join immediately for the full-time service, while class (II) members will report within forty-eight hours and will then be directed either to join for full-time service or to remain until further orders from their civil work.

Local authorities and water companies who have members of the Home Guard among their employee's will have to consider whether it is necessary for the maintenance of their services, that particular men should be placed in class (II) and also men so placed, maybe upon reporting to be allowed to return to and carry on with their ordinary duties. Even in an emergency, there will be services of local authorities and water companies which must continue, and the Government could not contemplate the breakdown of such services by reason of the placing in class (1) of any employee of a local authority who is a member of the Home Guard, or through a requirement that a class (II) member of the Home Guard shall leave his work on reporting for duty. It is considered by the Minister and the Army Council that it should ordinarily, be possible for the local authority or water company in consultation with the appropriate officer of the Home Guard, to secure the proper classification of the men in question, as between classes (I) and (II) and (not less important) within class (II) It is provided in the Army Council instructions on this matter, the purport of which was given in the press on the 23rd January, that where there is a difference of opinion between a man's employer, and the appropriate officer of the Home Guard, the difference shall be referred to the Manager of the Local Employment Exchange, where local authorities and water companies are concerned, the Minister is confident that the number of cases which have to be so referred will be small, but he has arranged with the Minister of Labour and National Service that Exchange Managers shall be instructed to give special attention to any cases which arise affecting local authorities and water companies, and if in any doubt on such a case shall consult the Senior Regional Officer of the Ministry of Health.

This circular relates only to men who are already in the Home Guard, It does not apply to men who are subsequently enlisted voluntarily, or under compulsory powers, about whom further circular will be sent at a later date.

I am, Sir,
Your obedient Servant.
(SIGNED) R. B. CROSS Assistant Secretary.

'Unquote'

Sun. 1st Feb. **MALAYA / SINGAPORE:**

All British soldiers had crossed the Causeway from Johore Bahru onto Singapore Island, to prevent the Japanese an easy entrance onto the Island. The Causeway to be blown up and the fight to save the Colony of Singapore began. General Percival estimated that he had a force of 85,000 men including 15,000 administrative and non-combatant troops which included the last arrival of re-enforcement troops which were untrained and not ready for any battle? Comprised of - 13 British Battalions, 6 Australian, 17 Indian & 2 Malaysian. The morale of the troops was very low and had little faith in their leaders, many deserters hid in the city. The Japanese did not attack immediately, but took a few days to mass its troops on the Johore side of the Causeway, ready for the intended invasion of Singapore.

ooOoo

SOUTH WEST ENGLAND:

Western Morning News reports:

February -

Potato and Carrot Pancake. - 1lb potatoes, 1lb of Carrots, boiled together, strain, save water for soup, mash and fry slowly to a deliciously crisp crust.

Don't Travel by train unless necessary for your work.

ooOoo

Mon. 9th Feb. **SINGAPORE:**

At dawn the Japanese V & XVII Division's had all landed on the west side of Singapore Island. Using the same tactics used further up in Malaya, gradually infiltrated across the island towards Singapore, again they met stiff opposition from the defending British Forces. Nevertheless, there were too many of them, Singapore City became overcrowded. Along with the massing troops, refugees from Malaya, and the fleeing inhabitants of the Islands. The aerial bombing by the Japanese hit the oil tanks setting them ablaze, causing black clouds of acrid smoke to hang over the city. During the period from the ninth until the fifteenth, the final evacuation of Singapore took place, on a similar scale to that of Dunkirk in 1940. Small boats of the British and Dutch Navies or, any other vessel that could ferry the fleeing refugees to the Port of Batavia (now Jakarta) the Capital City of Sumatra. The scene was chaotic, as other boats tried to navigate out into the open sea, away from the mayhem that followed. Dead bodies from ships that had been sunk floated in the oily waters of the harbour.

Tue. 10th Feb.

A survivor of the Battleship HMS *Prince of Wales,* died in Singapore, his fate at the hands of the Japanese unknown.

Royal Marine. VICTOR HAROLD SMART Age 24.

CWG. PLYMOUTH NAVAL MEMORIAL Panel 103 Col 2.

[Author's note: HMS. *Jupiter & Stronghold* were recalled to Singapore to act as escorts to the S.S. Gorgan & Empire Star, and departed loaded with fleeing refugees en route to Batavia. *Jupiter* took on board another 122 refugees, whilst *Stronghold* took on 50 more].

Fri. 13th Feb. Known as '**Black Friday'.**

The Japanese advancing across the Island, shelling and using mortar bombs entered Queen Alexandra's Hospital, it was crammed full with injured men and any civilians who had been unfortunate enough to receive injuries. The Japanese ran amok sparing no-one, shooting and bayoneting any one in their path, even doctors and nurses were killed.

Their atrocities became known as the 'Alexander Hospital Masaacre.'

Also on the same day-

The Evacuation of Singapore: In the final hours of the evacuation Vice Rear Admiral Spooner was just about to leave, having done what he said he would do, (organised as many escapees as possible, under the circumstances). Just before midnight the *ML310* set sail with a party of Senior Service Personnel consisting: of Vice Rear Admiral E. J. Spooner, *HMS Sultan (Shore Base),* Air-Vice Marshal C. W. H. Pulford, 6 (six) Navy Officer's, 2 (two) Army Officer, 19 (nineteen) Naval ratings, 6 (six) Royal Marines, 8 (eight) Army, and another number of military personnel. The type of motor launch was only designed and capable of carrying a max of 7 personnel and with the number in excess of 40 one can only imagine the magnitude of the then evacuation. It is assumed in theory by the Author, that The Admiral and Naval Personnel were from HMS *Sultan,* amongst whom was a Torpoint sailor:

D/LX 21632. L/Std. JOSEPH GARFIELD EUSTACE.

The *ML.310*, cast off from the Telok Ayer Wharf, with the intention to reach Batavia. A course was set south, steering for Muntok or Bangka Island, off the shores of Sumatra. During the outward journey, the steering gear failed, causing her to steer off course before it run aground. Next day she was re-floated and lay off an island for the rest of the day. The ML310 must have traveled approx. 170 plus nautical miles South of Singapore, when approaching Bangka Island, they spotted the mast and funnels of

3 (three) Japanese Cruisers and 3 (three) Destroyers. The ML310 turned around and headed back towards the Tia group of Islands, but they had been sighted and were fired upon, shells landed close in their wake, the Japanese launched a seaplane, which dropped several bombs around them. Fortunately missing them, before once again, they ran aground on a coral reef, wh ich was a blessing in disguise? With the exception of the ML Crew Master and crew, they waded ashore and hid in the jungle. 1(one) Japanese Destroyer arrived and shelled the ML and launched a small boat whose crew before they left, put the ML310 out of commission. The party was to spend the next three months as castaways. Although not members of the above escaping party, during the evacuation of Singapore the following **2 soldiers** from Torpoint escaped:

843596. Grn. LEONARD BARTLETT CHAPPELL.

7th. Coastal Regt. Royal Artillery Singapore.

&

1020192. Sgt. WILFRED GEORGE SHEAFF.

3rd. Lt. A.A. Regt. Hong Kong And Singapore Royal Artillery.

[Authors Note: The assumed fate to these 2 Torpoint soldiers will be referred to later.]

& in-

TORPOINT:

2 HE bombs and four Fire Pot Bombs, landed at Millbrook Lake, no damage.

Sat. 14th Feb. **SINGAPORE:**

A Torpoint sailor from HMS. *Sultan,* Shore Base Singapore, died cause of death at the hands of the Japanese unknown.

D/MX 50022. E.R.A. ALFRED TREWERN. Age 23.

CWG. PLYMOUTH NAVAL MEMORIAL Panel 69 Col 1.

[Author's Note: It is not clear if this sailor was being treated for wounds received or otherwise, in the Queen Alexandra's Hospital. The massacre that did happen lasted for nearly three days, whilst the Japanese were on the rampage it is a strong possibility that his demise was linked to that period of time. It is strongly recommended that further reading of a recently published book "No Mercy From the Japanese" by the Author John Wyatt a FEPOW, who was witness to the massacre, being hospitalized for treatment to his wounds. Somehow he escaped, but was captured, interned in Changi before being sent to work on the Burma Railway, he survived that and was sent to Japan traveling on one of the Hell Ships. His harrowing story reveals more about life as a FEPOW than anything scripted within this book].

Sun. 15th Feb.

General Percival Commander in Chief Malaya, brought a disastrous period of history for the British Military, to an end when he signed The Documents of Surrender at 1810 hrs. in a room of the Ford Factory at Bukit Timah.

After only 73 (seventy-three) days since the Japanese invaded Malaya it was all over. Captivity for the remaining thousands was inevitable. Amongst those captured was Torpoint soldier:

Trp. 4133377. WILLIAM CYRIL RICHARDS. Age 31.

5th Btn. The Loyal Regt. Reconnaissance Corps.

[Authors Note: The Loyal Regiment were based at Jahore over the Causeway and in Singapore. Whether his capture occurred during the fighting in Malaya or in Singapore, it is not known, possibly the latter, after the *Loyal*'s had withdrawn from Jahore, he became a POW in the hands of the Japanese (fate to be referred to later)].

Also

1413555. S/SGT. WILLIAM HICK. Age 38.
Royal Artillery (fate to be referred to later).

ooOoo

Sun. 22nd Feb. **TORPOINT:**
Torpoint sailor. **CPO. WILLIAM HORACE SLEEP. Age unknown**
HMS *Drake.* Died. Cause unknown.
TORPOINT HORSOM CEMETERY SEC. C GRAVE 454.

The Far East:

THE BATTLE OF THE JAVA SEA
January to March 1942

DUTCH EAST INDIES:

The onward push by the Japanese forces to invade and secure the Islands of the Dutch East Indies, was relentless. By the end of February it was almost completely surrounded, at that moment in time, it was reported that the Japanese Navy had: 14 Cruisers, 55 Destroyers, 25 Submarines, 5 Aircraft Carriers, and 6 Sea-craft carriers active in East Indian waters.

Wed. 25th Feb.

The Invasion Fleet of the Japanese 16th Army, was on its way to attack the Northern part of Sumatra. Arranged in two flotillas, were 60 Troop Carriers, supported by at least two more, 10,000 ton Cruisers armed with 8 inch guns, together with 13 Destroyers, and several Submarines in front of the Troop Carriers.

Fri. 27th Feb. **SUMATRA - JAVA SEA:**

Trying to head off the invasion, an Allied Naval Force in the area was under the strategic control of Admiral Elfish of the Royal Netherlands Navy. Consisting of: HMS. *Exeter,* (survivor of the Battle of the river Plate in Dec.1939), HMS. *Electra & Encounter,* HMAS. *Perth*, RDN. *Kortenaer* USS. *Houston.* Also under the command of the Dutch Admiral Dormann, were the RDN. *De Ruyter, Evertsen & Java,* HMS. *Jupiter & Stronghold* HMAS. *Yarra* & USS. *Pope,* all sailing North of Surabaya. Approximately halfway between Bawean Island and Surabaya at 16:15 p.m., the Naval force made contact with the Japanese force. At extreme range, joint action commenced. Almost at once one of the Japanese destroyers launched an attack, but was driven off by the firepower of the allied cruisers. Shells from HMAS. *Perth* hit one of the enemy ships. Soon after the other Japanese destroyer flotilla launched a torpedo attack. While the necessary action was being taken to avoid these torpedoes, only one of the torpedoes took effect, sinking the Dutch destroyer RDN. *Kortenaer.* An 8-inch shell which penetrated into its boiler room, hit HMS. *Exeter* reducing her speed, and forcing her to drop out of line. Under cover of a smoke-screen the Japanese destroyers turned about. The three British destroyers were ordered to counter-attack, HMS. *Jupiter* reported only seeing two enemy destroyers, both of which she engaged with gunfire. After HMS. *Electra* had disappeared into the smoke screen, she was not seen again, it is presumed she was sunk. As soon as the allied destroyers with the exception of HMS. *Exeter,* who was unable to keep up, drew clear of the smoke they again engaged with the enemy, this time at a shorter range. Less than half an hour later, the enemy Cruisers retreated under cover of a smoke-screen. One, a heavy 8 inch Gun Cruiser had been hit and was burning fiercely. Admiral Doorman, turned his force around and chased the enemy to the northeast, but in the failing light failed to regain touch with them.

After nightfall, the allied cruisers sighted four enemy ships to the west, Admiral Doorman anticipated the Japanese Convoy to be due north, and in order to engage them planned to sail around them, but this was found to be impractical, because of the high speed the enemy was traveling, and so subsequently, turned his force south towards the coast of Java, intending to sweep up the coast to the west. At 23:30 p.m. when the allied cruisers were about 12 miles north of Rembang, two enemy cruisers were sighted between the Allied ships and the coast, they were immediately engaged and scored a number of hits. Two Japanese ships the *Nachi & Haguro* engaged the *De Ruyter & Java.* The *De Ruyter* was hit by one shell, immediately afterward the *De Ruyter* made a large alteration of course, presumably to avoid torpedoes fired by the enemy. The allied ships were reforming, when underwater explosions occurred simultaneously, in both the *De Ruyter & Java.* They sank at once. North of Java the overwhelming Japanese forces were in command of the sea and air. The Allied command was faced with the problem of extricating the remaining allied ships from a very dangerous situation. The way to Australia was barred by the 600 miles long Island of Java with both the Straits at either end, in control by the enemy.

Sat. 28th Feb.

At 07:00 in the morning HMAS. *Perth* who had received some damage, reached and anchored at Tanjong Priok. After dark *Perth* sailed out, with the intention of passing through the Sunda Straits during the hours of darkness, however a report received at 01:00 from *Perth* indicated she had come in contact off St. Nicholas Point with a force of Japanese ships. HMS. *Electra was* set a-blaze by gunfire and later, HMS. *Jupiter* was blown up when she in-advertently crossed a minefield. *Perth* accompanied by *Houston*, broke off the battle and headed for the Sunda Straits. *Perth* sent a further report, stating they had ran into another Japanese convoy and engaged in a fierce battle with four Japanese ships. After that nothing was received from *Perth,* or from USS. *Houston* both assumed sunk.
The same night the damaged HMS. *Exeter* accompanied by HMS. *Encounter* & the USS. *Pope* left Surabaya bound for Australia.

Sun. 1st Mar.

At forenoon on Sunday, a report from HMS. *Exeter* stated, she had sighted three enemy cruisers steering towards her. No further reports were received from HMS Exeter, *Encounter,* or the USS. *Pope.* All three were presumed sunk. Amongst those who lost their lives in the battle aboard HMS. *Exeter* was a Torpoint sailor:
D/MX 62594. E.R.A. WILLIAM ARTHUR WEEKS. Age 24.
CWG. PLYMOUTH NAVAL MEMORIAL. Panel 71 Col.2.

Mon. 2nd Mar.

When going though the Sunda Straits, the DRN. *Evertsen* HMS. *Stronghold* & the Sloop HMAS.*Yarra* met a similar fate. *Evertsen* was hit and beached, whilst *Stronghold & Yarra* were hit and sunk. *Stronghold* received hit after hit, before it stopped and was abandoned. Killed on board was a Torpoint sailor:

D/K 65707. C/Sto. JOSEPH SAMUEL CARTER. Age 35.
CWG. PLYMOUTH NAVAL MEMORIAL Panel 69 Col. 1.
[Author's note:] On Sunday May 18th 2008 the Sunday *Times* reported the finding of the wrecks of HMS. *Exeter* & HMS *Encounter.* Originally, a team of American and Australian divers found them sometime during 2007. The report stated that the two ships plus the USS. *Pope,* sank not three but nine Japanese warships during the so called Second battle of Java. All three ships were sunk, HMS. *Exeter* was to lose 50 crew members. The 650 survivors were captured and became POW's. 152 died in captivity. HMS. *Encounter* lost eight-crew members and 149 survivors became POW's, 38 died in captivity. To date the wreck of the USS. *Pope,* (in which 1 member of the crew was killed, the fate of the rest of the crew is not recorded), has not been located. The finding and identification of the two British shipwrecks was only recently confirmed. They were found lying in about 200 feet of water, 90 miles north of Bawean Island, 60 miles from the sinking position given by Captain Oliver of the *Exeter* in his book published after the war. It can only be assumed that its located position is the last resting place of a Torpoint sailor:
D/MX 62594. E.R.A. WILLIAM ARTHUR WEEKS.

Tue. 3rd Mar. **AUSTRALIA NORTHERN TERRITORY:**
9 Japanese fighter-bombers raided the town of Broome in Western Australia, in a 15 min attack on the Flying Boat Base, (then being used to ferry soldiers and refugees from Sinapore), 23 American, Dutch and British Aircraft were destroyed and approximately 70 people were killed. One (1) American bomber managed to take off, only to be shot down some way out to sea, of the 33 men on board only 1 (one) survived. It is assumed that the following two Torpoint soldiers, who were passengers on that plane, were amongst those killed or drowned.
9435967. Grn. LEONARD BARTLETT CHAPPELL. Age 28.
7TH. Coast Regt. Royal Artillery.
CWG. SINGAPORE WAR MEMORIAL.

Also
1020192. Sgt. WILFRED GEORGE SHEAFF. Age 32.
3rd. Lt. A.A. Regt. Hong Kong and Singapore Royal Artillery.
CWG. SINGAPORE WAR MEMORIAL.

Thu. 5th. Mar. **NORTH AFRICA:**
Drv. Bert Rowe sent this Forces letter after receiving his Mothers letter dated 30/11/41posted 3 months before.

.

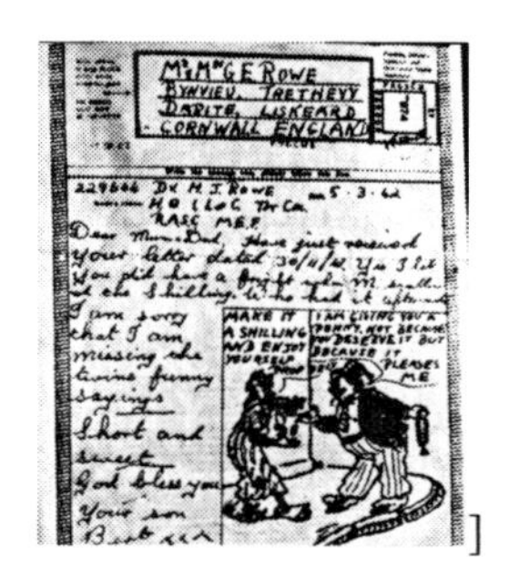
Mr & Mrs G E ROWE
BYNVIEW, TRETHEVY
DARITE, LISKEARD
CORNWALL ENGLAND

229646 Dr H J ROWE 5·3·42
HQ 1 LoC Tr Co.
RASC M.E.F.
Dear Mum & Dad, Have just received your letter dated 30/11/41. [illegible]
I am sorry that I am missing the [illegible] funny sayings
Short and sweet
God bless you
Your son
Bert xxx

]

Sun. 29th Mar.**ICELAND - BARENTS SEA:**

19 merchant ships in Artic Convoy PQ 13 set sail from Iceland for Russia, 5 were sunk and German torpedoes crippled their principal escort the cruiser HMS. *Trinidad.* During that engagement a Torpoint sailor was killed:

D/MX 47383. Shpt. 2nd /Cl. HAROLD GEORGE CROCKER. Age 29.
CWG. PLYMOUTH NAVAL MEMORIAL Panel 71 Col 1.

Sun. 5th Apr. **INDIAN OCEAN:**

5 Japanese Aircraft Carriers that had taken part in the attack on Pearl Harbour attacked and sunk ships. The armed merchant ship *Hector,* the Destroyer HMS. *Tenedos,* plus 2 British Cruisers HMS. *Cornwall & Dorset.*
On board HMS. *Cornwall* a Torpoint sailor was killed:

D/LX 20267. Std. RICHARD EARNEST PEARCE. Age 34.
CWG. PLYMOUTH WAR MEMORIAL Panel 72, Column 2

Thu. 9th Apr. **CEYLON - TRINCOMALEE:**

The Japanese bombed Colombo the Capital of Ceylon, and the North Eastern Port of Trincomalee, where the destroyer HMS. *Vampire* and the Aircraft Carrier HMS. *Hermes* were bombed and sunk, 300 men on board Hermes died in the attack amongst them was a Torpoint sailor:

FAA / FX75629. L/AF. KENNETH WILLIAM ARTHUR ENNOR. Age 19.
CWG. LEE- ON SOLENT MEMORIAL Bat 3 Panel 3.

Sat. 25th Apr.**TORPOINT:**

In the early hours of the morning, a lone plane dropped 1 (one) bomb on HMS. *Raleigh.* No casualties.

Sun. 26th Apr.

In another sharp raid 3 (three) bombs were dropped at Rame Head. No other details.

Thu. 30th Apr.**RUSSIA - BARENTS SEA:**

Whilst HMS. *Edinburgh was* escorting Merchant Ships on the Russian Convoys, carrying supplies from Reykjawik in Iceland to Archangel in Russia, the ship was attacked and sunk by German Torpedo Bombers. On board HMS. *Edinburgh*, one of the sailors that died was Torpoint sailor:

D/K 22286. L/S. WILLIAM PAPE. Age 46.
CWG. PLYMOUTH NAVAL MEMORIAL Panel 69 Column 3.

Wed. 13th May.

A further engagement with the Germans by the cruiser HMS. *Trinidad* east of Bear Island, as it escorted allied Merchant Ships in convoy from Iceland to Archangel, let off torpedoes, unfortunately through bad weather and a faulty Gyro on one of *Trinidad's* torpedoes, it traveled a full circle hitting the *Trinidad* and sank her. Eighty (80) sailors were killed, 20 of them survivors of HMS. *Edinburgh* which had been sunk two weeks previously. One of the crew of HMS. *Trinidad* killed was a Torpoint sailor:

D/MX 51509. C.E.R.A. REGINALD ALFRED EVANS. Age 28.
CWG. PLYMOUTH MEMORIAL Panel 68 Col 3.

Fri. 15th May.**SOUTH AFRICA - INDIAN OCEAN:**

Having rounded the Cape of Good Hope whilst steaming eastwards on her way to join the Far East Fleet, HMS. *Hecla,* accompanied by HMS. *Gambia* and the South African Navy minesweepers *Southern Barrier & Terje.* Whilst off the Cape of Agulhas *Hecla* struck a mine, she was taken undertow by *Gambia* into Simons Town South Africa for repairs. The explosion, which occurred under her huge workshop and storeroom, caused the death of 24 crew members, amongst those killed was a Torpoint sailor:

D/MX 66242. E.R.A. ERNEST HENRY HOAR. Age 25.
CWG. PLYMOUTH NAVAL MEMORIAL Panel 71 Col 2.

Fri. 22nd May. **SUMATRA - TJBIA Islands:**

To continue the story of the castaways on the Island of Tjbia, they were like Robinson Crusoe's, scraping a form of living out of the jungle, existing on fruit and just edible vegetation. They succumbed to illness and gradually all fell foul of it, including fever, specifically Malaria, a vicious and probably cerebral strain. After nine weeks of isolation and depravity, having repaired a small fishing boat, a small party set off to seek help, morale was low and eventually 1 Naval Officer died, followed by 18 others including Rear-Admiral Spooner, Air Vice Marshal Pullford, and possibly it is assumed, a Torpoint sailor:

D/LX 216323. L/S. JOSEPH EUSTACE. Age 31.
CWG. JAKARTA WAR CEMETERY SUMATRA 1 .F. 21.
[Authors Note: It was not until three weeks later that the Japanese landed and took the remainder of the party into captivity to become Prisoners of War, maybe to work on the infamous Thai Burma Railway.

May 1942. **SINGAPORE / SIAM:**

Similar to the fate of the POW's in Hong Kong, The Japanese in Singapore had no idea what to do with the 127,000 allied prisoners they had amassed and en-capsulated since the disastrous defeat in Malaya and Singapore, when approxately 9,000 allied troops were killed and wounded. Whilst those who did not escape were captured, other Indian Forces cried wolf and joined in with the Japanese and became guards to their ex-comrades in arms. However, that is another story. The Japanese were faced with a few problems mainly the feeding of so many, where to keep them, mainly in Changi Jail where the conditions were atrocious. The fact that their conquering armies would be deployed to the north to strengthen their Northern Armies already fighting in Burma and Assam, where the British XIV Army, 'Wingate's Chindits' were fighting and harassing the Japanese. Malaya, Siam, and a great area of Burma was totally occupied by the Japanese, their biggest problem was transporting supplies to troops in those areas. In October, they came up with an ingenious idea to extend the single line railway, which ran from Singapore up to Bangkok (Siam), onto Moulmein in Burma crossing the border at Three Pagodas Pass the distance of approximately 300 miles through arduous and mountainous country. Construction work to be finished in 18 months, scheduled work rate per day: 1.8 miles and without any equipment, an impossible task. Who better to be employed to do the labour than the POW's on hand? They would be off their hands, and gainfully employed. As the work progressed, they would set up their own labour camps, their food would be grown locally. Their plan was swiftly put into action. The POW's were assembled into battalions of about 600 men and then put on a train to begin their 900 mile journey north to the Town of Ban Pong in Siam. They were packed into a small steel box truck, 30 men per truck. (understanding the humidity and heat of Malaya) Upon their arrival some 4/5 days later most were in a poor condition, thirsty and near starvation. Their first job was to set up a Labour Camp and begin work on the railway. Amongst those transported was a Torpoint soldier:

Trp. 4133377. WILLIAM CYRIL RICHARDS. Age 31.

5th. Bttn. The Loyal Regt. Reconnaissance Corps.

[Authors Note: When he was transported is open to speculation, his fate to be referred to later.]

TORPOINT:

Norman Beavers MBE. recalls:

After a year at Millbrook our family moved back to Torpoint to try and restart life. Although the war was still going on, dad was anxious to repair our house, but as the Albion Road School was still closed I was not able to continue my education, so for nearly two years I had no schooling, something I was to regret in later life. At the age of fourteen I joined the Civil Defence as a messenger and was fitted out with a uniform, steel helmet and a respirator. My post was Montpellier Terrace. We were still having air raids but on a smaller scale, bombs were still being dropped and we were still at war. I was paid nine pence for every appearance I made during air raids. Mum thought this was very wrong and called it "blood money"!

ooOoo

Sat. 30th May. **GERMANY - COLOGNE:**

The Germans suffered a physical and psychological blow when 1,000 Royal Air Force bombers dropped 1,455 tons of bombs on the German city of Cologne. It was to be the first 1,000 bomber raid of the war. This was far superior to the heaviest bombing raid that happened on April 16th 1941, when the Luftwaffe dropped 440 tons of bombs on London.

Sat. 6th Jun. **INDIA - CALCUTTA:**

Torpoint Soldier died. Cause unknown, possibly decease

1866610. WOII. ERIC CHARLES BUSH-PEARCE. Age 30.

Royal Engineers .

CWG. BHOWANIPORE CEMETERY CALCUTTA INDIA.

Thu. 11th Jun. **NORTH AFRICA - LIBYA:**

During the battles around Tobruk, Rommel ordered a double break-out from the area known as the 'Cauldron', in a series of devastating attacks against the 2nd & 4th British Armoured Brigades. During the tank battle that ensued, a Torpoint solder was killed:

316236. SGT. JOHN PEACH. Age 30.

Royal Dragoon/ Royal Armoured Corps.

CWG. ALAMEIN CEMETERY Col 15.

[Authors Note:] John Peach recalls:

June 1942 more bad news, dad had been informed that his younger brother Stan had been killed while serving with the Army in North Africa. His comrades had buried him where he had fallen, unfortunately like many others, his body could not be recovered after the war. However his name is on column 15 at the El Alamein Military Cemetery, situated near Alexandria. He was quite a good footballer and before the war he was Center Forward for Torpoint St. James.

Mon. 15th Jun.**MEDITERRANEAN SEA - South of CRETE:**

The Cruiser HMS. *Hermione,* one of three escort ship operating under the code name "Operation Vigorous" running supplies to Malta, was attacked by *U205.* Torpedoes hit her and she sank within 20 Minutes survivors were picked up. by other ships in the convoy.

Tue. 16th Jun.

It can be assumed that Torpoint sailor **David Rule** a crew member of HMS. *Hermione,* was rescued but died the following day:

D/K 57090. C/MECH. DAVID RULE. Age 41.

CWG. PLYMOUTH NAVAL MEMORIAL Panel 69 Col. 1.

Sat. 4th Jul. **RUSSIA - BARENTS SEA:**

The minesweeper HMS. *Niger* sailed from Murmansk with convoy QP13 on escort duties. After sailing into foul weather, the convoy lost their bearings and strayed into an enemy minefield. On the 5th July late at night in dense fog, *Niger* hit a mine blew up and sank.

Killed or drowned on board were 2 Torpoint sailors:

D/J 108986. P.O. CLIFTON JAMES BANKS. Age 33.

Panel 63 Col. 2.

&

D/M 34614 Eng. Rm. Art. 1st. Cl. WILLIAM LESLIE STANTON. Age 54

Panel 69 Col. 1.

BOTH AT CWG. PLYMOUTH NAVAL MEMORIAL.

Thu. 1st Oct. **EAST CHINA SEA – DAQU SHAN Islands:**

A torpedo hit the Japanese merchant vessel *SS Lisbon Maru,* one of ***"The Ships from Hell"*** which began to sink, on board were 1,816 British prisoners of war being taken from Hong Kong to Japan. When the prisoners tried to leave the sinking ship, the Japanese had the hatches battened down. As the ship went down, hundreds attempted to break out, the Japanese fired on them. Those who managed to jump into the water and tried to climb up the ropes of four other Japanese ships close by, were kicked back into the sea. More than 840 were killed or drowned, the rest were picked up by small patrol vessels, boats, or by sympathetic Chinese, and were taken prisoner and shipped back to Japan.

[Authors Note] At this point, it might be permissible to relate the history behind this drastic incident, and try to understand the horrors that were inflicted upon those unfortunate POW's, including one of Torpoint's sailors. Therefore, the following is transcribed from written work of two survivors. P.O. Telegraphist Alf Hunt (Ex HMS. *Cicala & MTB 12)* & Telegraphist Jack. H. Hughieson *(MTB 08),* who pieced together the events from extracts taken from the following:

"The Knight of the Bushido" By Lord Russell of Liverpool

"Guest of the Emperor" by Martin Weeden

" Extracts from the Log Book of *'USS 'Grouper"*

By kind permission of the FEPOW Association.

The sinking of the "LISBON MARU":

In the annuls of modern warfare the sinking of the "Lisbon Maru", as a result of which 1,000 officers and men lost their lives, does not perhaps rate as a horror story. There have been many incidents in which many more people have been killed in more brutal fashion, but it stands out as an un-necessary killing and a callous disregard for human lives, which could have been saved. Each of the survivors remembers with clarity his own part of this affair, but few know all the facts. The account which follows is based on the book by Martin Weeden 'Guest of the Emperor', the newspaper account of the War Crime Trial's of the Japanese and extracts from the log book of USS "Grouper", which torpedoed the "Lisbon Maru", newspaper accounts of the presentation to the Sing Pan Islanders who helped the prisoners, and the newspaper accounts of the 'Japan Times Weekly' dated 20th October 1942. "The Knights of the Bushido", By Lord Russell of Liverpool, personnel accounts written at the time, and personnel reminiscences.

One matter should be placed beyond doubt, the official Japanese account quoted the survivors as voicing indignation against the American submarine which sank the 'Lisbon Maru, this is quite untrue, The 'Lisbon Maru' was armed and carried Japanese troops as well as Prisoners of War, she bore no sign that she was a POW ship. The American submarine was fully justified in sinking her, and I have never heard any criticism of the Americans for their action.

The affair is worth recording for one other reason, the gallantry of a number of individuals, and the high standard of conduct of all the men. Some individual acts are recorded in these pages, but their were many others of which I have no personal knowledge. The general steadfastness was due in large measure to the leadership of Lt. Colonel H.W.M. Stewart O.B.E. M.C., the Commanding Officer of the Middlesex Regiment (The Diehards).

G. C. Hamilton.
Hong Kong.
1st February 1943:

ooOoo

PACIFIC Island OHAU - PEARL HARBOUR:

On leaving Pearl Harbour on her second patrol on the 28th August 1942, the 'USS *Grouper',* under the command of Lt./Com. Claren. E. Duke had her first 'kill' on 21st September, when the *'Tone Maru'* crossed her sights. On the 1st October she sighted an unmarked 7,000-ton freighter, the *'Lisbon Maru' which* had sailed from Hong Kong on the 27th September 1942.

Departure of the 'Lisbon Maru' from Hong Kong:

On that date 1,816 British prisoners of war were assembled on the parade ground of Shamshuipo camp Hong Kong. They were addressed by Lt. Hideo Wada of the Japanese Imperial Army through his interpreter Niimori Genichiro. You are going to be taken away from Hong Kong he said, to a beautiful country where you will be well looked after and well treated. I shall be in charge of the party, take care of your health and remember my face. Reactions amongst the POW's were mixed. After the initial shock of the surrender on Christmas Day 1941 had been absorbed, hopes had run high for an early release, but now it had become apparent that no relief was to be expected from the Chinese Army. Singapore and the Philippines had fallen to the Japanese, and the news from the European theatre was bad. Conditions in the main camp in Shamshuipo, and the Officers Camp in Argyle Street were poor. Quarters were crowded, with inadequate food, Medical supplies were scarce. A diphtheria epidemic had reached alarming proportions, and deaths were common. A few intrepid men had escaped, but reprisals on those that remained were so severe, and punishment of those who were caught was so savage that future escapes were doubtful, even for those who still retained sufficient stamina to make an attempt.

There were some who argued that a move to Japan, which seemed the obvious destination, would be an improvement since, (they believed) the Japanese Army would not wish to display its inhumanity to it's POW's and that consequently, better treatment might be expected. The more cynical doubted these ideas and would have preferred to stay in Hong Kong where, perhaps the chances of rescue and escape were slightly greater, but discussion was futile for the POW's had no choice of action.

On board the *'Lisbon Maru'* the men were divided into groups of 50, each group being in the charge of a Subaltern, while the whole party was commanded by Lieutenant Colonel H.W.M (Monkey) Stewart O.B.E., M.C., the Commanding Officer of the 1st Battalion of the Middlesex Regiment (The Diehards), assisted by a small number of officers. After an exhaustive but (as it turned out) ineffective medical examination, the prisoners were loaded on the 27th September into lighters from the pier at the corner of Shamshuipo camp, and taken out to a freighter of some 7,000 tons, the *'Lisbon Maru'* under the command of Captain Kyoda Shigaru, where they were accommodated in three holds. In No 1 hold nearest the bows, were the Royal Navy under the command of Lt. J.T. Pollock. In No 2 hold just in front of the bridge, were the 2nd Battalion of the Royal Scots, 1st Battalion Middlesex Regiment, and some smaller units, all under the command of Lieutenant-Colonel Stewart. In No 3 hold just behind the bridge, were the Royal Artillery under Major Pitt. Conditions were very crowded indeed, all men lying shoulder to shoulder on the floor of the hold, or on platforms erected at various heights. The officers, on a small between-decks half way up the hold, were similarly crowded.

There was not sufficient room for the men to be able to lie down all at the same time, so sleeping was to be achieved by rota. Food was adequate according to prisoners of war status, the usual rice and tea for breakfast with an evening meal of rice and possibly a small portion of corned beef, with a spoonful of vegetables. Drinking water was at a premium and was rationed, water for washing was non-existent. Some cigarettes were issued, a great luxury. The latrines consisted of wooden hatches hanging over the side, too few for the numbers on board. Within a very short time after boarding, the stench of sweating men and excreta became an intolerable burden, so the Japanese allowed sections of prisoners on deck for prescribed periods of time. Also on board were 778 Japanese soldiers, who occupied most of the deck space forward, with a guard of 25 under Lt. Hideo Wada.

For the first few days, the voyage had been uneventful apart from the natural grumbling of the men who so far had not been able to have much sleep, due to the heat, the oppressive atmosphere, the stench and the rolling movements of the ship. About half the men were issued with Kapok Life Belts. At the subsequent War Crimes trial, interpreter Niimori claimed that every man had a life belt, which he checked at each roll call. The ship sailed on the 27th September. There were four lifeboats and six life rafts, and according to the Captain it was decided that the four lifeboats and four of the life rafts should be set aside for the Japanese if required, leaving the remaining two life rafts for the 1,816 POW's.

The Torpedo Attack:

On the night of the 30th September 1942, the "USS *Grouper"* (SS214) of the 81st Division of the US Pacific Fleet Submarine Force, was engaged in the second War Patrol in an area to the south of Shanghai. It was a bright moonlight night, and at about 04:00 "*Grouper*" sighted about nine Sampans and a 7,000 ton freighter the '*Lisbon Maru*', the Commander decided that it was too bright for a surface attack, so he paced the target in order to determine her speed and course, "*Grouper*"then took up station ahead of the '*Lisbon Maru*' waiting for daylight. During the course of this action, "*Grouper*" passed within 4000 yards of two fishing vessels which were well lit. In No 2 hold Lieut. G.D. Fairbairn of the Royal Scots, duty officer of the day, visited the lower deck at 06:30 to rouse the men and ensure they rolled up their bedding and dressed for roll call at 07:00. As usual, several men visited the latrines on deck to beat the morning rush. At daylight, the '*Lisbon Maru*' altered course, this surprised "*Grouper*"who then dived to start her under water attack. At 07:04 "Grouper"fired three torpedoes at 3,200 yards her closest working range, but none reached their target.

The '*Lisbon Maru*' stayed on course, "*Grouper*"fired a fourth, and two minutes ten seconds later heard a loud explosion. "*Grouper*"came up to periscope depth and saw that the '*Lisbon Maru*' had veered about 500 to starboard and stopped. "*Grouper*" then lined up a beam to starboard of the '*Lisbon Maru*' for a bowshot, "Grouper's" Commander recorded, target meanwhile hoisted flag resembling 'Baker' and was firing at us with what sounded like a small-caliber gun, sharp explosions all around us. On board the '*Maru*' the POW's were very fearful, they did not know if the explosion, engine stoppage, and power failure, was due to internal breakdown or external attack. The Japanese were shouting wildly, and seemed very agitated, pushing all prisoners on deck back into the holds, including some sick who were permanently on deck in isolation. Then the ships gun began firing.

The account in the Japanese Weekly Times dated the 20th October 1942 was different. "We must rescue the British POW's", was the foremost thought which leaped to our minds when the ship met her disaster said Lt. Hideo Wada. "It was just the hour for the roll call of prisoners, somewhat taken aback that they were about to be stampeded, "don't worry Japanese planes and warships will come to your rescue" we told them. The commotion died down. It was encouraging to note that they had come to such trust in the Imperial Forces during their brief POW camp life.

By 08:45 "*Grouper*" was ready for a 00 gyro 800 track, range 1000 yards attack, "*Grouper*" fired a sixth torpedo with a six-foot depth setting, but again missed. The '*Lisbon Maru*' meanwhile had listed slightly to starboard, so "*Grouper*" went around to her port side in order to let off a stern tube. At 09:38 "*Grouper*" fired a 1800 gyro, 800 track range 1000 yards at zero depth setting, immediately diving to 100 feet. There was a loud explosion 40 seconds later, upon diving the Commander spotted a *Mitsubishi Davai 108* light bomber overhead, two minutes later three depth charges exploded, with no damage reported. The POW's did not feel this torpedo hitting, it may have been mixed in with the depth charges exploding nearby. The Japanese claimed to have destroyed the sixth torpedo. "It was just about 10:30 that I happened to discover the sixth torpedo rushing towards our vessel, said one of the '*Lisbon Maru's*' gunners," Colonel Moji gave us the order to fire at the torpedo, surprised beyond words, but faithful to the order, we charged our cannon with a shell aimed at the torpedo and fired. We then looked ahead and discovered that we had scored a direct hit. "*Grouper*" came up to periscope depth, the ship had disappeared, but the plane was still in sight, leaving the Commander assuming he had done the job.

In The Holds:

No one was allowed on deck for any reason, and for the next seven hours in the stifling heat the Japanese were un-cooperative, food and water were refused, as well as requests to visit the latrines. "*Grouper*" stayed in the vicinity all day, occasionally hearing depth charges, as did the POW's. At 19:05 visibility was poor and "*Grouper*" surfaced and left the area.

It was about this time that the Japanese began to batten down the hatches. Lt. Colonel Stewart the senior British officer on board began to remonstrate with the Japanese, requesting that they should at least remove one bulk of timber to help provide a little air. Captain Shigaru was arguing with Lt. Wada about the hatches being closed, but Wada insisted that his 25 guards could not control the 1,816 POW's. Under the circumstances at about 21:00 Lt. Wada came to the bridge and ordered Captain Shigaru to close the hatches completely. Wada was very threatening telling Captain Shigaru he had no authority to intervene in military matters. All the hatches were battened down and covered with tarpaulins, which were then roped down leaving the POW's in complete darkness.

At his trial in Hong Kong in October 1946, Captain Kyoda Shigaru, the master of the *'Lisbon Maru'* stated that the Japanese destroyer *'Kure'* arrived on the scene in the afternoon of the 1st October, ordering the transfer of all 778 Japanese troops to the destroyer at 17:00. While the transfer was taking place using two of the lifeboats the '*Toyokuni Maru*' under Captain Yano arrived. A conference was held on board the *'Lisbon Maru'* and the remaining troops were transferred to the *'Toyokuni Maru'*. The 25 guards along with 77 crew remained onboard, with arrangements for the *'Lisbon Maru'* to be towed to shallow waters. There was now no means of exit and no fresh airflow, the conditions worsened very rapidly, but through it, the men remained calm and obedient. They had not had any food for over 24 hours. Apart from the few early birds who went at 06:30 prior to the torpedo attack, they had been denied access to the latrines for over 24 hours as well. The men in No 2 hold had managed to get into contact with Royal Navy men in No 1 hold by tapping out in code on the bulkhead, and No 3 hold by voice via a vent. They learnt that conditions in No 1 hold were very similar to their own, while those in No 3 were getting desperate CQMS Henderson of the Royal Scots, his beard jutting out aggressively, encouraged non-swimmers like himself by insisting that now was their opportunity to learn!

No 3 hold was now taking water and the pumps had to be manned, reports came from No 2, that the men who had been manning the pumps rapidly lost consciousness owing to the extreme heat and lack of air. Each man would do about six strokes on the pump before fainting. In No 2 hold in similar conditions, they found that by lying flat and not moving they remained conscious. Reports came through that two men had died in No 1 hold from diphtheria.

The Breakout:

By dawn of the 2nd October, twenty-four hours after the torpedo had struck, the air in the holds was becoming dangerously foul, the ship began to lurch and stagger, it was evident that she was going to sink. Since all requests to the Japanese had been ignored or refused, Lt. Colonel Stewart authorized a small party to attempt to break out, principally to persuade the Japanese to at least give them a fighting chance. Lt. H.M. Howell had survived two previous shipwrecks, and so was put in charge of attempting to open the hatch. One of the men produced a butchers knife, which had not been detected by the Japanese, and Howell climbed the steel ladder in pitch darkness to attempt to cut an opening, trying to hold on with one hand, whilst thrusting the knife with the other, was too much and Howell gave up through lack of oxygen. At 8:10 on the 2nd October, Captain Shigaru sent a flag message to the *'Toyokuni Maru'* requesting permission for 'all' to abandon ship. The reply was that a ship would come along side and take off the Japanese guards and crew, but not the POW's. At 09:00 the ship gave a lurch, and Howell who had found a rickety wooden stair leading up to the hatch, tried again, this time succeeding.

Lt. Howell and Lt. Potter plus one or two others climbed onto the deck, reporting that they could see an Island. They saw some gunners trying to get through the porthole from No 3 hold onto the well deck. Howell and Potter unscrewed a bulkhead door and let them out. They then walked slowly to the bridge asking to be allowed to talk with the Captain of the ship. The Japanese opened fire with their rifles into the hold, killing one man and wounding Lieut. G.C. Hamilton. They fired again hitting Lt. Potter and one or two other ranks who had climbed onto the deck, Lt Potter subsequently died. The remaining men returned to the hold and reported to Colonel Stewart that the ship was very low in the water and evidently about to sink. Suddenly the ship lurched again and began sinking by the stern, the water rushing into the now open hold, the stern resting on a sand bank and the forward section remained protruding from the water for about an hour.

Colonel Stewart gave the order to abandon ship. The Japanese soldiers, who were standing by aboard ships alongside, now began to fire at the escaping prisoners, and at those swimming in the water. About three miles away there were some small Islands, Sing Pan Islands that were believed to be very rocky and dangerous, and the current was swiftly taking men in this direction. About four Japanese ships were standing by, but did not attempt to assist the prisoners. Ropes were dangled from the ships, and as prisoners tried to climb them, they were allowed to get within inches of the deck and were then kicked back over the side.

Later the Japanese policy changed, but not before several men had managed to get to the Islands, many were lost in the water or sent crashing onto the rocks. Others were picked up by Chinese Junks and Sampans and taken to the Islands. These Chinese treated the prisoners with great kindness, giving them what little food they had and some of their clothing. Then the Japanese landing parties came and gathering the prisoners together, they transferred them to Shanghai. Others were taken aboard Japanese craft, or put down the holds of other ships. Most of those recovered were naked and covered in oil. The night air was so cold that the prisoners sheltered under the tarpaulin. From then on they received four tack biscuits a day with some watered down milk and every third day a bowl of thin weak soup.

On the 5th Oct. all the prisoners who had been recaptured were assembled on the dock at Shanghai and a roll call was taken, of the original 1,816 prisoners 970 answered their names, 846 had perished.

Amongst those that were killed was Torpoint sailor:

D/MX 46040. C.E.R.A. LESLIE GEORGE PERKINS. Age 32.

CWG. PLYMOUTH NAVAL MEMORIAL Panel 68 Col 3.

It was learned later that six or seven men had managed to escape, assisted by the Chinese. 35 of the worst dysentery patients were left in Shanghai and the remainder were taken aboard the SS '*Shinsei Maru*' where five men later died. On arrival at Moji en route for Osaka 50, more very sick prisoners were dropped off at Kokura with a similar number at Hiroshima. 500 went to Kobe and the remainder to Osaka. 200 died during the first winter from diphtheria, diarrhea, pneumonia, and malnutrition. It had been the intention of the Japanese to let the prisoners drown, so that they would be able to say that the Americans, leaving them no chance to effect a rescue, had sunk the ship. It was only after the Japanese had watched the Chinese rescuing so many prisoners that it was decided that their original plan would not be believed. All the prisoners could have been saved had the Japanese transferred them

at the same time they had transferred their own troops. The *'Lisbon Maru'* was not marked in any way to indicate that she was carrying prisoners of war, which in it self was a contravention of the Geneva Agreement. For the families of those men who went aboard the *'Lisbon Maru'* on the 25th September no one will know exactly which men drowned, and which men survived to die later.
The Japanese did not keep any records.

ooOoo

STRAITS OF GIBRALTAR:

Arthur Corbidge recalls:

One weekend we sailed into the Mediterranean Sea,we always used go out into the Atlantic and then cut through the Straits of Gibraltar during darkness, as we new there were a lot of German spies in Spain. We sailed into the Mediterranean with The *Ark Royal, Valiant,* and our destroyers up to Genoa for that was the Germans main shipping port for North Africa supplies. So on the Sunday morning at 0800 hrs, we started to bombard and we sunk every ship in the harbour and blocked it completely. You can guess the amount of stuff that went in there. We finished at 0900 hrs, so that crippled poor old Rommel.

8th Nov. We assisted with the landing in North Africa, we landed troops into Algiers and Casablanca and right across North Africa. So it gave Rommel another headache for there was another front for him to look for, this they said finished the War in North Africa.

Sat. 14th Nov.**MEDITERANEAN SEA :**

The Italian ship *S.S. Scillian* was located 9 miles off Krait in Tunisia, by an unknown British Submarine who fired its torpedoes crippling the ship, surfacing, she continued to shell it until the *Scillian* sank. On board that ship was a Torpoint soldier, a POW captured by the Italians who was in transit with others, and was either killed or, drowned in the sinking, circumstances unknown.

7608991. Sgt. HEBER ERNEST TRAYS. Age 24.
Royal Army Ordnance Corps. Att. Royal *Artillery.*
CWG. ALAMEIN CEMETERY Col 83.

Thu. 3rd Dec. **ENGLISH CHANNEL:**

Whilst HMS. *Penylan was* on escort duty with Coastal Convoy PW-257*, a*t 06:30 hours 5 miles south of Start Point, a torpedo fired by a German Motor Torpedo Boat No. *S115* hit HMS. *Penylan* and sunk her. On board that ship was a Torpoint sailor**:**

D/J 98113. L/S. ERNEST. F. T. SEARLE. Age 37.
Details unknown, but assumed drowned.
CWG. TORPOINT HORSOM CEMETERY Row 36 Grave 761.

ooOoo

TORPOINT:

Henry Banks recalls:

Another time when I was driving for the Brewery, we were at the RAF base at St Eval, there was an air raid on and a dogfight was taking place over the airfield, one aircraft was smoking and came spiraling down. We were ordered to get into the shelter, but stood just inside so we could watch the action, suddenly bullets were hitting the wall just in front of us, they were coming from the aircraft that was spiraling down with its guns jammed, then there was an explosion, it had crashed somewhere on the airfield. Of course by this time, doing a driving job it was not easy to find your way around because ALL road signs were removed because of the war, so not to help the enemy. But I can honestly say that I never got lost once, there were little Army camps all over the place, especially in the big country houses and we covered the whole of Devon. At one time we had to drive up to a place called Colophon to collect the beer because the drew house had been hit, you see we were right next to the Devonport Dockyard or you might say in between North Yard and South Yard. The main building and spirit store were burnt out and destroyed during the Blitz.

After being deferred three times, I was called up and went in to The Royal Air Force.

ooOoo

SCOTLAND - ROSYTHE:

Arthur Corbidge recalls:

We then sailed to Rosythe and joined the Fleet in Scarpa. The next day the 16th December 1943 with the HMS *Queen Elizabeth* & HMS *Ocean we* sailed with a flotilla of destroyers for the Far East. I was absolutely dumbfounded to see the *Q.E.* I was paid off in Portsmouth in 1938 when she went in for a D2. refit, I served on her for 3 years and I month flying the flag of Admiral Sir Jack Fisher and Admiral Sir Dudley Pound. I quite agree I was luckier than some of the lads, for when I was in Rosythe my wife and I were staying in Queensferry, so I had another month of going ashore with her every other day.

ooOoo

1943
YEAR FOUR

SOUTH WEST ENGLAND:

Notes from Western Morning News:

Friday 1st January.
"Hit and Run raid on SW Town".
[Authors Note: Possibly the air attacks on Plymouth that were concentrated on around the periphery giving the city some respite from the spasmodic air raids]

Sunday 3rd January.
"Feathered trail" Stolen Chicken,trail of feathers led to defendant's hut. Ashes, Bones, possibly a Rabbit? Defendants story not believed. Bound over 15/- cost.

Monday 4th January."Raid on 2/1/43 on small SW market town (coastal). Shortly after noon on Saturday
It was reported that Food Rationing was to become tighter.

Tue. 5th Jan. **SCOTLAND – EDINBURGH:**
Torpoint soldier. Cause of death unknown.
Pte. 3055076. ALEXANDER Mc CAFFERY. Age 23.
Royal Scots.
CWG. (PIERSHILL) Cemetery. Sec. M. Grave 636.

SOUTH WEST ENGLAND:

Western Morning News report
Friday 8th January.
"Hit and run raid on SW town scattered residential districts. 7 Focke Wolf 190's swooped in from sea.

Sunday 10th January.
"12 killed others missing in raid on small SW coastal town. Rescue party searching through the night. Machine-gunned in the street Air Ministry people on the front at the SW coastal resort saw a German Plane shot down into the sea.(possibly Torquay) Report: 10/JG2 Focke Wolf 190, shot down by Flying Officer Small in a Typhoon of No. 266 Squadron, and crashed into the sea 500 yards off Teighmouth.

Monday 11th January.
"Bus Curfew" 9.30. p.m. Confusion, Cinema Programme finished at the same time. Police called to sort out the milling crowds. Many left behind.

Tuesday 12th January.
"54 year old Home Guard claimed to have served as a rear gunner". Regulations- "Raid on Duisburg. Military Medal for action against 1917. £50 pound fine plus £35 cost. Lost Job.
Use of Car for funeral "reasonable" carrying elderly people Technical Offence. £2 fine.

"Soldier fined £1 at Torpoint today for stealing a cycle lamp value 5/-. The lamp had been left on a bike inside a garage. Chairman of the Bench said it was ' a mean dirty trick' -
"10/- fine for failing to immobilize a car at Torpoint on the 30/11/42.

ooOoo

TORPOINT:
Notes of various Wartime experiences:

Joy Hanning: When I was born in 1943, it was the practice for women to stay in bed after the birth for about a week. When the air raid siren sounded my gran. dashed in and grabbed me and took me to the shelter and left my mother to fend for herself.

An Incendiary bomb was dropped at the Junction of Victoria Street, North road and kempton Terrace. Mr. Mitchell towner of the local corner shop (No 12 Merrifield Terrace), dashed out and threw a bag of sand over it, only to discover that he had picked up a bag of rice instead, His wife (Minnie) was not impressed!

Joyce and Minnie Carter worked for William's Restaurant in Plymouth. One evening at the end of their shift they arrived at the Torpoint Ferry in the middle of an air raid. The ferries' had stopped running so they were stranded on the Devonport side. They had been there sometime, when an Army lorry came down the hill and the officer in charge insisted that the ferry run across the river as the lorry contained ammunition for the Tregantle Fort. The ferryman had to take the lorry across, so all the civilians climbed onto the ferry as well. It was only after they had landed on the Torpoint side, that they realised how dangerous it had been to travel across with a lorry full of ammunition.

The Carter family who lived in Carbeile Terrace (Now Kempton Terrace), used to regularly walk out to Crafthole and stay with the Channing family at the Post Office to avoid the bombing at night, and walk back again in the morning, never knowing what they would find when they got back. Harry Carter used to come in a lot earlier than the rest of the family, as he was the baker at Graingers Bakery Fore Street (now it is the Chinese Takeaway)

Fri. 15th Jan. **NORTH AFRICA - LIBYA:**

Field Marshal Montgomery's 8th Army (The Desert Rats) in hot pursuit of Field Marshal Rommel's Panzeramee attacks Buerat, Rommel is then forced to retreat to Homs.

Thu. 21st Jan.

Homs is captured. Rommel continues his retreat further west to Medinine, fortunately the Anglo/American 1st Army advancing from Tunisia in the west trap Rommel in a pincer movement.

Thu. 28th Jan. **LIBYA - TRIPOLI:**

Tripoli the promised city, surrounded by green flourishing countryside, was captured from the fleeing Germans. It was a victory for the 8th Army who had seen nothing but miles and miles of desert sand. In celebration of this event.
Driver **BERT ROWE** sent a forces mail letter to his parents off the Capture of TRIPOLI much to the delight of the 8th. Army and Bert. as illustrated below.

Sat. 13th Feb. **TORPOINT:**

Air-raid at 2200 1 SC500Kg. landed at Home Farm Cremyll failed to explode. defused by BDS.

Fri. 5th Mar. **MOUTH OF RIVER THAMES:**

M.T.B. 667. was part of the 33rd Flotilla preparing to depart to the Mediterranean. It was in the area of Brightlingsea when the engine blew up and three sailors were killed, one of those was a Torpoint sailor:
D/JX 145641. PO. JAMES HEANEY. Age 22.
CWG. UPTON CROSS

Also on the same day-

SINGAPORE:

Prisoner of War .Torpoint soldier died. (no information on cause of death.)
1413555. S/Sgt. WILLIAM HICK. Age 38.
Royal Artillery,
CWG. SINGAPORE MEMORIAL Col 4.

Mon. 8th Mar. **NORTH AFRICA – LIBYA:**

With the 8th Army, pushing forward against the retreating Germans and Italians towards the Mareth Line in Tunisia. The 6th Battalion *Lincolnshire Regiment* arriving at 5.a.m took over positions on a feature, overlooking the Djebel Abiod-Tamera Road, a vital link for the Germans. A Regiment of the Corp's France d'Afrique had previously occupied the position. Their information was that the Germans were a considerable distance away. Having dug weapon pits, it was not long before an attack began. Mortars and heavy machine gun fire supported the Germans, being in considerable strength the initial attack lasted until midday, avoiding any penetration by the Germans. That night another attack developed, again it was repelled by the *Lincolns*, who inflicted heavy losses on the Germans, nevertheless they incurred losses themselves, one of those killed was a Torpoint soldier:

5341659. Pte. JOHN HARTLEY COWLING. Age 26.
CWG. TABAKA RAS RAJEL WAR CEMETERY.

On the same day-

A Torpoint airman based at RAF Berka II 38 SQD. died, cause unknown.

648319.F/SGT. (W.OP./AIR GN.) JACK WILLIAM BLYTH. Age 33.
Royal Air Force
CWG. BENGHAZI LIBYA 3 B 22-24

Thur. 18thMar.**MEDITERRANEAN SEA:**

On patrol with 'Q' Force HMS. *Lookout.* On board was a Torpoint sailor who died, circumstances and cause of death unknown.

D/JX 149505. L/S. NOEL CLIFTON PIDGEN. Age 23.
CWG. PLYMOUTH NAVAL MEMORIAL Panel 78 Col. 3.

Fri. 23rd Apr. **NORTH AFRICA - TUNISIA:**

Longstop Hill, was strategically located, overlooking the desert areas below. The Germans had been entrenched for some period of time. During a Battle with the American Army they captured the hill. The German's counter attacking, recaptured the hill. However, it was a vital vantage point, for the 8th Army in their advance across North Africa. From the 20th to the 25th a planned attack was made by. The Buffs, Royal West's and Argyll's, supported by artillery and tanks, fought a battle. In one heroic bayonet charge, Major John Anderson was awarded the V.C. Three days later the slaughter had ceased, when the hill was recaptured. The Argyll's, were to suffer badly, losing 9 Officers - 25 N.CO's and men, amongst those, was a Torpoint soldier:

14211282. Pte. WILLIAM EARL STROUD. Age 35.
8th Btn. Argyll and Sutherland Highlanders
CWG. MEDJEZ-EL-BAB. TUNISIA.

[Author's note: In a newspaper cutting, it refers to the Battle of Longstop Hill. A certain person, by the name of Spike Milligan, spoke about that battle in his book 'Milligan's War'. He along with his mate Edgington, were present during that battle, both with 'D' Battery 56th H. Regt. Royal Artillery, providing supporting fire. When they received orders to provide support, Milligan relates a surreal passage from his book. 'In the rush Edgington handed me a piece of paper, it read:
"Stalin's orders of the day:

a) Two Lagers. b) Packet of Crisps. c) Stalingrad" –
I said, 'This is vital information Comrade Edgington, this must never fall into enemy hands. This must be burned and you must swallow the ashes.'
Whereas Edgington, snatched the paper and ate it. 'Delicious' he said.
I said 'That's called the 'Readers Digest'].

EAST AFRICA - MOMBASA:

Arthur Corbidge recalls:

On the 20th April I was sent over to the *Q.E.* to take my Petty Officers Examination and this was a great honour for me seeing I done service on her as a boy. Ordinary Seaman and Able Seaman, then to be sent to her to pass for P.O. On the 19th August I was drafted from HMS *Renown* to Lanka Barracks, then by passenger ship to Mombassa where I joined HMS *Falmout*

ooOoo

Mon. 26th Apr. **TORPOINT:**
ARP. GEORGE RODLEY. Age 62 . 7, Coryton Terrace
Killed cause unknown.
TORPOINT HORSOM CEMETERY.

Mon. 10th May. **INDIA - RANCHI:**
Torpoint soldier died, cause unknown.
1058582. S/SGT. LEWIS ARTHUR GREET. Age 33.
28/76 Batt. 9th. Field Regt. Royal Artillery.
CWG. RANCHI CEMETERY INDIA 1.F.7

TORPOINT:

During the period May 22nd to the 29th of May, it was "Wings For Victory Week". The aim of Torpoint and the surrounding villages was to raise £40,000, enough money to build 2 Catalina Flying Boats. As can be seen from the following programme, the suggested events for raising the money, indicates the different targets set, and the method by which events were organized. (Document supplied by Freda Hawken with thanks).

Norman Beaver MBE. recalls:

Col.Thompson was the Garrison Commander for Plymouth and district and always appeared at Warships Week, Spitfire Week and other fund raising events. It was of course good propaganda and it was usual to have contingents of the Royal Navy, The Army and the Royal Air Force to march past, we boy's loved it but I must say we were sure that Hitler would never come to.

Wed. 13th May.**PLYMOUTH:**

During a night-time raid on Plymouth. Beaufighters of 125 Squadron, then operating out of Exeter engaged German planes 20 miles off the coast, two of the attacking force, A Dornier Do 217 of 1/KG2 and A Junkers Ju.88 of 9/ KG6, were shot down into the sea. A third plane another Ju. 88. caught fire over the sea and crashed into the grounds of Beaumont House Penlee Gardens Stoke, which then was a WRNS hostel. Two of its crew was killed and a third one baled out who was captured. A fourth plane another Junker Ju.88 of 7/KG6 was also damaged in the melee and crash-landed at Frittiscombe Devon. One crew member was killed one seriously injured and taken prisoner and the third baled out over the sea.

Sun 16th.May. **GERMANY - RUHR VALLEY:**

RAF squadron 617 (The Dam Buster Squadron) Using the bouncing bomb technique bombed the Mohne; Eder & Sorpe dams the main source of power for the munitions factories located in the Ruhr Valley. Although the Dams were breeched drowning many Germans they were quickly blocked thus stemming the massive flow of waters to a trickle. A young lad from Millbrook **F/Sgt (Air Gunner) Albert Whurr.** Although not actually a crewmember during the bombing of the dams, did later serve in 617 Squadron. In 1947 he was involved in an air crash in Egypt and subsequently died from his injuries in 1948. [Authors Note: Information was given by his sister Mrs. Barbara Hocking (nee Whurr)].

Sun. 29th May.**SCOTLAND - KILBRANNAN SOUND:**

HM Sub. *Untamed* failed to surface off of Campbelltown Scotland. A Sub-Mariner from Torpoint was drowned.

D/JX 151254. PO. WILFRED TIPPETT. Age 22.

CWG. DUNOON CAMPBELLTOWN CEMETERY. ARGYLLSHIRE.

Thu. 14th Jun. **TORPOINT:**

Torpoint suffered the effects of a direct hit on the Devonport Dockyard.

Fri. 25th Jun.

During another sharp air raid an unexploded Ack Ack shell, from the Rame Artillery landed at Shallow Pond Tregantle.

Fri. 30th Jul.

Spitfires of 165 Squadron, shot down 1 Ju. 88 and two Focke-Wulf 190 south of Plymouth.

ooOoo

John Peach recalls:

Another pastime was playing in the bombed houses. Near us were Corryton and Tremayne Terrace's now York Road). There were many houses there that had been destroyed, but they were ideal places for climbing, jumping from windows and making camps. Looking back now I suppose our pursuits were dangerous, but the only casualty I remember was John Smith. A large piece of timber had fallen, cutting his head rather badly. He was dispatched off to Dr. Jones to be treated, returning later proudly displaying a large bandage.

Another favorite play area was the old workhouse (Now Marine Drive flats). It had been standing empty before the outbreak of war. With its long passageways and large rooms it was ideal for playing hide and seek and other such games. Similar pastime would be put to use in Cambridge Fields where a large air-raid shelter had been built.

Now for a confession!! A friend (who shall remain nameless) and I were walking past Port Rouge (now Four Seasons) when we noticed a fire alarm. It was set in a wall with a glass cover. Temptation overcome us, so we broke the glass and pushed the alarm button. Then realising what we had done, we took to our heels. My friend went in one direction and I up to Victoria Street. The Fire Engine duly arrived to be told that it was a false alarm but two boys had been seen running towards Victoria Street. One of the firemen began house enquiries, making his way even closer to number 15, I was looking out from behind the curtain shaking with fear. He was only a couple of doors away, when the fire engine was recalled to deal with a genuine alarm. Saved by the bell you might say however, I was suitably punished and rightly so.

ooOoo

SOUTH WEST ENGLAND:

Western Morning News report:

Monday 9th August.

Still no trace of U.S. missing soldiers(lost early hours of Friday) Experienced fishermen think that until the present neap tides start to feel the influence of the next Spring Tides, they will not be found.

ooOoo

Mon. 9th Aug. **TORPOINT:**

Air- raid on Torpoint. Artillery Ack-Ack in action. 2 Unexploded Ack Ack shells possibly from Burroughs Farm site landed: 1 at St John's Lake the other at St Anne's Farm Crafthole.

SOUTH WEST ENGLAND:

Western Morning news Report.

Tuesday 10th August. Man fined £4 at Torpoint today for blackout offences in a hut at Freathy Whitsands. Man owned several huts at Whitsands, which he let out to irresponsible young people, so that police had to patrol the area at weekends. Most of the blackout cases were due to negligence of youngsters(who were also fined).

Thursday the 12th August.
Raid over SW coastal town, 1 Plane destroyed some fatalities, early hours of Wednesday.

Plymouth had one of its worst raid from the civilian points of view since 1941 heavy raids. 9 o'clock, brief start, but false alarm - two Spitfires. People went back to bed. 12.30. sirens started again but alert lasted only 10 minutes. People sent back to bed again Shortly after a plane came roaring in, low, dropping flares. Within four minutes, bombs dropping. Sirens wailed again, many people caught before they reach shelters.

Nine Bodies of U.S. soldiers found (5 still missing).

ooOoo

Thu. 12thAug. **PLYMOUTH:**

Sharp attacks were made on Plymouth by 17 Bombers. Damage was caused by HE's and fires. 42 people killed.

.

Fri. 13thAug.

Plymouth attacked. On this occasion, the Plymouth Defence's were caught napping, due to our own RAF Bombers flying well to the east of Plymouth, returning from their own bombing raids. The barrage balloons were down and the Ack-Ack batteries were on semi alert. The Germans using the same tactics as our own pilots, flew in with the returning RAF Bombers, seventeen German planes, having crossed the coast, broke away and headed directly south west coming in over Plympton. One single aircraft, came in very low and dropped flares for the following raiders to make low level attacks, and drop their bombs across the city, over Devonport and Torpoint. Bomb loads were scattered across a wide area, from Laire to Devonport. The bombs were both HE and Incendiary. Many of the HE bombs did not explode upon impact, so there were many UBX's to deal with. Incendiary bombs rained down on Mount Edgecumbe, Barnpool, Lyner, and Antony. One house was damaged and one person injured in Wilcove. 1- 50Kg UXB landed at Beech Wood Mount Edgecumbe, and was like most of the others defused by the BDS. The German losses that night was One Ju.88 from 2/KG6 shot down by a Beufighter, from 125 Squadron by Sgt's Miller and Bone, crashed into the sea, eight miles south east of Plymouth.

August 1943 **BURMA:**

An engineering survey, carried out before the war of the area, revealed it was not feasible to build a railway line, due to its mountainous and impossible terrain. The cost of attempting such a project would be enormous. The Japanese started work on the Thai Railway back in May 1942. They had begun their construction programme from both ends, using the forced labour of POW's from Sumatra and those being transported by boat to the northern point at Moulmein. As already stated, the POW's from Singapore started on the southern point at Ban Pong, a branch line to the East of Rangoon. The first 20-miles was covered over flat open land to the town of Kanchanaburi, where it met up at the junction of two rivers, Mar Maeklong and the Kwai Noi. The River Maeklong was eventually bridged, and work progressed along ancient trading routes, through the Kwai valley up and over the mountains at Three Pagodas Pass into Burma. Camps were set up at various intervals, to allow work to be carried out as swiftly as humanly possible, normally each camp held about 100 or 200 men sleeping in 2 long houses thatched with attap, an individual had about 2 feet of space to sleep in. The POW's were marched through the jungles to the next camp and so on. The way the railway was laid was hacked out by hand, clearing the surrounding jungle to about 8 feet wide, using bill hooks, saws and rope. A large trunk or clump of bamboo would take a group of 20 men, a day to remove. Embankments were made with soil, shale or stones. A man was expected to move one cubic metre of soil per day. Crowbars chipped away with hammers at any rocky overhangs. All work was done by hand. The famous 'Bridge over the River Kwai' possibly a myth, was the construction of a cantilever bridge which spanned the Mekhong River, was made out of tree trunks, and bound by rattan creepers out of the jungle. During its construction, hundreds of POW's were employed, and took months to build. It was never used, being replaced by a concrete and iron bridge, only to be bombed out of use by the RAF. The two ends of the railway finally joined up near the frontier late in 1943. Nevertheless, it was not the Japanese who built the Thai Railway, it was those soldiers, sailors and airmen who became Japanese POW's.

The privation these POW's were to suffer has gone down in the annuls of history. They died from starvation, exhaustion, sickness, decease, despair, accidents, and the brutality of the Japanese. Also a Cholera epidemic, which began in July 1943, slew thousands in a few weeks. As there was no medicines to sustain the Cholera, from the parties which were transported from Singapore in April 1943, by the end of August 25% were dead and by December it had risen to 40%. The dead were either buried or cremated. Working amongst those unfortunate POW's who died, (circumstances of death unknown) on Friday August 14th was a Torpoint soldier:

4133377. Trp. WILLIAM CYRIL RICHARDS. Age **31.**

5th Btn. The Loyal Regt. Reconnaissance Corps.

CWG. THANBYUZAYAT MYANMAR, BURMA B3 CD.

[Authors Note: Only those Allied POW's who died on the Siam/Burma Railway are remembered with honour at this cemetery. See picture below that details the different stages that the POW's stayed at during their horrific journey].

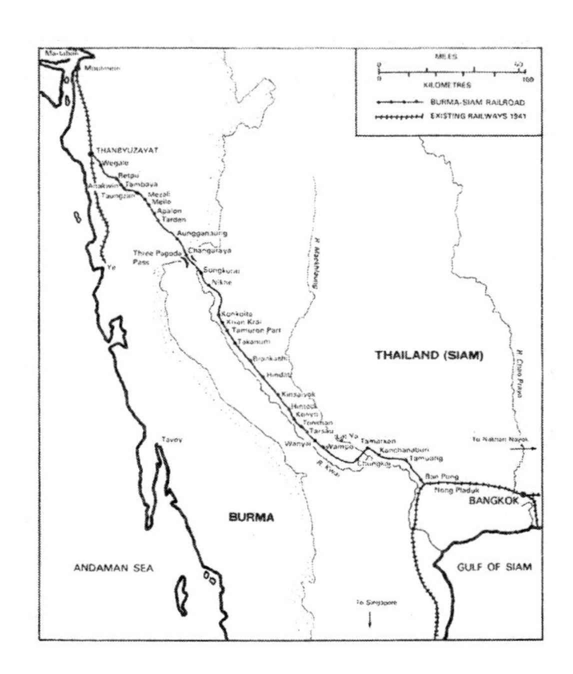

SOUTH WEST ENGLAND:

Western Morning News Report:

Friday 14th August.

Still searching for a woman missing in Wednesday's raid. Sad scenes at the mortuary. A father had to identify two children age 7 and 4. A young woman had to identify her parents and other relatives and has lost her home. Some bombs fell on fields. Those bombed went to Public Assistance Dept. and were given money and clothing coupons.

Monday 16th August.

Funeral held for raid victims, victims included wife of Home Guard member. Home guard members attended the funeral. The Boy's Brigade sounded The Last Post for National Fire Service personnel who were killed 2 men and part-time firewoman.

Tuesday 24th August.

After 73 years, Trams to be withdrawn in Plymouth, and replaced by Buses.

Stone on railway 11 year old boy bound over stone was between the catch points.

YORKSHIRE – LEEDS:

Fred Timms recalls:

What odds would a present day person give you, for the chance of speaking to husband, wife and daughter for five minutes, and wishing them a safe journey home to Leeds, only thirty months later to become a guest in their home for five days. Well it happened to me!

After the mass burial service at Horsom Cemetery for the soldiers and sailors, killed at the end of April, when a German bomb hit them as they were taking cover in the air-raid shelters at HMS *Raleigh. The relatives that attended the service were allowed into the NAFFI to obtain cigarettes, chocolate and clear gums, before leaving to journey back to their homes. As I was on duty that day, I met some of the relatives and said good-bye, before they left for their return journey to Leeds.*

In October 1943 I was in Leeds on a days leave, that evening we went to the Robin Pub in Boar Lane outside the railway station. I was having a conversation with Paddy the barman, it was about 7.p.m. and clocking off time for the day shift from the Vickers Tank Factory, when in walked three girls, they ordered a pint each and the nearest one too me turned and said. 'Canada would you pay for mine', Paddy laughed out loud and said 'he's not a Canadian', whereupon the girl replied. 'Well he does not speak English'. I spoke to her again, and one of the other girls she had come in with said to me. You come from Devon or Cornwall don't you? to which I replied 'Torpoint', In her Yorkshire accent she said to me, 'My brother was killed in HMS *Raleigh and she, along with her mum and dad, had stayed overnight in to attend the funeral service at Horsom Cemetery the next day', I stood there and downed my drink, placed the pint pot on the bar, she immediately told Paddy to fill it up again. Turning to me said after you drink that up your coming home to meet my mum and dad and tell them how those Torpoint Ferries work, but bear in mind there will be nothing for you at the end of it! I already have a boyfriend'.*

Over the next four weeks, I had a bed in their spare room available whenever I was in Leeds.

[Authors note: Having studied the CWG Records the only Seaman who came from Leeds was O/S. J. Schofield age 20. I believe the family in question was Mr. & Mrs. Albert & Jane Schofield. it was their son Jack that was killed on the 28th. April 1941.]

ooOoo

Fri. 27th Aug. **ATLANTIC:**

During a U-Boat search off Cape Ortegal west of Vigo Spain, the Canadian 5th Support Group, were relieved by the 1st Support Group, consisting of the sloops HMS. *Egret, Pelican,* and the Frigates HMS. *Jed, Rother, Spey & Penelope,* also the Cruiser HMS. *Bermuda* was relieved by the Canadian destroyer HMCS. *Arthabascan* and the British destroyer HMS. *Grenville.* They were attacked by 18 Dornier's Do 217's, which carried Heinschel Glider bombs. *Athabascan* was heavily damaged and *Egret* was hit by a bomb and sank with the loss of 194 of her crew. One of those drowned was a Torpoint sailor:

 # Unknown W/ENG. REGINALD WALTER HAILES. Age 39.

CWG. PORTSMOUTH MEMORIAL PANEL 73. Co 1.

Fri. 22nd Oct. **AEGEAN SEA:**

Having being given orders to take on escort duties between Malta and Haifa during the month of September, during October HMS. *Hurworth,* carried out mine sweeps and the bombardment of a German held island in the Aegean Sea. During a supply run to the Greek Island of Leos, together with the Greek Destroyer *Adrias,* they ran into a newly laid minefield, *Adrias* lost her bow, whilst *Hurworth* broke in two and sank within fifteen minutes. Amongst those drowned was a Torpoint sailor:

D/MX 52902. E /ART. 2nd/Cl. FREDRICK WILLIAM STACEY. Age 27.
CWG. PLYMOUTH NAVAL MEMORIAL Panel 82 Col. 3.

Sat. 23rd Oct. **ENGLISH CHANNEL:**

Six British destroyers, accompanied by the new Light Cruiser HMS. *Charybidis* embarked on 'Operation Tunnel' hoping to catch a German Merchant Ship on its way from the French port of Brest, into the English Channel. However they were surprised when caught by the Merchant Ships escorts. Two torpedoes sank the *Charybidis* with the loss of 462 men, amongst them was a Torpoint sailor:

D/K 62154. MECH. 2/Cl. FRANK BRADFORD. Age 38.
CWG. ST. PETER PORT (FOULON) CEMETERY A.M. GRAVE 54.

On one of the destroyers HMS. *Limbourne,* 42 men were killed. Many of the bodies were washed up onto the beaches of the Channel Islands. Their bodies were buried by the Germans with full military honors. As a mark of defiance 5,000 Channel Islanders made their way to the cemetery to pay their respects.

Also on the same day-

WALES – PEMBROKESHIRE:

Torpoint airman of 236 Sqd. based at RAF Carew Cheriton Dyfed Pembrokeshire, was on board a light Blenheim Bomber that was lost in a flying accident.

922912. SGT. (OBS.) STEWART JAMES LAMERTON. Age unknown.
CWG. St CONSTANTIN CHURCHYARD.

Tue. 16th Nov. **TORPOINT:**

In the early morning, using the same tactics as they had employed on their previous visit in June, flying in with our own returning RAF planes. The Luftwaffe swept in from the north east, flying towards the south west, 15 planes attacked Plymouth. This time the Gunners were ready for them, sending up a barrage, but the bombers after dropping their bombs with disastrous effect, got away. 14 HE bombs fell in and around the Torpoint area and about 100 Incendiary bombs fell at Terrill Farm, causing one hayrick to ignite. At Fodder, Cawsands 2 persons were injured. At Carbeile Farm, outbuildings and a hay elevator. At Mill Lane off Carbeile Road electric cables were down. Unexploded Ack Ack shell at Rame Gun Site was defused by BDS.

Fireman killed in Torpoint (No other details) But it assumed that during the attack carried out it claimed the life of the named Fireman below

LEONARD WYBORN. Age unknown

ooOoo

Record Log No. 5187 incidents reported on Tuesday 16/11/43 - Incident 73:

05.00~ Torpoint.~ Sirens sounded warning. Torpoint reported HE. and Inc. bombs. Fires in Devonport Area.
05.55. Torpoint.~ HE. bomb in Carbiele Road the final figure for Torpoint being 14. It is estimated that about 500lbs of various types of bombs were dropped damage to property slight, road surface damage, and electric cables down. Situation report as at 18.00 hrs 16/11/43 In all 14 HE. bombs, fell in and around Torpoint. The most damage to property was caused to the farmhouse at Carbeile the property of Mr. Parkins. Nine houses received minor damage.

This is an excerpt from Betty Kellar's book "Trouble in the Amen Corner". Betty Kellar at the time of this incident lived at 35, Clarence Road. The incident was the only bombing raid, that took place in Torpoint during the month of November.
'Quote'

One November night we were wakened abruptly by the siren, the drone of planes overhead and the noisy explosion of bombs intermingled with the heavy gunfire all happening at once. There was no time to come gradually to our senses. We all shot out of bed, feeling for our dressing gowns in the dark shadows of the bedroom.

The first thing Gan (this is how they called their granny, as described in her book) did was to fling open the curtain. White moonlight flooded the room together with the bright lights flares being dropped by the bombers. We huddled together on mum and Gan's bed, at first too stunned by the din to utter a word.

Gan was the first to pull herself together.' This ones on Devonport', she had to raise her voice to make herself heard.' They're after the Dockyard again'. Her voice broke our dazed silence and six year old Jill began to whimper, Mum drew Jill's head into the muffling folds of her dressing gown.

For once, Sir Percy Blakeney was unable to stiffen our backbones (a fictitious character often quoted by our grandma from the book The Scarlet Pimpernel). Sitting next to Gan I heard her invoke him, but I don't think anyone else did. So his demands that we were brave and not let the League down were ineffective. I could feel Diane pressing close to me, feel her warmth through our thin dressing gowns, and a trembling I wasn't sure was hers or mine.

The gunfire became heavier but, as Gan shouted in our ears 'it was our own it will be from the ships in the harbour she told us' and from the incessant clamour in our ears, she must have been right. Above the din we heard a new sound, and mum lost her nerve.

It was the first time we children had seen fear betrayed by an adult, and for us it was more traumatic than the raid itself. We heard a stick of bombs approaching us, the shrill whistle as one came right down above us, and mum cried out, her voice cracked with fear. 'Oh mum this is it'.

I can't remember hearing the explosion when the bomb landed several streets away, over-riding everything was Gan's reaction. She shouted at mum 'Of course its not, you silly little blighter, don't let me hear such tommyrot'. The shock of her berating mum as she frequently did us, drove everything else from my mind.

"Unquote".

SOUTH WEST ENGLAND:
Western Morning News Report:

Wednesday 17th November.
Raid on south west town. Many people saved by Anderson Shelters. Yesterday morning, people buried in their homes and dug out by the Rescue Squads. Family escaped by being in the shelter. Germans claim raid was on Plymouth. Early morning, a number of incidents scattered over residential areas. At dawn, police and rescue squads still searching for buried victims. No tapping heard by rescue squads,later two bodies brought out. Direct hit on house, people buried in the cellar. Two married women were in the kitchen next door to the bombed house, when they heard the plane screaming down, they immediately scrambled for the cupboard under the stairs, as their kitchen disappeared beneath the rubble of their neighbours house.
In another area, a HE dropped in the road outside a house occupied by girls, who were unhurt. A man who was fire-watching outside was hit by bomb splinters and taken to hospital. On the other side of road, a bomb damaged a Salvation Army hostel (blast) - bomb dropped in the front garden, 8 people killed, others trapped in this road.

Raid started shortly before dawn - short sharp raid. Raiders dropped flares, also helped by moonlight. They were challenged by heavy barrage. One plane may have crashed into sea. HE's, Incendiaries and Oil bombs dropped. Fires started, put out by NFS.
Attackers followed their usual pattern of sweeping in over the coast to the east,then turning dropping their bombs at speed,and racing out to sea.
13 month old baby killed. Also woman killed, but 2 men brought out alive. House next door had a lucky escape - 7 people in an Anderson Shelter, including a woman and her 2 children,12 and 2 years. (This was where another house had a direct hit, burying people in the cellar).

In another district, rescue squad digging for a man and woman. The woman was alive earlier yesterday, but later no sound was heard from her. She is the wife of a police officer, who was expected home yesterday,and a niece of a local police officer. Buried man is a tenant. It is believed that the woman (Mrs. Simons) was out in the street helping to extinguish an Incendiary bomb and had just returned to the house for water when it had a direct hit (HE). Woman who lived next door missing.

A home guard officer feared killed (his mother died of shock in the shelter during the last air raid on the town). A baby, 5 months old in hospital, badly injured, her 36 year old mother killed.
A number of HE's fell on western outskirts of an adjoining town - little damage, no casualties. A HE fell in another area, all extinguished.
Thursday 18th November.
Still digging for victims, those dug out were dead.

ooOoo

Wed. 24th.Nov. **ITALY:**

Drv. Bert Rowe had time to send Christmas Greetings Home

ooOoo

Mon. 6th Dec. **TORPOINT:**

At 1703 in Torpoint a sharp raid, 1 50Kg. landed at Glebe Farm Sheviock failed to explode, defused by BDS.

John Peach recalls:

I have pleasant memories of one Christmas. Toys and the like were at a premium, so to my great joy I unwrapped my parcel, a friend of dad's had made four aeroplanes out of lead. They looked wonderful all suitably painted. I had countless hours of playing make believe air battles.

ooOoo

SCOTLAND – SCARPA FLOW:

War Diary by L/Telegraphist Banham:

One bleak day in December 1943, when I left the good ship "Speedwell" after having been on her for 4.1/2 years, my feelings were rather mixed. I had had a very comfortable time during my stay and seen many different places and of course had seen quite a few actions, even if only small scale ones. So I did not wish to leave the old ship but on the other hand, a change is as good for you as they say, and as I had to

go, I was prepared for anything, as I had never been to barracks and had only served on the one ship. So away I went, not feeling too cheerful at leaving my friends who I had been with for so long. After the long boat and train journey (I was at Scarpa) arrived at the barracks at Chatham. There I had to go through "joining up" as it was called, which entails going round about a dozen different places, giving various particulars, and carting your bag and hammock backwards and forwards all over the place, by the time you have finished you are about 'all in'. However I was able to get away on 10 days leave the same day that I had arrived, so I did pretty well. I certainly was glad to get away, as I had quite enough of barracks already, though perhaps it is not so bad there, when you consider there are about three times the number of naval ratings there than the place was ever meant to accommodate.

On my return from a most pleasant leave, I hung around "depot" for a few days and then went to Cookham Camp, which is where most of the communication branch are billeted, and is really a training place or signal school. This entailed more "joining routine" etc., then I was settled in a Nissen Hut with about 20 other ratings. It was more comfortable here than at depot, except that being in a rather exposed position the camp was very cold and damp, but its advantages outweighed the disadvantages in my opinion. I was a few days settling down, and just as I thought I was going to be comfortable there for a few weeks anyway, I got my draft chit to *HMS Ajax*.

That night 24th December 1943, I went ashore to have a look round Portsmouth, phone up home, and go to the pictures, as we were sailing on Xmas Day for Scarpa. As it turned out I should have stopped on board as the next day I wakened with a very thick head and a temperature, I didn't take much notice of it at first, thinking that it was just my usual cold, but after struggling through dinner, (not our proper Xmas dinner as that had been postponed until we reached Scarpa) and doing my first watch, I felt so bad I had to go to the sick-bay, where they found my temperature was "way-up" and they made me turn in right away. There I remained for about eight days, it was apparently flu as I was sweating and coughing and had a bad chest for about a week before it began to clear up. I certainly felt rather a fool, my first trip in a fresh ship and I did it in the sick-bay.

After a fairly decent trip we arrived in Scarpa which I had only left about three weeks previously after leaving my old ship. I was feeling a little better and was praying my taste buds would return so that I could enjoy my Xmas dinner. It did almost, and I quite enjoyed the very nice menu for that day. We started off with grape fruit and egg and bacon for breakfast, dinner was tomato soup, a very good helping of chicken and turkey, with peas cabbage and baked potatoes, followed by a very nice helping of Xmas pudding and custard. There was tinned fruit and cake for tea, then soup and cold ham for supper.

ooOoo

1944
YEAR FIVE

SOUTH WEST ENGLAND:

Not long after America had entered into the war in December 1941, advance parties of the American Forces arrived in England. however it was not until July 1942 that the main bodies of the American Army and Air Force first arrived.

One of the many American Army Divisions was the 29th Infantry Division. Originally formed as an Infantry Division in World War I with its scource of men, coming from Maryland, Virginia and Pennsylvania, whose menfolk had fought on opposite sides during the American Civil War, subsequently they were nicknamed "The Blue and Gray" Division. Initially they arrived in Scotland, then transported to and re-formed in Wiltshire, before they arrived at their British destinations of Devon and Cornwall, their final deployment prior to the future Invasion of France. Plans for this invasion had been formulated many months or even years before, were unknown and 'Top Secret'.

The South Coast of England, became the launch pad and one large garrison area, with many English, Canadian, Australian, plus other Commonwealth troops, including the Americans, Polish and other European troops, began their training carrying out numerous war exercise's, in preparation for the future Invasion. Devon and Cornwall witnessed the first American G.I. (General Issue) troops of the 29TH Infantry Division Head Quarters were located at Tavistock Devon, and consisted of 9 Battalions, three in the 115th, three in the 116th, and three in the 175th. The 3 Battalions of the 115th were re-located in Cornwall at

TORPOINT:

The 1st Battalions Head Quarters was at Tregangle Fort, the 2nd Head Quarters at Launceston, and the 3rd at Bodmin. The 115th with its troops originally from Virginia, known as the 115th 'Stonewall Brigade, set up camps in Torpoint and its surrounding area, as far down as Downderry, around the Rame Peninsular, at Fort Tregantle, Filhawn Fort, Scarsdon Fort, and Picklecombe Fort. The closest American camp to Torpoint was located in the woods, by the Antony Gates, opposite Burroughs Farm, were Coloured CB (Construction Battalion) Troops were camped, as well as Picklecombe Fort. Their main job was to construct and lay 'Hard Roads' to all vantage points where later, the Americans would embark on their way to the D-Day Landings. Still in evidence is the Hard Road from Antony Gate down to Jupiter Point? known as 'Anthony Passage'. Support Groups of the 115th were located at Bake Camp near Trevolfoot.

Billeted at Fort Tregantle Head Quarters was The Heavy Weight Boxing Champion, Joe Louis. nicknamed the "Brown Bomber", along with two other boxing Champions of the world, - Jackie Wilson Lightweight Champion and Sugar Ray Robinson Middleweight Champion, all three stayed here for a period of time. (Most probably all three did travel on the Torpoint Ferry). They were over here on Morale Boosting Missions, so never did get to join in on 'D-Day'.

Freda recalls:

When Hitler and Co. provided us with more air raids, the authorities moved a lot of us out to Mount Pelier High school. The idea being, that if one half got hit the other half could take over. What a change It was, a lovely school with a big canteen where we could

buy a home cooked dinner. During the lunch time they put on ENS concerts, once we were entertained by the Black Gospel Singers of the American Army and sometimes our own boys put on a show for us. We were one big happy family and well looked after.

Later before D-Day we had a lot of American troops billeted down at Antony Drive they had built a concrete road from the top end of Antony Road right the way down to Jupiter Point, which is still there today, and no concrete cancer, the Yanks certainly knew how to do it. One of their buildings is still down at Jupiter Point located in the Naval quarters.

[NB. Freda's husband: P.O. Reginald Hawken, served aboard HMS *Blankney* in home waters, the Mediterranean, the Artic seas, including the Normandy Landings. For his services on the Russian Convoys he was awarded by the Soviet Union, The Great Jubilee Medal commemorating the 40th Anniversary of the Patriotic War].

ooOoo

Thu. 6th Jan. **ENGLISH CHANNEL:**

The Merchant vessel *M.V. Underwood (London) sailing* from the Clyde, destination Portsmouth, was attacked by a German 'E' Boat torpedoed and sunk at 49 degrees 57 seconds north, 5 degrees 28 seconds east off of the Lizards. 15 crew members were lost, including 3 gunners. Among those that perished was a Torpoint Merchant Seaman:

A/B. LEONARD ADAMS. Age 28.
CWG. TOWER HILL MEMORIAL Panel 113.

Tue. 8th Feb. **TORPOINT:**

At HMS *Raleigh a* Torpoint sailor died:

D/237760. CPO. ARTHUR MARTIN RILEY. Age 52. (no other details)
CWG. TORPOINT HORSOM CEMETERY. Row 10 Grave 903

ooOoo

Another story submitted, was by Jim Smith (Inst. Lt. Com. MBE, RN. Rtd), who arrived in Torpoint in 1942 to start an Apprentice Artificer Course at *Fisgard.* Jim liked Torpoint so much that he returned after the war, and now lives in Wilcove. The following are excerpts from his own book, and provide an idea of what is was like when the Americans visited Torpoint.

MARYFIELD HOUSE:

In March 1944 was used as overflow accommodation for Warrant Officers working in *Fisgard* and *Raleigh*. I was newly promoted Acting Warrant schoolmaster (H.O) Royal Navy aged 21 years, billeted with a group of Free Dutch Warrant Officers, as there was no room for us in the Warrant Officer's Mess in *Raleigh.* I worked in *Fisgard*, had my meals in *Raleigh* and shared a bedroom in Maryfield House. The Dutch spoke good English and we got on very well together. Most had escaped from the 'nazi-occupied' Holland and were passionately devoted to their families and their country. When Holland was liberated they gave an enormous party in *Raleigh,* and Maryfield House, largely based on their Bols Gin, I recall it went on for 2 days at least.

ANTONY HOUSE:

The house was used as the WRNS Quarters and buses operated a frequent service between there and *Fisgard & Raleigh* picking up people, male and female along the way I caught an early morning bus at the top of School Lane (Antony passage) Directly opposite the American Camp entrance

The surrounding woods were full of American troops under canvas, with their tracked vehicles, all ready for the D-Day landings. The road down to Jupiter Point (of excellent construction and still good as ever today), had already been built by the Americans for their tanks, armoured cars and lorries. The foreshore at Jupiter Point and nearby beaches at Cremyll for example, was used as practice areas for landings. Even today in 1999 (ref: Jims Book) at Cremyll or along the lovely cliff top walk from the Rising Sun Pub at Kingsand towards Picklecombe Fort, you can find reminders of these mock landings, concrete slabs up to one yard square, composed of six or nine blocks and looking like pieces from a giant chocolate bar. They were part of the emergency hard surface ramps, down which heavy vehicles drove onto the assorted landing craft, beached ready to embark and transport the invasion forces across to Normandy.

In 1944 the American troops obviously knew where they were going and what the task was. They were very well paid by our standards and had a high disposable income to lavish on ladies they pursued. Their uniforms were smart and well cut and their generosity and determination to enjoy themselves before facing unknown future horrors across the Channel, made them popular with some local girls. Having the WRNS Quarters full of nubile, desirable females only yards away from their tents, must have presented a challenge to American know how and integrity, to outsmart Navy security and the strict non-fraternising-on-site rule. So did some enterprising love tryst in the bushes go on in 1944?, we shall never know. But oh, what stories those surviving trees in Antony House woods could tell us, *'if only they could speak'*

THE LOCAL WATERING HOLES:

The 'New Inn' at Wilcove (now the Wilcove Inn), the Ring O' Bells at Antony, the St. John's Inn, and the New Inn at Crafthole (now the Finnygook Inn), were all popular jaunts for naval personnel on runs ashore in 1944. Petrol was rationed until 1953 I believe, and private cars were rare, so Shank's pony or bus was the normal mode of transport to and from the pubs. Many Americans frequented these places also, and they usually got on very well with the landlords and locals as they spent freely and learned to play darts, shove-halfpenny and bar skittles. The Wilcove pub was largely patronized by Navy and Merchant Navy personnel, and the Ring O' Bells was often full of Americans and their girl friends. Occasionally, there was a punch-up between their service men and ours, usually sparked off by excess alcohol or some Brits. resenting the Yanks obvious ability to 'pull' the ladies. But this was the norm in all of south England ports at that time, so the odd fracas was accepted as the price to be paid for effective war-time collaboration between allies.

ooOoo

Thu. 2nd Mar. **BAY OF BISCAY:**

On the 22nd February H.M.L.S.T. *362,* part of a Convoy No. SL149, left Bizerta heading for Gibraltar, where they joined up with another convoy No. MKS40, sailing north bound for Liverpool. Whilst crossing the Bay of Biscay, German U-Boats attacked them. Several ships were hit including H.M.L.S.T.*362,* which sank at grid ref- 48o.N.17o.23'W. On board that ship either killed or drowned was a Torpoint sailor:

D/J 110980. RICHARD NORMAN SCOREY. Age 35.
CWG. PLYMOUTH WAR MEMORIAL Panel 87 Col 2.

Wed. 8th Mar. **PORTSMOUTH:**

At the shore base of HMS. *Gannet*, a Torpoint sailor:Died (No details)

D/SX 20. Ch/Yeoman of SIG. WILLIAN HARRY PARKER. Age 57
CWG. TORPOINT HORSOM CEMETERY Row 10 Grave 90

Wed. 29th Feb. **BURMA – RANGOON:**

Whilst on a bombing raid on Rangoon, a B24 Liberator Bomber '*Darling Diana'*, was hit by Japanese artillery and crashed, the crew of eight perished. One of the crew on board that plane was a young Royal Air Force lad from Mount Edgecumbe:

1659085. Sgt. ANTONY DESMOND RIVERSADALE BURGESS. AGE 19.
Royal Air Force 159 Sqdn. Grave Unknown.
COMMEMORATED ON THE SINGAPORE MEMORIAL COL. 435.

Fri. 31st Mar. **GERMANY:**

A crewmember of *Lancaster DV311* based at 61 Sqdn. Coninsby Lincolnshire, was killed during enemy action over Germany. He was a Torpoint airman:

1602927. SGT. (AIR GRN.) REGINALD THOMAS WEVILL. Age 21.
Royal Air Force Volunteer Reserve
CWG. HANOVER NIEDERSACHSEN GERMANY 8 J 5.

Sat. 1st Apr. **SOUTH WEST ENGLAND:**

In preparation for the forthcoming 'unknown invasion' the following warning was issued by the newspapers. Including other out of dates reports:

South Western News report
From April 1st 1944
'Prohibited Zones' along a coastal front extending in a ten mile belt in land, were to come into force, people who did not reside within the belt were prevented entering them or being there after April 1st. Everyone

over the age of sixteen must carry an Identity Card, a £5 pound fine would issued for any infringement against non carrying of Identity Cards and passes. Binoculars and telescopes must not be used by any unauthorized person. Letter boxes would be sealed up.

Saturday 8th April
More than two thirds of Cornwall affected by the ban on travelling to a protected area. A third not protected from Mawgan Parth to Devon border.

Tuesday 18th April.
Lax behavior on the part of young women must be checked - Government increasing pressure on recruiting women police, which Cornish Police resisted. Letter from Home Secretary asking about it. 'In view of lax conduct on the part of young women'. Chief Constable against women police. He said they'd have to be sent out in pairs, and in a car after dark. A sub committee appointed to go into the matter,(which had been debated for the last 3or4years),only two voted for an amendment, so Chairman said that nothing could be done.

Wednesday 19th April.
Case brought against a sale of rabbits in Devon without authority. Solicitor for Ministry of Food said the case was brought mainly as a warning - 'There is a great deal of illegal and underhand traffic going on and the authorities want to try and stamp it out'. Case dismissed. Defending solicitor was about the most trumpery and rotten that the Ministry had brought for a long time. 'And that is saying something'.

ooOoo

Tue. 4th Apr. **INDIA – KOHIMA:**

The unexpected landing of Japanese parachutists, happened at Kohima in India, where the local Garrison of 150 held on tenaciously to as much of the town as they could, until two and a half weeks later, reinforcements arrived to support them. In between times the Royal Air Force bombers from bases in Assam, flew more than two thousand sorties against the Japanese besiegers, whose losses were in the thousands. Then the battle for Kohima began.

The following is an extract of 'The action that took place at Kohima', and refers to the fighting during the battle, Probably the best eye witness account of an action.

As obtained from the Light Infantry Museum Durham City. and.is retyped with their permission.

'Quote'

"Here is an extract from a letter from an Officer of the 2nd Battalion. It is an account of the attack by the 2nd Div. On KOHIMA. And the latter advance down the road to IMPAL, 6th Brigade, seems to lead the Division when there is any real trouble, and the 2nd Battalion usually leads the 6th. They did magnificently? and as someone said. " The casualties they suffered were only proportionate to the results that they achieved". I have seen a good many of them in the last couple of months, and they are all very cheerful and pleased with themselves out here".

2nd Battalion The Durham Light Infantry S.E.A.C. (South East Asia Command).

THE DEFENCE OF SUMMERHOUSE HILL KOHIMA:

(Dated 28th August 1943)

On 17th of April, the Brigade had concentrated at M.S.42, about four miles from Kohima. By the 21st "B"&"D" Companys, and the Royal Berks. had relieved the Garrison of Summerhouse Hill, the Royal Berkshire Regiment on the east and south and the Battalion on the north and west except for Summerhouse Hill, the whole of Kohima was in Japanese hands.

The Hill had to be seen to be believed. The garrison of about 200 strong had been completely surrounded for about three weeks. They had been pushed back after each Japanese attack until they were crowded together on the last remaining feature. They had been unable to evacuate any of their wounded. They had been supplied by air, and the whole area was littered with parachutes, ammunition, water containers, dead mules etc. Quite a lot of stuff was still hanging in the trees, but Japanese snipers just wouldn't let you get them down. Our forward positions were overlooked by Kuki's Picquet the next feature which was Japanese held, and therefore movement was more than a little risky. Only the perimeter's were tactically sited and the rest were deep 'funk' holes.

On the morning of the 22nd, it was decided that my Company "D" should attack Kuki's Picquet, the next-door feature at dawn the following day, rumour had it that the Japanese were pulling out but why, no one could understand. "A"&"C" Company's, were then ordered up on to the hill, "C" to take over from "D" who were to lie up for the night, and "A" to come into reserve to exploit what successes were gained. The relief was completed under a heavy smoke screen, without incident, and we settled down for a quite night.

The dispositions were as follows, "C" Company were facing the Japanese on Kuki's Picquet, "D" were in non tactical holes just behind, "B"&"A" were on a plateau about 100 feet below.

Just before 'stand to', my attack which had been put in elsewhere by the Royal Berkshire Regiment and the Royal Welsh Fusiliers had failed. I heaved a sigh of relief, as I didn't believe in this 'pulling out' theory.

About 1830 the Japanese put over about 20 rounds of 75mm and a few spring grenades, most of which landed on the forward platoon of "C" Company. There were quite a few casualties and it was unpleasant, but just the Japanese's nightly hate.

All was quite again and as the Commanding Officer told me to have a good night's sleep, I settled down to it.

Then about 0140 the Japanese opened up on "C" company again with mortars and spring grenade. I turned over and said to myself that it was nothing to do with me and tried to go to sleep again. It just didn't work and the noise increased.

The "C" company platoon on the forward slope were taking a good hammering. Japanese automatics had all our Light Machine Guns pinpointed, and they were losing men fast.

By now quite a few trees were on fire, an ammunition dump was hit and the place looked like Blackpool on a summer night, plus a firework display.

Things were getting pretty serious. The Japanese lengthened their range, mixing smoke and High Explosive, and at the same time attacked the unfortunate platoon of "C" Company in great strength. The Japanese came up the slope shoulder to shoulder, the leading wave wearing respirators and throwing phosphorous grenades. They were knocked down but as soon as one man fell another took his place. The inevitable happened and the Japanese broke through the centre.

Jack Ailey, the platoon commander was fairly badly hit and the position on the left and right was very confused. I managed to get my company to form a line about "C" company Head Quarters, and we held the Japanese there. Every now and then we managed to push forward a little but our casualties were heavy. We were now lying shoulder to shoulder and were suffering very badly from spring grenades. Martin Wilson, second-in-command of "C" company was badly hit but refused to be moved till the others had been evacuated.

All line had gone and most of the wireless sets, our gunner at the observation post was killed and it took us nearly two hours to get any defensive fire.

About 0400 we started to counter-attack the right flank. Bill Watson "D" Company was killed leading one of these. He was last seen clubbing Japs. with the butt-end of a Bren. Willie Lockhart second-in-command of "D", was also killed by a burst from an automatic.

The Japanese were taking a pretty good beating too, and we could hear then shouting and screaming just below us. They seemed to have had just about enough and some officer was trying to reorganize them to attack again.

There was a short lull. Roger Stock, Officer in Charge "C" Company and I had a cigarette together and talked of Teesdale and our next leave.

The Japanese attacked again. That was the last I saw of Roger, he went forward to his hard-pressed company, and I back too collect the clerks and cook. When I returned I was told that Roger had been killed and Pat Rome wounded.

The Japanese didn't get any further but they were holding on to what they had got. I went across to Battalion Head Quarters to put them in the picture and saw that John Steel and Tom Claque were O.K. They told me Gibbs-Kennett had been killed attacking a Japanese position single-handed.

I saw the Royal Berkshire Company Commander on our left and everything was quiet with them, I nearly got shot by his batman for my trouble.

At about 0500 hrs the Commanding Officer ordered "A" Company up from down below to try and regain the lost ground. They went in with great dash, retook two positions but failed on the third, largely due to the fact that they only arrived the previous evening and hadn't seen the ground before. The Japanese from Kuki's Picquet opened up with all they had and "A" Company had to come back. Peter Stockton was killed, Baker and Sean Kelley, who was commanding "A" Company were wounded.

We then dug in on the line "D" Company was holding. Martin Wilson died from wounds during the morning.

The 23rd was spent licking our wounds and strengthening our positions. Tony Shuttle, Cedric Cowan, 'Ding Dong' Bell, Conkey Greenwell and John Rolland arrived up to reinforce us. "A" Company took over the forward positions and "C" & "D" became one Company. With one platoon on the right, one forming a second line behind "A" Company, with the third platoon in reserve.

The 24th to 26th was quiet except for sniping. All food and water was supplied by air. Tommy Benwick managed to get up all the ammunition we wanted in carrions supported by tanks.

Battalion Head Quarters had moved slightly down the hill between "B2 Company and us and a platoon of "D" Company had taken over the right hand platoon of the Royal Berkshire Regiment.

During the afternoon of the 27th the "D" Company platoon was heavily mortared and the Commanding Officer relieved them by a platoon of "A" Company.

About midnight the fun started again if you can call it that. All positions were mortared with the main concentrations on the left hand platoon "A" Company. The Japanese drill for the attack was the same as for the 23rd, and they attacked with about 2 companies the "A" Company platoon on the left. The leading man carried bags full of grenades but no weapons. They again broke through owing to weight of numbers and got on the plateau on the top of the hill, here they went round and round shouting 'Tojo' and blessing the Mikado (it was the old boys birthday). Finally they settled down to dig in on the plateau but not in very great strength.

The Commanding Officer ordered 'Conky' Greenwell and Battle Patrol, and a Composite Force under Tony Shuttle to put in a counter attack. This went in on 2 sides at first light. 'Conky' went over the top blowing his horn, a great sound, and they caught the Japs. with their pants down. The Japanese packed up and ran and as luck would have it, found cover in our own smoke, which was blanketing 'Kuki's Piquet. The defensive fire was first class 3.7's 25 pounders, and our mortars fired off and on through the night. Our mortars fired 1300 rounds and caused the Japanese heavy casualties.

On the 30th, we were relieved by the Royal Welsh Fusiliers, and went down for 48 hours rest.

Unquote'.

ooOoo

Sun. 23rd Apr.**KOHIMA.**

During the days fighting a Torpoint soldier was killed in action:

53773. Major. REGINALD GIBBS-KENNETT. Age 31.

Durham Light Infantry.

CWG. KOHIMA MEMORIAL KOHIMA 12 A.7.

Fri. 30th Apr.**PLYMOUTH:**

Plymouth attacked. This time the main target was the shipping anchored in Plymouth Harbour, HMS. *King George V* along with other ships. This raid was to be the first and last that the Germans carried out, using what then was the first Radio Controlled Bombs, which could be steered onto their targets. 12 Dormer's Do.217s released 1500kg Fritz-X armour piecing bombs. The defences put up such a dense smoke screen, that none of the bombs hit their intended targets. Two bombs landed at Laire, and another two landed at Stoke. In all 14 bombs fell during that night, 10 fell on Government property, in Cremyll and one 1000 kg. Parachute bomb landed at West Antony Farm but failed to explode, UXB was defused the following day by the BDS. One at Penpell Farm Stoke Climsland, and one at Glebe Farm Havelock, no damage was caused anywhere. During the attack, four German planes were destroyed: A Junkers Ju.88 of 5/KG6, A Focke-Wulf 190 of 3/SKG10.

A Mosquito piloted by Sq/L D.J. Williams and F/O C. J. Kirkpatrick of 406 Squadron, shot down a Dornier Do 217 of StabIII/KG100. The plane crashed into the sea off the Sound. Two survivors came ashore in Whitsand Bay and were captured. The same crew of the Mosquito's of 406 Squadron shot down another Dornier Do217 of 9/KG100. It crashed at Pasture Farm Blackawton Devon. All crew members killed.

TORPOINT:

Record Log No. 5187 incidents reported on 30/4/44 – Incident #. unknown:

03.10~ Torpoint.~ Siren sounded 03.34 Kingsands reported the dropping of bombs in the vicinity of the Breakwater. Situation reported as at 14.35 hrs 30/4/44 In all 14. HE. bombs fell, 12 exploded,2 UXB, one West Antony Farm Torpoint, one at Glebe Farm

SOUTH WEST ENGLAND:

Western Morning News:

After nearly 6 months respite (last raid 16/11/43), raid in early hours 3.15. and lasted about 70 minutes. Between 30 and 35 aircraft. One plane brought down in the sea.From one raider, most of the crew escaped by parachute,and members of the Home Guard controlling Whitsands collected them as they made their way ashore in rubber dinghies. Raid hit Mile House region,as well as Plymouth (Twyford's retrospective account).

Monday 1st May.

Germans claimed Plymouth bombed, the centre of concentrated attacks. First bombers reached Plymouth 3.30 am and for 20 minutes a large number of HE's and Incendiaries bombs were dropped. Germans also claimed attacks were made on shipping concentrating off the south west coast. A number of people killed and injured, and twenty cows.

Large Number of Planes over Dover,People thought invasion had started. Three planes,some damage.

ooOoo

Fri. 26th May.**IRAQ - HABBANIYA**

After running out of fuel, Dakota *KG494* crashed in stormy weather near Habbaniya Iraq. A member of its crew was a Torpoint airman:

574148. FT/SGT. EDWIN GEORGE WILLIAM BROAD. Age 22.

Royal Air Force

CWG. HABBANIYA CEMETERY IRAQ.

SOUTH WEST ENGLAND:

Western Morning News report:

Monday 29/30th May.

Planes flew along the coast, Spying for invasion activity (ships).

ooOoo

TORPOINT:

Norman Beaver MBE. recalls:

Another outstanding memory of the war was the arrival of the Americans, and their ability to boast and share their candy with us. A few days before D-Day some of my school friends and I walked past HMS. *Raleigh,* which was occupied by the G.I's and so renamed "Fort *Raleigh*"! Here the Yanks were confined before boarding for The Normandy Landings. Also Landing Craft were being loaded from the Ferry Beach at Torpoint. Of course now, as adults we understand how serious those times were and that many men would never return to their respective countries.

(Author's note: March-June 1944)?

John Peach recalls:

Torpoint was to see a large American presence in the area. Preparations for the D-Day landings, saw the occupancy of Tregantle Fort, among other places, hundreds of soldiers could be seen lining the Ferry beaches, waiting to board the war ships at anchor in the Hamoaze. At last the war was going our way.

ooOoo

Thur. 1st Jun. **TORPOINT / HAMOAZE:**

Anchored in the river Tamar, Lyner, Hamoaze and the waterways surrounding the shores of Torpoint, were numerous Landing Ship Tanks (LST's), and Landing Craft (LCT's). The American 115th Battalion with all its men, armoured vehicles and artillery equipment, on the Torpoint side of the Hamoaze, were due to embark on the waiting craft. Torpoint woke up to see the departure of the American troops from the surrounding area. HMS *Raleigh* had become a dispersal point for their departure. From there they marched down to the Torpoint slipway, to board landing crafts, which took them out to the waiting Troopships, anchored in the River Tamar. Other dispersal points for American troops, was at Jupiter Point, and Cremyll. Once they, their equipment, armoured vehicles, etc., had been loaded aboard the Troopships, they departed on their way to Southampton, where the Invasion Fleet were gathering, before finally setting sail to the French coast of Normandy.

Thur. 1st. Jun.

The following photos of U.S. GIs leaving Torpoint en-route to the assembly point of the vast Invasion Fleet heading for the Normandy Beaches. The first photo also illustrates the devastation caused by the earlier bombing.

Column of GIs line up in Ferry Street (now the Ferry Lanes)
Photo taken from the top of Ferry Toll gate

GI's waiting for Landing Craft on Slipway

GI's Boarding Landing Crafts thence to be taken to the Troopships in the Sound

Loading supplies & equipment at Cremyll

Convoy of half tracks ammunition and tanks being loaded

Mon. 5th Jun. **FRANCE - NORMANDY**

Operation 'OVERLORD' began late in the evening at 11.55. British Infantry men, members of the 6th Airborne Division, landed by Gliders at the French Village of B'enouville, 6 miles North of Caen. Amongst those infantry men was Harry Webber, from Millbrook, in the Devon & Dorset Regiment. From Torpoint, tank driver Cyril Price. 23rd Hussars Regiment - 11th Armoured Div. 28th Armoured Brigade.

Tues 6th Jun. **D-Day - INVASION DAY:**

As part of the massive invasion force, and the intended spearhead for driving the Germans north, and finally out of France, back to Germany. The invasion fleet sailed for the beaches in Normandy, of Utah, Omaha, (American Objectives), and Gold, Juno and Sword (British and Commonwealth Objectives). The invasion forces were met with much ferocity from the Germans. With their superior power, abundant supplies of ordinance, they took the beaches, but not without sustaining heavy casualties.

[Author's note: In November 2008, a party of nine from the Torpoint Conservative Club and Members of the Royal British Legion made a three-day trip to visit the Cemeteries of Normandy. There, they laid nine wreaths donated from different Torpoint Association's and Military Regiments. In the museum at Arromanche, there was a life size model of a GI of the American 115th Infantry Division who was about to leave a Landing Craft his name was:
Private Harry Porley. Stated on the wall was his comments that read:

'As our boat touched sand and the ramp lowered,
I became a visitor to hell.'

One cannot imagine the horrors that he and others faced, as they fought their way up the beaches of Normandy. However, the nine wreaths laid at different cemeteries had a poignant connection with Torpoint].

As the invading armies advanced inland, they drove the Germans away from their defensive positions along the French coast. By the 13th of June, the Americans had captured Nantes, approx 230 miles inland, across the River Loire. Not far away was a small village called Montaigu, this very quickly was to be taken by the Americans. However, Montaigu was the site of a secret weapon, and perhaps was, the first VI weapon site to be discovered by the allied forces. A very significant discovery in respect to **PLYMOUTH** and the surrounding area, the reason will be revealed later.

As part of Hitler's continuing strategy to wipe out England. His German scientist had been secretly developing other forms of bombs. These became to be known as, the VI and VII. Although Torpoint was never to receive any of these items of destruction, they did however, get involved in different way. It might be worth stating a few facts about the VI and VII, Hitler's "Revenge Weapons".

The V1 Oder Vergeltungswaffe Eins (Revenge Weapon 1), popularly known as the Doodlebug or Buzz bomb. A pilot-less, mid wing monoplane, with a wingspan of 17ft. 6inch. Overall length-25feet 4.1/2 inches. Designed to travel a distance of approx 130miles, at a height of 6,500 feet. Its flying time was 25-30 mins duration. A gyroscopic unit that operated it governed the direction, altitude, and range of flight automatically, and the air operated rudder and elevator, which stabilized the bomb. Constructed out of thin sheet steel and plywood, it was capable of carrying a warhead of 850kg of High Explosives. Its engine was a petrol fed, pulse jet, mixed with compressed air as an oxidizer, the sound of its engine brought fear amongst the waiting populace below, because of its pulsating exhaust, that gave of a rapid stuttering sound, which when its fuel run out, just cut-out, due to its loaded front weight, and immediately fell sharply and silently towards the ground. There was a pregnant pause, and dreaded wait, before with an almighty bang, it exploded upon impact, causing serious destruction and many casualties, mostly fatal as it hit houses.

After the D-Day Landings and the advance of the Allied forces, VI sites, were over-run by the Americans, which happened to be the first noticeable evidence, that they had been intended for launching in the direction of Plymouth. In all the inaccuracy of the Flying Bombs, landing on a specific target, were negligible, if the Germans had launched them before their discovery at Montaigu. The probability being, one or more would have been aimed at Plymouth. Could well have exploded in **TORPOINT.** However, that was not the case. When the Germans did retreat, it was only a matter of days, before they unleashed their Flying Bombs further up the coast of France, in the direction of London and the Home Counties.

Mon 13th Jun. **SOUTH EAST ENGLAND:**

Following the invasion at Normandy, the first four Doodlebugs landed on England mainly in the home counties around London. It was the start of the second Blitz on London. These Flying bomb attacks continued, and gained intensity as the days went by. **The daily bombs that landed on London and the home counties between the 13th June to the 1st of September was 102.**

It was then that "The Third Evacuation Plan" began. 'Evacuation Rivulet' Evacuees from Laondon and the surrounding Home Counties took refuge in the South West. Torpoint was then to receive and become a place of solace to many London refugees as listed Later.

The following two sketches, illustrate the reality of its likelihood of the Germans VI programme Landing in Plymouth and its surrounding areas

[Authors Collage with Kind permission of Before and After the Battle]

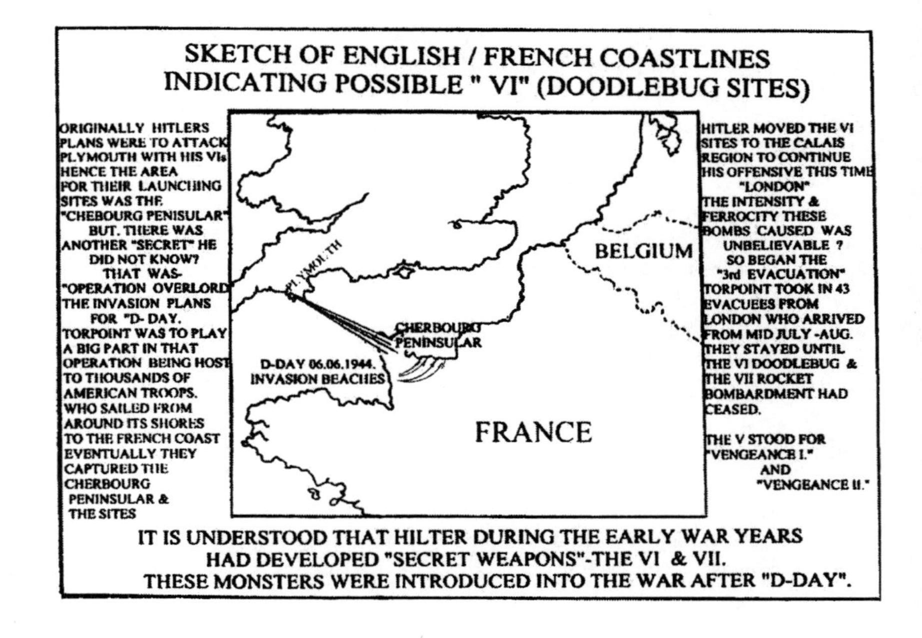

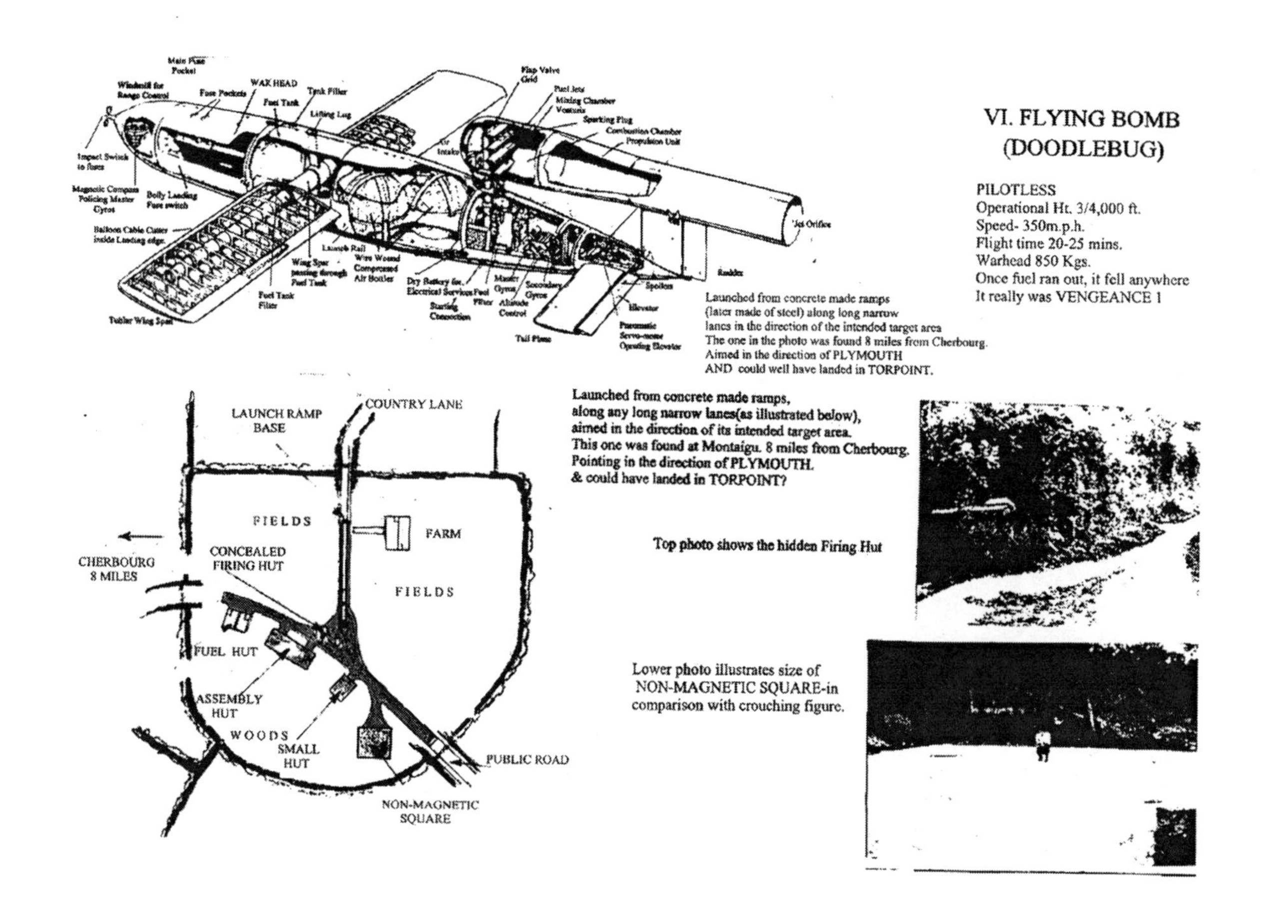

VI. FLYING BOMB (DOODLEBUG)

PILOTLESS
Operational Ht. 3/4,000 ft.
Speed- 350m.p.h.
Flight time 20-25 mins.
Warhead 850 Kgs.
Once fuel ran out, it fell anywhere
It really was VENGEANCE 1

Launched from concrete made ramps
(later made of steel) along long narrow
lanes in the direction of the intended target area
The one in the photo was found 8 miles from Cherbourg.
Aimed in the direction of PLYMOUTH
AND could well have landed in TORPOINT.

Launched from concrete made ramps,
along any long narrow lanes(as illustrated below),
aimed in the direction of its intended target area.
This one was found at Montaigu. 8 miles from Cherbourg.
Pointing in the direction of PLYMOUTH.
& could have landed in TORPOINT?

Top photo shows the hidden Firing Hut

Lower photo illustrates size of
NON-MAGNETIC SQUARE-in
comparison with crouching figure.

Thu. 15th Jun. **ENGLISH CHANNEL:**

One of the ships taking part in the sea defensive operation, supporting the D-Day Landings, was HMS. *Mourne* which was sunk by a U boat off the West Cortin Peninsula, onboard that ship killed or, drowned was a Torpoint sailor:

D/JX 339013. A/B. ERNEST JOHN PALMER. Age 21.
CWG. PLYMOUTH NAVAL MEMORIAL Panel 87 Col 1.

Sun. 8th Jul. **TORPOINT:**

The second evacuation plan, Code name **'Operation Rivulet'**. Began and Torpoint became host to a number of besieged Londoners and the Home counties The first person to arrive from London in Torpoint, was a Mrs. A. L. Bragoli. She was billeted out to 18, Fore Street. Her date of return to London is not known.

Over the following weeks other evacuees were to arrive in Torpoint a total number of 42, were to billeted out in various addresses these are as follows:

Wed. 12th July	Mrs. B. L. Whittaker (from Croydon) to 54, Macey Street Returned to London on the 3rd November 1944
Fri. 14th July	Mrs. F. Hutchins (from Leytonstone) to 1, Chapeldown Terrace Returned to London on 6th October 1944
Date unknown	Mrs. G. F. Breeze (from Epsom) to 97, Clarence Road Returned to London on 9th October 1944
Sat. 15th July	Mrs. M. Downing (from Twickenham) to 3, Chapel Row Returned to London on 9th October 1944
Mon. 17th July	Mrs. C. J. Armitage (from Dagenham) to 11, Waterloo Road Returned to London on 28th January 1945
Date unknown	Mrs. D. Duchy (from Dagenham) to 5, Arthur Terrace Left for Padstow date unknown
Tues. 18th July	Mrs. T. M. Arpons (from London) to 3, King Street Returned to London on 22nd January 1945
Wed. 19th July	Mrs. A. G. Webb (from Esher) to 54, Clarence Road Returned to London on 11th May 1945
Thur. 20th July	Baxter J. W. (13 yrs. old from London) to 16, The Cresent Returned to London on 18th October 1944
Tues. 25th July	Mrs. G. M. Mills (from London) to 11. Montpellier Terrace Returned to London on 1st. October 1944
Date unknown	Mrs. K. M. Dawnes (from Rochester) to 21, Mt. Edgecombe Terrace Returned 9th to London in November 1944
Date unknown	Mrs. J.G. Mitchell (from Chingford) to 10, Harvey Street Returned to London on 27th October 1944
Date unknown	Miss. Burnell Shula (9 yrs. old from London) to 1, Gorian Terrace Returned to London on 27th May 1945

Fri. 27th July	Mrs. J.J.S (from Malden) to 42, Clarence Road Returned to Malden on 25th April 1945
Date unknown	Mr. George Good (from Thurock) to 56, Macey Street (deceased)
Sun. 30th July	Mrs. D. Angled (from Hendon) to 3, Lytherton Terrace Returned to Hendon on 23rd August 1944
Tues. 1st Aug.	Mrs. A. Bristow (from London) to 35, Clarence Road Returned to London on 16th October 1944
Wed. 2nd Aug.	Mr. & Mrs. A.G. Lane (from Godstone) to 4, Park Road Returned to Godstone on 3rd October 1944
Date unknown	Mrs. R. H. Williams (from Southgate) to 7, Clarence Road Returned to Southgate on 19th August 1944
Date unknown	Mrs. D. B. R. Williams (from London) to 13, The Cresent Returned to London on 6th October 1944
Fri. 4th Aug.	Mr. & Mrs. H.T. Gould (from Harrow) to Jubilee Inn 17, Fore Street Returned to Harrow on 14th October 1944
Date unknown	Mrs. J.G. Ashwell (from Beckenham) to 32, Clarence Road Returned date not known
Thur. 10th Aug.	Mrs. L. G. Glenville (from London) to 5, Gale Terrace Returned date not known
Fri. 11th Aug.	Mrs. K. G. Wyles (from London) to 4, Lytherton Terrace Returned to London on 8th November 1944
Date unknown	Mrs. C.G. Hoonton (from London) to 4, Lytherton Terrace Returned to London on 8th November 1944
Sat. 12th Aug.	Mr. & Mrs. G. Swanson (from London) to 2, Kingsway Terrace Returned to London on 26th August 1944
Date unknown	Mrs. G. Lawrence (from Poplar) to 3, Grovenor Terrace Returned to Poplar on 10th December 1944
Sun. 13th Aug.	Mrs. V.M. Hoat (from London) to 19, The Cresent Returned to London on 18th October 1944

ooOoo

ATLANTIC:

War Diary by L/Telegraphist Banham:

10th July 1944:

Well here we at sea again ploughing our way through the Atlantic at 25knots. en route for Gibraltar.

After returning from our little part in the invasion, we went into dock for new guns and a few minor repairs, and were fortunate enough to get 7 days leave which was much enjoyed, and very welcome after our rather strenuous three weeks off the French coast.

It was expected that we would be returning over there for more bombarding or perhaps new landings, but it was no great surprise to hear we were going to the Mediterranean again, as it is possible that landings will be made on the south coast of France, or further East in the Greece area. So we are on our way, to what we can only guess! July 10th 1944.

CEYLON – COLOMBO:

Arthur Corbidge recalls*:*

On the 19th August I was drafted from *Renown* to Lanka Barracks in Colombo then by passenger to Mombassa where I joined HMS. *Falmouth*. A town class Frigate. We use to do convoy duties from Aden to Durban. One voyage I will never forget, it was when we had to escort HMS *Valiant* to Capetown, she had to go around the Cape as she could not be trusted to go through the Suez Canal as she was in the Floating Dock in Trinco when the dock turned over and apparently done some damage to her and she had to make her own way back to the U.K. for refit, but I did hear she was scrapped instead. While we were going to Durban we was escorted by the South African Air force doing Submarine Patrol. We were about 16 hours sailing out of Durban and over came the plane. I was the duty Petty Officer of the watch and was on the bridge checking the look-outs, when I saw the aircraft acting rather dangerously, I drew it to the attention of the Officer of the watch and ?then to the Sea boat and manned it ready. Suddenly it crashed off our Port bow, we rushed to it lowering the Sea boat the same time, and within minutes I had hold of one of the crews hand he was still alive but only just, we put him in the stern sheets and grabbed another but he was dead, but as we pulled him in so Johnny sharko took his left leg, we went to pick up another member of the crew, but we were too late the sharks had got him. We steamed at full speed for Durban but the Pilot was dead before we got there. The warning went all over Durban & all the beaches were cleared, for the sharks were following us into the harbour. After we attended the enquiry we proceeded to Capetown for 8 weeks for a refit, then I went to Pretoria for 2 weeks leave.

We were lucky, just after I had joined her we were told the Captain was going to be relieved and the new Captain was a Lt. Com. Cutler. He was coming from Trincomalee, I knew him and had served with him when he was in command of the barracks in Trinco. He was a very strict disciplinarian but very fair. I spoke to my messmates and warned them to watch certain points, and also about allowing the lads to call them 'Knocker' and 'Geordie'. One was called White and the other Haddle, and if they were caught, the new Captain would say 'If you like to be familiar with your ratings then join them'. So they took notice and we never had any complaints.

ooOoo

TORPOINT:

More evacuees arrived from London:

Mon. 21st Aug. Ivy Dagger (London) to 25, Fore Street
Returned to London on 29th October 1944
Kemp. Leslie. R. (9 yrs. London) to 49, Clarence Road
Kemp. Edward. D. (8 yrs. London) to 49, Clarence Road
Kemp. Barry. G. (6 yrs. London) to 49, Clarence Road
Kemp. David. L. (3 yrs. London) to 49, Clarence Road
All four brothers Returned to London on 17th March 1945

Tue. 5th Sept. Mrs. H.G. Else. (Poplar) to 1, North Road
Returned to Poplar on 14th October 1944

Fri. 8th Sept. Mrs. V. Hooker (London) to 57, Clarence Road
Returned to London on 14th October 1944
Mrs. C. M. English (Ilford) to Merton Carbeile Road
Returned to Ilford on 24th October 1944

Mon. 2nd Oct. Mr. & Mrs. A . Pollen (London) to 6, Park Road
Returned to London on 22nd November1944.

Wed. 20th Dec. Harriette Arney (Leyton) to 8, Clarence Road
Returned to Leyton on 17th February

ooOoo

1945
YEAR SIX

TORPOINT:

Mon. 22nd Jan. Mrs. A. Patience (London) to 3, Park Street
Returned to London on 3rd March 1945

Thu. 8th Feb. **GERMANY WEST FAHLAN :**

After the Battle of the Bulge, with the advancing Allies determination to get to Berlin The German Army was hampered by The R.A.F destroying their supply lines to the rear, however they put up a stiff resistance around the Reichswald Barrier towards Cleve and Udem. The Scottish 15th. Division was engaged in the thick of it, but sustained losses, among those killed was Torpoint soldier:

2570025. Cpl. CHRISTOPHER NEWTON. Age 28.
9th *Cameron Highlanders Scottish Rifles.*
CWG. REICHSWALD KLEVE NORDRHEIN WEST FAHLAN 54 F 10.

TORPOINT:

The following evacuees arrived in Torpoint:

Tue. 27th. Mar. Cain James (13 yrs. London) to Salamanca House
Returned to London on 23rd August 1945

Sun. 1st. Apr. Howard Hubbard (16 yrs. London) to 4, Park Street
Return to London unknown

ooOoo

Norman Beavers. MBE. recalls:

The war with Germany was coming to an end, and one of my last memories of the war was the grounding of the *James Egan Lane* off Wiggle beach, This American Liberty ship was down in the stern with two thirds Of her above water, never then did we ever suspect she would end up as recreation for todays scuba divers.

Now back at school, what did the future hold for me on leaving school? Employment In the Torpoint and Rame Peninsular was in the Royal Dockyard, and to become an apprentice one had to pass the entrance examination. As I have already explained I was not much of a academic, having lost quite a lot of school time. Dad insisted that I should become an apprentice of sorts and was ready to find a master outside of the Dockyard if I failed the entrance exam. Much to my surprise I passed. If I remember correctly I was around 158 out of 200 apprentices that were accepted. Now having no idea what trade to take, the name "ship–fitter" looked promising, so I became No. 34947 and started working life as a Dockyard Matie. Although the war with Germany was over, Japan had yet to surrender, but there was little feeling that we were still at war.

Mon. 30th Apr.**GERMANY: BERLIN:**

Adolf Hitler German Dictator commits suicide, together with his mistress Eva Braun, finally bringing to an end the **Third Reich**

&

END OF THE SECOND WORLD WAR IN EUROPE.

Mon. 7th May. **TORPOINT:**
Jim Smith MBE. recalls:

The land campaign in Europe ended with unconditional German surrender on 7th May 1945 and the following Day. All over the continent people gave vent to their feelings of joy and relief in fantastic parties, an seen in documentary films on T.V. In the signal 'Splice the mainbrace' was received from Admiralty, an order guaranteed to make the Lower Deck smile. It was a traditional way of authorizing the issue of an extra tot of rum to officers and ratings over 20 years old. It was also a rare instruction given to mark some great national event, or exceptionally, it was ordered by the ship's captain to reward men at the successful end of some very arduous task. Such as splicing the mainbrace on a square-rigged sailing ship, or coaling ship in the days of steam.

Tuesday MAY 8th 1945

John Peach recalls:

Now for the happy conclusion. After nearly six years of extreme hardship, loss of homes, and even greater loss of life, the war with Germany was at last at an end. On the Morning of May 8th 1945 after hearing the news on the radio, Mum came into our room, gave us a hug and probably weeping a little said **" Its all over, the war is over".**

ooOoo

Victory In Europe Celebrations took place on the Torpoint Foreshore.

Bonfire being built on Torpoint shore line
(where the Rowing club stands today.
Note the Gasometer in background)

Dancing outside the Kings Head.

Wednesday May 9th.

Official ouside Service

Sunday May 13th.

Celebrations on Foreshore

ooOoo

PLYMOUTH:

Mrs Marjorie Harwood recalls

I was very proud to be one of the NAAFI Contingent, to march in the V.E. and Victory Parade in Plymouth. We had to practice marching for two weeks before, with the Regimental Sgt. It seemed a long way to march from the Plymouth Public Library before we came to the Royal Parade. When we saw the 'Saluting Base' heard the order 'eyes right' our hearts were bursting with joy and pride, 'we had done it, we had won'. No more bombing, fighting, and loss of life. We thanked God we were free. Peace at last. But we had the Japanese to contend with after that. We were not happy until our men were home form the Far East.

ooOoo

EAST AFRICA INDIAN OCEAN:

Arthur Corbidge recalls:

We sailed from Capetown to Durban then on to Mauritius, then on to Rangoon in Burma. Rangoon was a nice run ashore but very dangerous to land, the rivers were very fast running and full of poisonous fish and if you fell in you never lived, we lost one young lad. We used to go out on patrols along the coast for about a week then come in, refuel, and take on provisions. We had approximately 20 Somalis on board, they used to do duties in the mess and also on deck, and in the morning they always scrubbed the Quarterdeck and dried it before we ever turned to, but this morning the provisions boat came along side to deliver the spuds, so they were taken off the deck job and loaded the spuds on board, so the deck was still wet when we turned to. Georgie told one of the lads to squeegee down the deck, but it so happened he told the wrong one, he was a Rhodesian and he refused to do it and said 'I'm not clearing up after a coloured man', so naturally he was charged with "disobedience of orders". He was taken before the O.O.W. (Officer of the Watch) and then to the O.O.D.) Officer of the Day) and he still refused to do it and was put under escort and charged with "Direct Disobedience of Orders". When we went to sea that day they allowed him to carry on with his normal duties. He was on watch in the Asdic Office when he asked the Officer of the Watch if he could be relieved to go to the toilet, down he went and about five minutes after we got a shout from aft, "MAN OVERBOARD" He had thrown himself overboard. We searched around for him, but all we found was a piece of a singlet covered with blood, so we guessed right away that he had been cut up by the propellers. We went back to Rangoon and were then ordered to proceed to Star Island with a load of pieces of equipment to build a prefabricated lighthouse, which the Japs had destroyed. We were ashore and had erected it, we had settled for the night ready to return to the ship in the morning, when we received a signal to return immediately. We rushed to the whaler and were pulling to the ship when the motor-boat took us in tow. When we were about half way back rockets and verie lights started to fly, we thought naturally we were being attacked with the Japs but there was no gunfire which seemed queer. So when we got alongside they hoisted us straight away, we were secured for sea, then we were told the Japs had surrendered and we were sailing for Singapore.

ooOoo

Thur. 26th Jul. **LONDON:**

The coalition Government that had been the centre of the Government throughout the period of the war was disbanded. After voting had been counted it was declared the Labour Government had won a sweeping victory over the Tories and Clement Atlee was declared leader of the Labour Government.

Mon. 30th Jul. **TORPOINT:**

The Royal Navy withdrew its supplementary manning of the Torpoint Ferries, and with so many Torpoint men still enlisted in the services there became a shortage of manpower, the ferries could not be fully manned and with the departure of many female employees, who wanted to return to domestic chores, it was not possible to maintain a full service, therefore only one ferry was in operation for several months, until male employees became more available.

ooOoo

Mon. 6th Aug. **JAPAN – HOROSHIMA:**

The first Atomic Bomb was dropped by the Americans on the Japanese city of Hiroshima laying it to waste, the devastation of its power was awesome and a definite warning to all.

<u>SO BEGAN THE AGE OF THE ATOMIC BOMB</u>

Thur. 9th Aug. **JAPAN – NAGASAKI:**

A second Atomic Bomb was dropped by the Americans this time on the Japanese city of Nagasaki, again laying it to waste..

Tues. 14th Aug.

The Japanese Empire surrenders unconditionally.

Thur. 16th Aug.

The war against Japan is declared over, bringing to an end.

WORLD WAR II

ooOoo

TORPOINT:
With the Victory in the Far East More celebrations!

Thursday 16th August

Thanksgiven Service
Gathering at bottom of Harvey Street

Floral Dance

Childrens Street party on the waterfront.

V- Table layout between Pole & Cowan Terrace's
Note the lack of cars?

Childrens Street Party at Pole & Cowen Terrece (now Buller Road)
Mums & the Old Folk serve the Spam & Jam sandwiches

[Authors Note: The celebrations in Britain did carry on for some time, nevertheless there were many Servicemen still serving overseas in many different countries and on different seas as related by Arthur Corbidge:]

MALAYA Straits of MALLACA:

Arthur Corbidge recalls:

We arrived in the Straits of Malacca, where we had to wait for the Pilot, as there were a lot of mines about. On our way to Singapore, I was ordered by the Captain to find something to use as a Jackstaff for when we entered Singapore. I hunted amongst the timber in the timber rack in the port waist and it seemed my luck was in. I found the actual Jackstaff with the Crown attached, with five of the lads we sandpapered the staff and re-varnished it. When we entered Singapore on the 7th September 1945, if you knew anything about the peacetime Navy you would understand how the ship and the ships company felt, for Singapore was HMS Falmouth's home, she was well known in Singapore before the war as the 'White Lady' as she was painted overall white with a yellow funnel and yellow masts, she was the Commander in Chief China Fleets Yacht. We sailed in and joined with HMS *Rotherham* commanded by Captain H.W. Biggs DSO & HMS *Sussex* flying the flag of Vice Admiral C.S. Holland C.B., they had arrived on the 4th and had received the surrender of the Japanese Fleet and the Japanese Army. After we had anchored, we hoisted the Jack in its proper place. I cannot be sure, but I would estimate we were one of the first to do so after the war. So when we had completed anchoring, the Captain said 'Hoist the Flags' and up they went. IVOR, MONKEY, TACKLINE, BAKER, APPLE, CHARLIE, KATIE. Which reads 'I'M BACK'. Vice Admiral Holland came aboard and welcomed the ship back, we were so proud.

ooOoo

Sun. 8th Sept. **JAPAN – ASAKA:**

After years in captivity as a FEPOW.(Far East Prisoner of War.)
A Torpoint soldier died. Cause unknown:

1415975. S/SGT. GERALD GOLLEDGE. Age 40.

1st. Hong Kong Regt. Hong Kong and Singapore Royal Artillery.

CWG. SAI WAN BAY MEMORIAL HONG KONG.

ooOoo

PORTSMOUTH:

Jim Smith MBE. recalls:

On leaving Fisgard, I joined a new 17.000-ton light Fleet Aircraft Carrier HMS. *Vengeance*, which left Portsmouth with no aircraft on board, at high speed via the short route (the Suez Canal) for Singapore and Hong Kong. There we embarked battered aircraft, Army and Navy vehicles, plus a group of equally damaged service men and civilians from the nearby hospitals, airfields and camps. It was a heart-rending, scene as some struggled to climb the ships steep gangways and we saw the heavy price of victory paid by some unlucky personnel in the Far East War. We returned home slowly by the scenic route, stopping at Ceylon, the South African ports of Durban, Port Elizabeth, Capetown, Freetown and Gibraltar. At Capetown, the ship's captain was invited to send a detachment to take part in the end of War Victory Parade and he led it personally through the streets of this beautiful city. The passengers were distributed in several messes, with special medical support and supervision and 'Jack' was as compassionate and hospitable as ever.

It was rumored that the messes ran a weigh gained competition (with unofficial gambling on the winner of course) to fatten up the guests before we docked in Pompey. Because we carried no serviceable aircraft, there were plenty of deck-hockey games and exercise sessions in the sunshine on the flight deck to get them fit as well as fat. For those who had not participated before, there was the usual hilarious and raucous Crossing the Line Ceremony as we crossed the Equator. In Belfast, we off-loaded most aircraft for repair, in Plymouth, we landed stores and personnel and we returned to Portsmouth looking like a container ship with the flight-deck full of lorries and store boxes. Then our priority passengers were landed first for a check up at R.N. Hospital Haslar, Gosport before going on leave.

TORPOINT:

Freda recalls:

I am proud of my generation, a proud and noble lot. To see how the people of Plymouth carried on in the Blitz, my dear friends at work, quite a few of them had Telegrams to say their husbands were dead or 'believed missing'. But they still came to work, to fight the good fight, they could not let their men down, and carried on working the milling, and drilling machines, some were fitters. They say that cigarettes are not good for you, Not them, some of the girls got a lot of comfort from them. One girl whose husband was a Pilot in the Air Force, one day said to me "if I see a shooting star I know he will be coming back" two others went down with the Glorious and quite a few went over on D-Day and got killed. I lost four cousins, three in the Navy and one fire fighting in Plymouth, also several friends.

I could not be happy when the war ended, I remembered the dear boys that would no be coming back, but I was thankful that there were no more air raids. The lights were on again after years of darkness, To sleep in your own bed peacefully again, but I have never forgotten those men that made it possible that we enjoy so much today. We must never lose sight of it and let us not forget the boys that gave everything in the war. Since our boys are among the best in the world, let us support them wherever they may be.

I remember doing my compulsory Fire Guard Training at Mile House, I passed but they never called me, they said I had enough to do, But I would know what to do if the need ever arose again. When Edward abdicated and left, our lovely King and Queen who took us on, and stayed with us through times of great strife, and kept our chins and spirits up;* and the people never forgot.

I remember when Gerald (Pidgen DFC & BAR) came to see us just after we had been bombed out. He said. Don't you worry Aunt Nell. I'll give the B.......'s hell when I go over I'll go right down the Beam we will show them, That's just what he did He was a dare devil

ooOoo

1946
AFTERMATH.

SINGAPORE:

Arthur Corbidge recalls:

We left Singapore on the 10th and sailed for Bombay where we stayed until January 6th 1946. When we left for Bahrain, we sailed around different Islands in the Gulf, the most important one to me was Muscat where I painted the ships name on the rock. There was at least 300 ships names there dating back to the early 1700's. When I finished doing it I looked up and right above our ship was *H.M.S DIANA* and the initials J. W. C. 1905. Therefore, I put my initials under the 'Falmouth's A.L.C. 1946. When I got home I told my dad, he replied 'Yes I also did that in 1905.

I left HMS *Falmouth* and went by army transport overland to Bagdad, then onto Haifa then down to Cairo, onto Alexandria and back to Port Said where I joined a Tank Landing Craft to sail home, sailing onroute to Malta she developed boiler trouble and had to discharge us in Malta. From there we then sailed on a Troopship to Toulon France, then on by train to Dunkirk, across to England and by rail to Devonport arriving there on the 4th April. Yes, I saw my wife again after 2 years and 4 months.

During my 25 years in the Navy, 19 of those years spent on overseas service, Yes? 19 years can any of you beat that? .... I think it's a record?

ooOoo

Fri. 18th Jan.**PLYMOUTH:**

A Torpoint soldier died possibly from his wounds:

5615760. SGT. CHARLES DEAN LEACH. Age 31.

1st Duke of Cornwall Light Infantry.

CWG. PLYMOUTH EFFORD CEMETERY No. 7017.

February **GERMANY:**

Sir John Carew Pole, who at the time was in command of the 2nd Army Re-inforcements, upon the disbandment of the Northwest European Campaign, an Altar that had rendered service to countless numbers of soldiers throughout the remainder of the war, rather than it be broken up and burnt, upon his instructions was brought back to his Maryfield Church. The History of the Altar began in Normandy at the Army Rest camp in Bouffay close to Bayeux.

Soldiers made the Altar including a Cross and two candlesticks, from wood salvaged from the bar of a shell-torn Café. The shield painted in Blue and White the colours of the 2nd. Army was dedicated at the camp by the Rev. William Sergeant. C.F. Rector of Needwood Staffs. Following the advance of the Army the Altar was used in the Garrison Church, Bourg Leopold, Belgium from the 11th December until 8th April 1945. From there it was transported to the garrison Church, Emsdetten Westphalia Germany until July 1945. It now resides in Maryfield Church and is still used at Remembrance Service in St Giles Plymouth and St James's Torpoint...

[Authors note: This extract was taken from a story written by Marjorie Harwood about the History of Maryfield Church]

TORPOINT
German and Italian
PRISONERS OF WAR

Many Captured German and Italian prisoners of war were sent back to England to serve their rest of the war behind barbed wire in various POW Camps throughout the U.K. Like our own POW's they tried to escape without much success. However, many of the Axis POW's were put to work during their enforced stay. They became workers assisting on the many farms and did agricultural tasks across the land, including clearing the beaches of barbed wire plus other obstacles. and as required they were dispersed to camps across the length and breath of the country side.

One such camp was Bake at Trevolfoot. This had been the home of the American 2nd Battalion 115th Inf. Regt. up to the D - Day Invasion, and was later utilized to house the many prisoners that were only too willing to work on the land, others who objected were kept behind barbed wire until they were finally released back to the own homeland. The POW's who found themselves in Bake Camp worked on the farms in and around Torpoint Urban District. One Market Gardener Albert Carter employed several of the POW's to work on his land at Wilcove.

The following is a letter issued by CCC No 4 Divisional Office Liskeard.
Wed. 14th August.

Dear Sir,
Operation Prisoners:

The County Surveyor has approved of you employing 4 Prisoners of War in your district on hedge cutting etc, and he has obtained the necessary sanctions.

1. I have arranged with the O. C Bake, for these men to be in 2 gangs each with 1 man who can speak some English.
2. The men will be collected by lorry at approximately 06.45 and returned to camp about 17.45 or 18.00 hrs.
3. The cost of haulage will be deducted against the cost of the men's Labour.
4. Only the time actually worked by the men will be signed for viz. 83/4. hours, the same time as our own men. The men will not be worked on Saturdays.
5. It will be necessary for the County man in charge of each gang to sign time worked on a Daily Time Sheet (spare attached) which the prisoner in charge will produce each day.
6. In the event of a prisoner receiving any injury, give normal First Aid and then arrange to return him to camp if the injury prevents him working .
7. I have arranged with the O.C Camp to commence collection on Monday the 19th August.
8. Will you please arrange for the collection and delivery lorry as expeditiously as possible.
9. The Sgt. In charge at Bake is Sgt. Ridley and the phone number is St. Germans 220.
10. The Prisoners bring their mid-day meal with them.
11. Before the end of the 4 weeks period let me have your report on the prisoners work, and if you would like to extend the time & if you would like the numbers increased let me know.

Yours faithfully

Divisional Surveyor
Pto.

Copy of memorandum as received from Head Quarters at Truro for the information and attention of each of the FOUR District Surveyors:-

Copy:- P.O.W. Labour:

"Kindly note that if any P.O.W. labour is employed, their
"Transportation costs should be charged to Recoverable
"Expenditure, with a Job No. and when these costs are recovered
"from the payments made for the labour employed, the amounts
"deducted must be shown in the allocation as a Credit to
"Recoverable Expenditure, using the same Job No."

County Hall
Truro 1/10/1946.

ooOoo

TORPOINT

Sat. 22nd. Feb 1947.

Torpoint Urban District Council invited all the returning servicemen to a Celebration Dinner and Entertainment held in the Council Hall in gratitude for their success in the defeat of the enemy. One such person to return and was invited was H. J. Rowe, he was demobbed from the army in June/July 1946 after serving his wartime in the Desert and Italy. He was a driver in the Royal Army Service Corps. And had been a St. John Ambulance driver in Torpoint before being called up. However he did survive to return to Torpoint. Norman Beaver MBE. Knew Mr. Rowe as a colleague during his time in the St John Ambulance and relates the following.

Norman Beaver MBE. recalls:

There was also a Certificate dated 8th June 1946, awarded by His Majesty King George VI to all the boys and girls who went through the war, on the reverse side was a history of important dates throughout the war years.

8th June, 1946

TO-DAY, AS WE CELEBRATE VICTORY, I send this personal message to you and all other boys and girls at school. For you have shared in the hardships and dangers of a total war and you have shared no less in the triumph of the Allied Nations.

I know you will always feel proud to belong to a country which was capable of such supreme effort; proud, too, of parents and elder brothers and sisters who by their courage, endurance and enterprise brought victory. May these qualities be yours as you grow up and join in the common effort to establish among the nations of the world unity and peace.

George R.I.

[Authors Note: Presented with this award was a small gold gilded cross medal with a Red White and Blue ribbon that was worn during the Victory celebrations later that year. I lost mine many years ago.]

At the beginning of the war there were approximately 980 houses in Torpoint during the Blitz of 1941 112 houses were demolished or, deemed unfit to live in another 700 were damaged but repairable. In the years after the end of the war, the number of families in Torpoint who had been left homeless, found accommodation in the disussed army huts and barracks that had been left intact. Mike Pearns MBE.ISM., family were resettled in the army huts vacated at Borough Farm as did Betty Kellars family, until the building of Pre-Fabricated homes were erected in the vicinity of the west end of North Road, down as far as the bombed out ruins of the old Workhouse. It became known as Mount Edgecumbe Estate. The houses that had been damaged and repairable were repaired, but those that were beyond repair were cleared of debris and new houses or, flats rebuilt in their place. The Ferry Toll Gate was removed (the two top side stones now reside outside the entrance to Carbeile School). The water frontage changed drastically, the area was cleared, including the demolition of the old Gasometer formally known as Rendals Park, and part is now used as a car park for the Rowing Club, on the opposite side across the ferry lanes, a new Police Station was built, behind that the Torpoint Library, in fact all that area has now been rebuilt. Another good example is York Road (formerly Coryton Terrace) the row of houses up from the Torpoint Council Chambers possibly 12 in all. Gradually the town rebuilt itself and its residents came to terms with the normal state of the country of severe rationing that did not end until early in 1952.

In 1974 after the re-organisation of the Cornwall District Councils, the old Torpoint Urban District Council ceased to exist. During the seventies new Housing Estates were to spring up at the Mount Edgecumbe Estate, Bungalows replaced the pre-fabricated ones. In 1984 wth the closure of the Chatham Naval Dockyard many of its workers and their families transferred to Devonport, as these families began to arrive to work in the dockyard and in Plymouth City, more housing was required. With the building programme well underway including the housing estate known as the Goad Estate providing good new housing facilities within easy reach of the City Centre. As a point of interest the origin of the named Goad Avenue was in commeoration of the heroism of Torpointer:

Capt.Roger Phillip Goad. GC. MBE.

A senior Metropolitan Police Bomb disposal expert who was posthuously awarded the George Cross after his brave attempt to defuse a IRA bomb fitted with an anti handling device planted in a shop doorway in Church Street Kensingon on London on 29th August 1975. Torpoint residents specificaaly requested the Avenue to be named Goad in honour of his scarifice.

Torpoint became a viable place to settle down and to cope with the ever increasing road traffic, the ferries introduced a third ferry, in addition the construction of the Tamar Bridge eased the flow of traffic through Torpoint via the ferries, nevertheless in the Nineties the three ferries were 'stretched' a complete new section was welded into the middle, increasing their carrying capacity of cars from approx. 32 to 54. A new Gateways (now Sainsbury's) Supermarket and Garage was opened in Antony Road. HMS *Raleigh* flourished and expanded to what it is now, possible the largest Training Establishment for the Royal Navy.

At the turn of the century, three new 'State of the Art' Ferries replaced the old ones. A new Fire Station was built adjacent to the Torpoint Community College built earlier under the Building Scheme along with Carbiele Junior School. Over the years the town has prospered to become a thriving hospitable township. As for evidence of the war years, little remains except the difference in the stonewall coping of front wall gardens bordering old Terraced houses. The blocks of flats in Harvey Street and Macey Street. The wire fencing that replaced the dry wall in the field adjacent to the Defiance Rugby Field opposite the Oil Tanks. Possibly the boarded up section at the rear corner of Cornestone Church facing the old Torpoint School, that has never been built upon. In Cambridge Field opposite the children's swings etc., the long mound at the top end covers the remains of a wartime shelter.

Evidence is still there if you care to look for it?

ooOoo

A song about Torpoint. (Composer Anoymous) circa 1947? Someone provided this prior to the 1939-1945 Torpoint Exhibition in Torpoint Library 2005.

THE BALLAD OF TORPOINT.

EVERY man sings of the place he loves best,
Say's it's a corner of heaven.
Bonnie Loch Lomond, or home in the West,
Old Glasgie toon, or red Devon,
Dear old Manhattan, or Naples so blue-
Here's a new place that I'll mention to you.

It's a corner of heaven set down in the \West,
Is Torpoint by the sea.
For the storm weary matelot a haven of rest
Is Torpoint by the sea.
It's famous in story, it's famous in song.
The locals all love it, and they can't be wrong,
And when I have missed the last ferry I long
For Torpoint by the sea.

The buildings are noble, and gracious in style,
In Torpoint by the sea.
Our famous Council Chambers' a notable pile
In Torpoint by the sea.
The Waterfront 's Spacious, with sands, rocks and crabs;
There's the Splendid Y.M. where the Art his bun grabs;
But better than all are the lovely pre-fabs.
In Torpoint by the sea.

We're very well furnished with pubs and such things.
In Torpoint by he sea.
And I think the best pint may be drunk at the King's
In Torpoint by the sea.
The Standard, the Wheelers, the old Jubilee,
The Queen's and East Cornwall are good for a spree;
(A Chief Stoker gave these details to me)
In Torpoint by the sea.

The locals have pinched all the best-looking girls
In Torpoint by the sea.
The very complexions, the peroxide curls,
In Torpoint by the sea.
The big chaps in "H" Class and P.O. Apps. deft
Of the second rank beauties their mates have bereft,
And the rest of us have to put up with what's left
In Torpoint by the sea.

The people are gay, and delightful to meet.
In Torpoint by the sea.
There's Brooking and Bevan, with sisters so sweet,
In Torpoint by the sea.
While as celebrities, lummy, there's lots-
The Shorings and Arnolds and other big pots;
So come along gentlemen, drink up your tots
In Torpoint by the sea.
ooOoo

ROLL OF HONOUR

Containing the names of the people of Torpoint who made the supreme sacrifice during the Second World War.

Known Prisoners of War
who died in captivity at the bloody hands of the Japanese
LEONARD BARTLETT CHAPPELL
GERALD GOLLEDGE
LESLIE GEORGE PERKINGS
WILFRED GEORGE SHEAFF
LESLIE EUSTACE
ALFRED TREWERN
JOSEPH SAMUEL CARTER
WILLIAM HICK
HEBER ERNEST TRAYS (ITALIAN POW)

ROYAL NAVY

ATKEY MBE.	James William Harry	BANKS	Clifton James
BOLTON	William Thomas	BOWMAN	George A. F
BRADFORD	Frank	CARR	Arthur Ronald Walter
CARROLL	Peter W.	CARTER	Samuel Joseph
CROCKER	Fredrick John	CROCKER	Harold George
CROCKER	Thomas William	DRAKE	Edward Henry
ENNOR	Kenneth William Arthur	EUSTACE	Sydney J. Garfield
EVANS	Reginald Alfred	FISHER	Frank
HAILES	Reginald Walter	HEALY	Daniel Edward
HEANEY	James	HENDER	Horace
HOAR	Ernest Henry	HOUSEHOLD	Ernest Edward
JELLEY	Nelson	LAMERTON	Stewart James
LANCHBURY	Charles William	LAUNDRY	Richard W. George
LEACH	Fredrick Victor	LOVICK	Francis
LOVICK	Leonard Horace	LOWINGS	George W. Richard
MARTIN	Reilley Arthur	MILLETT	Arthur Leslie
NETHERCOTT	John James	NERTHERCOTT	Thomas Frederick
OLIVER	Aubrey George	ORR	John
PALMER	Ernest John	PAPE	William
PARKER	William Harry	PEARCE	Richard Ernest
PERKINS	Leslie George	PIDGEN	Fernley
PIDGEN	Leonard Albert	PIDGEN	Noel Clifton
RILEY	Arthur Martin	RILEY	Edward William
RULE	David	SCOREY	Richard Norman
SEARLE	Ernest F.T.	SLEEP	WilliamBassett
STACEY	Fredrick William	STANTON	WilliamLeslie
STRICKLAND	Harold	THOMAS	Cecil Holt
TIPPETT	Wilfred	TREWERN	Alfred
WAGGOTT	Andrew Hall	WATERS	Cyril Henry
WAYE	Thomes Alfred	WEEKS	William Arthur
WHITING	Fredrick Alexander.		

ROYAL MARINES

ROBERTS	John Crispin	SMART	Victor Harold

WOMEN'S ROYAL NAVY SERVICE

SPURNWAY Phyllis

ARMY

BUSH-PEARCE	Eric Charles	CHAPPEL	Leonard B.
COWLING	John Hartley	GIBBS-KENNETT	Reginald E.
GOLLEDGE	Gerald	GREET	Arthur
HICK	Charles William	LEACH	Charles Dean
McCAFFERY	Alexander	MUDGE	Charles John
NEWTON	Christopher	PEACH	Stanley John
PEARCE	Eric	RICHARDS	William Cyril
SHEAFF	Wilfred George	STARBROOK	Jack
TRAYS	Heber Ernest.	STROUD	William Earl

AUXILLARY TERRITORIAL SERVICE

1 Unknown

ROYAL AIR FORCE

BLYTH	Jack William	BROAD	Edward Charles
BROAD	George William	LAMERTON	Stewart
WATERS	Cyril Henry	WEVILL	Reginald Thomas
WILTSHIRE	Samuel Derry		

MERCHANT NAVY

ADAMS Stanley Leonard

NATIONAL FIRE SERVICE

LEACH William Henry

TORPOINT FERRIES

MAHONEY Jeremiah

THE DOCKYARD MALTA G. C.

CREWS Raymond Robert

DEVONPORT ROYAL DOCKYARD

BISHOP William Gilber

TORPOINT CIVILIANS

BROWN	Samuel Emery	CAREY	Arthur James
CAREY	Edith Mary	CONNING	Arthur Edwin
CONNING	Barbara	CONNING	Brian
CONNING	Ruth	CURWOOD	Poppy Emma
DEVONSHIRE	Arthur Augustus	DOWNING	Vida
ETHERINGTON	Eric	EVANS	Herbert Arthur
HOAR	Albert Benjeman	NORTHCOTT	Muriel Lillian
O'GORMAN	Arthur Ernest	PARKER	Alfred A. John
PEACH	William Thomas	PUCKEY	Charles
PUCKEY	Mabel	ROBBINS	Henry
RODLEY	George	WESTLAKE	Colin
WESTLAKE	David	WESTLAKE	Eunita Clarice
WYBORN	Leonard		

Possibly Mrs. A. Roberts.?

BIBLIOGRAPHY

The following list of Newspapers, Books & Museums that have been referred to for extracts of information in the complilation of this book:
Australian War Memorials.
Churchill - The Second World War.
Commonwealth War Graves Commision.
Cornwall At War by Peter Hancock.
Cornwall's Record Office.
Cornish Studies Library.
Great Aircraft of the World. Pub. Colour Library Books
Her Majesty's Stationary Office
HMS Raliegh Publicity.
Imperial War Museum.
It Came To Our Door. by H. P. Twyford
Kelly's Directory.
National Archives.
No Mercy From The Japanese. by John Wyatt
Operation Cornwall by Viv. Acton & Derek Carter
Purnell's Second World War Publication.
Plymouth Central Library Naval History Department.
Royal Artillery Museum.
Singapores Dunkirk. by Geoffrey Brooke.
St James Church Torpoint.
Sinking of the Lisbon Maru. by Alf Hart & J.H. Hughieson
The Battle of Britain. by Richard Hough & Dennis Richard
The Blitz Then and Now. - After The Battle Publications
The Durham Light Infantry Museum.
The FEPOW Association.
The German Embassy.
The Making of a Cornish Town. By Gladys & F. L. Harris
The Polish Institute & Sikorski Museum.
The RAF Historical Branch.
The RAF Museum Hendon.
The Second World War. (USA Publication by Martin Gilbert)
The Western Morning News.
The German Embassy.
Torpoint Archives.
Torpoint Ferries. - A History & Review
Torpoint Library.
Trouble in the Amen Corner- Trouble in the Teacups. By Betty Kellar
U.S. Army Heritage & Education Centre.
Various Internet Sites.